ON BECOMING A
LEADERSHIP COACH

ON BECOMING A LEADERSHIP COACH

A HOLISTIC APPROACH TO COACHING EXCELLENCE

SECOND EDITION

EDITED BY

CHRISTINE WAHL, CLARICE SCRIBER, AND BETH BLOOMFIELD

palgrave
macmillan

First published in 2013 by
PALGRAVE MACMILLAN®
in the United States—a division of St. Martin's Press LLC,
175 Fifth Avenue, New York, NY 10010.

Where this book is distributed in the UK, Europe and the rest of the world,
this is by Palgrave Macmillan, a division of Macmillan Publishers Limited,
registered in England, company number 785998, of Houndmills,
Basingstoke, Hampshire RG21 6XS.

Palgrave Macmillan is the global academic imprint of the above companies
and has companies and representatives throughout the world.

Palgrave® and Macmillan® are registered trademarks in the United States,
the United Kingdom, Europe and other countries.

ISBN: 978–1–137–32288–3

Library of Congress Cataloging-in-Publication Data

    On becoming a leadership coach : a holistic approach to coaching
excellence / edited by Christine Wahl, Clarice Scriber, and Beth
Bloomfield.—Second edition.
      pages cm
    ISBN 978–1–137–32288–3 (alk. paper)
     1. Executives—Training of. 2. Executive coaching. 3. Leadership.
4. Employees—Coaching of. I. Wahl, Christine. II. Scriber, Clarice.
III. Bloomfield, Beth.

HD30.4.O5 2013
658.4′092—dc23   2013005944

A catalogue record of the book is available from the British Library.

Design by Newgen Knowledge Works (P) Ltd., Chennai, India.

First edition: September 2013

10 9 8 7 6 5 4 3 2 1

For all who believe in the rigor of practice and the possibilities for our remarkable profession.

CONTENTS

FIGURES AND TABLES

FIGURES

TABLES

INTRODUCTION

Possibility. Sustainability. Agility. Reality. Opportunity. Quality.
Authenticity. Ability. Capacity. Stability. Productivity. Curiosity.
Rationality. Emotionality. Resiliency. Dignity. Integrity. Humanity.

MEANINGS THAT WE ASSOCIATE WITH the words above have tremendous connection to the work we do as coaches of leaders. Coaching leaders is a heart-and-soul, mind-and-body endeavor that holistically focuses on a leader's desired results. It requires our leader clients to step onto the challenging path of reshaping their current boundaries and recrafting the borders of their lives. Such work is uncomfortable yet emboldening, freeing yet grounding. The work has the impact of bringing leaders back to a person they know well—themselves.

So much of coaching leaders is to help them remember their best version of "self" as well as the version of "self" they aspire to. We call this authenticity, and we need more of it from our leaders.

The chapters in *On Becoming a Leadership Coach: A Holistic Approach to Coaching Excellence* are written by coaches who are or who have been on the faculty of the Leadership Coaching Certificate Program at Georgetown University. The chapters cover topics that cover heart and soul, body and mind. When we wrote the first edition of this book, we intended to share the current thinking about the multiple aspects of the art and discipline of coaching leaders from the perspective of the edgy and inquiring minds of the faculty. This second edition reflects our updated thinking and offers new topics for coaches to reflect on and revisions of the thinking in some of the original chapters.

While aimed at coaches who wish to continue their own development by offering them concepts and tools to work with, this book will appeal to anyone in the business of listening to others and helping them clear and forge a path. So, consultants, psychologists, leaders, managers, clergy, and entrepreneurs will get something useful from any chapters they are drawn to. The book is a primer for being with others who wish to understand themselves better to find greater personal and professional fulfillment. As Joseph Campbell so eloquently states, "one way or another, we all have to find what best fosters the flowering of our humanity in this contemporary life and dedicate ourselves to that." In terms of coaching leaders, we believe Campbell's thought is our imperative. Our business leaders shape the world.

To support leaders in achieving and sustaining results in the most humane way, coaches need to work from various stances, including "being" with their clients and really seeing them; "doing" things with and for their clients that will forward a client's progress; and "using" tools, concepts, models that apply appropriately to a leader's work on any given day. Leaders will always be in the perfect position to create the future. They affect business, economics, global productivity, and ultimately global mindsets, and they do this through the "who" they embody daily. Their "who" is affected by their level of self-awareness and self-compassion, and it touches and influences all of the people in their orbit. It is from their "who" or way of being that their actions flow, and from their actions they work to achieve the right results to benefit the whole—their organizations and, ultimately, the larger systems within which their organizations live—to include the health of our planet and cosmos.

As members of the coaching faculty at Georgetown University, we are infinitely committed to our own development and to pushing the edges of what is possible, inviting new ways to think about the transformations needed in our world and what that means for the coaching we bring to leaders. Our students help us develop, and we are ever grateful for their conversations with us, which continue to loop and generate insight and action. We all have teachers and guides who inspire our lives and to whom we are grateful. And of course, we are grateful to Georgetown University administrators for the leap of faith they took when they supported the start of our program in 2000 and for their continued support as we grow and transform as an entity.

In this second edition, we hope you will find inspiration, insight, and validation, and that you will continue to explore your own edges and bring your passion forward.

We need everyone's thoughtful, positive spark to bring more peaceful ways of being that help us navigate the polarization that will always keep people separate from others. I have always said that every coach is an ambassador for bringing generosity, curiosity, generativity, challenge, and kindness into the world of achieving in the workplace, so as to bring these ways of being into the awareness of leaders. Joseph Campbell writes, and I agree with him, "I don't believe people are looking for the meaning of life as much as they are looking for the experience of being alive." When we, as coaches, listen deeply to find the wholehearted aliveness in our clients, we help them tap into that experience of being alive.

May you, the reader, be graced with time to reflect on the ideas in this book, time and support to engage in personal and professional renewal, and resolve to make a difference in the lives—the "being alive"—of those you touch. Your presence makes a difference.

CHRISTINE WAHL

PART I

BEING

CHAPTER 1

ON BECOMING
A LEADERSHIP COACH

NEIL STROUL AND CHRISTINE WAHL

THE OPERATIVE WORD IN THE TITLE of this chapter is "becoming." Human beings always become something. Those who like to learn set their intention to becoming a new and learned version of their self. Those who are mindful find ways to learn from the multiple events, surprises, and disappointments that comprise daily life; they also know they will never really "arrive" at a place of achieving "becoming"—like a river that continues to flow, the lessons are too numerous, our time is too short.

A model we wrote about for the inaugural edition of *Choice*,[1] a publication devoted to the blossoming field of professional coaching, serves us here. We explored coaching through three distinct perspectives—Being versus Doing versus Using. In this chapter, we take the model in a new direction, exploring the three perspectives in the question of how one *becomes* a leadership coach.

Before moving into the model, we want to emphasize that becoming a leadership coach demands certain knowledge in addition to knowing the fundamentals of coaching. Leaders today are challenged to the max. Stakes are high. Competition in the marketplace is a fast-paced game. The spotlight is constant, and it is sometimes hot. The business world seems to require that leaders be beyond human, demanding 24/7 accessibility, perfection, up-to-the-minute knowledge, vision, stamina, emotional agility, and people savvy. Leadership coaches must have experience in organizations, systems, and change and must possess business acumen to have any credibility with leaders in today's organizations. Leadership coaches must understand and know how to work with pressured leaders in today's complicated systems and, as such, have highly developed distinctions of their own about what it means to be a leader.

The original conception of "becoming" was introduced in 1955 by Gordon Allport,[2] who found the then-prevalent conceptions of adult personality development to be lacking. Although Allport's framework is beyond the scope of this article, we do want to acknowledge his ideas that we humans continue to evolve and develop across the span of our lives, that each of us represents a unique self, continually integrating new experiences that are reflected in who we "be." Regardless of what might be apparently stable traits, we are continually *becoming*. The "who" that we "be" has the possibility of continued growth and development.

First, we believe that coaches need to develop their own voice, rigor, and conception of coaching, by blending what they learn from the experts in the field through training and experience with their own way of applying what they learn. As teachers in the field of coaching, we expose our students to many different formulations about coaching, and from their learning, we ask them to extract and integrate for themselves those ideas that are resonant with who they are as unique individuals. Coaches have a professional obligation to aspire to become masters of their own discipline and to engage in continual self-development. Our becoming reflects our being. Our being informs our doing. The tools and techniques we use are an extension of our being. *Being* is the cornerstone.

ON BECOMING A COACH: BEING

Although we encourage our student coaches to formulate a highly personalized understanding of coaching, that is not to say that we don't subscribe to several key principles. Coaching is a personalized vehicle for supporting clients in "stepping up and into" their own development. Development involves transformations based on increasing one's awareness. Through coaching, clients discover possibilities that were previously unavailable to them, given the way they had constructed their world; the clients' current state of awareness constrained the range of possibilities available to them. Awareness is not the same as insight. Awareness is dynamic. In the moment, what are we able to notice? Expanding awareness involves the capacity to shift what we notice and how we think so that we see our possibilities through new eyes.

Emerging awareness, seeing new perspectives, and noticing how and what we notice—these threads collectively generate a living tapestry we call *being*. To help aspiring coaches explore their being, we rely on several conceptual tools.

BODIES OF DISTINCTION

The first concept is "body of distinctions," which is a widely used concept in coach training. A body of distinctions equates to highly personalized frames of reference, or mental models, that serve as heuristics that determine what a person is able to notice. The idea that each of us possesses a highly personalized body of distinctions has been applied in music, cultural anthropology, philosophy, and now coaching. The idea of distinctions is best understood through illustrations.

Imagine standing on a bluff overlooking a desert landscape. Imagine allowing your gaze to slowly scan your surroundings. What might you notice? Sand? Vastness? Scrub vegetation? Blowing winds alternating with silence? Then, imagine being joined by a Saharan tribesman. What might the tribesman notice? Not only would he notice features of the landscape that escaped your notice, but he might also employ a dramatically different vocabulary to express what he notices. Much of what he is able to notice is informed by his body of distinctions. The tribesman would see the patterns in the sand, take clues from the vegetation. These might tell him of recent visitors to the area, or upcoming weather. He would be able to tell a story about the landscape that you would not be able to tell, based on the differences in your knowledge, or bodies of distinction.

Two individuals stand before a third person. We ask each individual, "What do you notice?" Would their descriptions be similar? If one individual is a fashion consultant and the other is a fitness trainer, might they focus on different features and express themselves through different vocabularies? Our bodies of distinctions will often draw our attention to different features of what we observe.

Are the words "red" and "green" in your vocabulary? If we show you two identical items, except one is painted red and the other green, would you be able to distinguish one from the other on the basis of color? If so, you have the distinction of red versus green. Similarly, we could ask someone who suffers from red-green color blindness the same question, and although such a person's vocabulary may have the words red and green, the person doesn't truly operate with the red-green distinction.

Generally, our bodies of distinction work in the background, operating implicitly. Yet, as we said in our introduction, all of us are unique individuals with unique histories and, therefore, unique bodies of distinction. Unless we consciously choose to make these distinctions explicit, we may never recognize that we may "see" yet not truly notice. Generally, we are inclined to attach significance to what we notice only to the degree that the significance meets one of these conditions: One, it is already present in our preexisting body of distinctions, or, two, we are engaged in some form of learning that is intended to expand or modify our current body of distinctions. The immense implication is that, as often as not, our experiences are determined not only by features of events in real time, but also by preconceptions and conditioned tendencies that shape our experience.

For all of us, our "structural determinism" is at work. The idea of structural determinism was initially proposed by the research biologists Humberto Maturana and Francisco Varela.[3] Structural determinism represents that experience involves an interaction, and that experience is not "pure." Rather, our experience is to some degree determined by both the nature of our biological/physical structure and the recognition that prior experience shapes what we are able to experience in the present. We are all Pavlov's dog, creatures of habit, repositories of our individual conditioning histories, reflexively salivating to our own wide, highly personalized array of tones and bells. If we are able to learn to notice how we notice, we will also be able to reclaim greater control of our experience. How do we learn to explicitly recognize our body of distinctions?

Our bodies of distinction operate implicitly. We don't experience our distinctions directly, or with awareness, though we do experience the effects of them. Part of the early work of becoming a coach is to learn how to bring our bodies of distinction to the surface, to make them explicit. To help aspiring coaches expose their distinctions, we work with the concept of "stories."

We experience our lives as extending through time, as a subjective narrative. Said a different way, your life is a story. The idea of story suggests the creative nature of our experience of our lives. We do not necessarily choose the circumstances of our lives, but we can choose the stories regarding how we "hold" and interpret those experiences. We not only live life, we also explain it. We communicate our lives to others through the stories that we tell. We are meaning making creatures. Subjectively, the various events and experiences of life are connected to each other through time and through a series of linkages of causes and effects. At the most basic level, a story is nothing more than our account of the relationship between some effect or result that we notice, and what we perceive as the cause. The stories you live and the stories you tell are a window into your body of distinctions.

For all of us, the common factor in our stories is we ourselves. We are the recurring character—the hero. We are the constant thread. Initiating the process of examining our own stories, becoming genuinely curious about who we are and how we conduct ourselves, and shifting away from relating to our stories as journalistic reports of news to seeing them as expressions of our creative self allow us to examine the dynamic way we as storytellers create our story. Coaches must be able to distinguish their stories! The intent at this stage is to raise awareness rather than to generate insight.

As a coach, as we achieve a better grasp of our way of being in our stories, we are able to see that we are both author and actor. For any adult, seeing oneself as both author and actor constitutes a major step into one's own development, being able to make meaning from the viewpoint of a curious observer, where the self becomes both subject and object. To do this, a coach must become genuinely curious about his or her self and learn to tolerate discomfort, as aspects of self that had previously been hidden from view are now available for personal scrutiny and learning. Later, when a coach engages with clients, this same curiosity becomes part of the coaching relationship in service of clients, helping them to explore their stories and how their stories inform their thinking, feelings, decisions, and actions.

For aspiring coaches, learning how your stories reveal your body of distinctions represents an accessible framework for perceiving "who you be" and for creating new awareness. This new level of awareness is the beginning of a walk into infinity in terms of the possibility for personal learning. In other words, once the awareness muscle is exposed and consciously used, it is regenerative ad infinitum.

From an examined state of being and an ability to be present, coaches have the ability to choose from a wider array of responses and actions to benefit their clients. Lacking this level of engagement internally, which comes from being able to be aware of stories and their impact on how a coach sees and makes sense of the world, the coach runs the risk of having the story in charge versus being in charge of the story.

ON BECOMING A COACH: DOING

Coaching is a highly personalized process for development in which the coach, as the instrument of coaching, plays a critical role. Development, in our view, is an "inside out" process. For both the client and the coach, "who you be" is the bedrock on which "what you do" rests. Our premise is that for coaches to share in this journey with a client, it must be a journey on which they themselves have already embarked and with which they are fully engaged. The coach's personal journey into greater self-awareness informs how the coach works with a client who is on a similar path. Still, being is only one part of the coach's craft; without it, the coach ends up relying on tools and techniques that don't work well on human beings. The coach has to learn and accept his human-being-ness to be able to move beyond the use of simplistic tools and techniques.

Coaches engage with clients primarily through conversation. Yet not all conversations are created equal. The first distinction that we address is that coaching conversations, although they might be interesting, must be purposeful. A simply "interesting" conversation does not constitute a coaching conversation. To be purposeful, coaching conversations focus dialogue on the client's development. To do this, the coach must be *present to the client*. In other words, when a coach enters into a conversation with a client, the coach must have already cleared his mind of distractions and attained a quiet-minded stance, thereby being open and engaged in the moment—or being present, with the client. Being present helps the coach to keep the purpose of the conversation front and center.

Boundaries are critical in a coaching relationship. Being in condition to coach by having worked on one's own awareness steers the coach to be able to listen for the client's struggles and successes, and it keeps the coach from overidentifying or imagining that the client's struggles are solved by sharing "solutions" from the coach's own life. We often see new coaches "doing" too much! It is easy for them to fall into the trap of believing that their worth comes only if they resolve the client's struggles. Au contraire. Developing good boundaries begins with the coach believing that the client is already capable of resolving issues, once the client is able to open up to a wider lens view of the challenge. Only in this way will the client learn and develop from the "inside-out"—therefore, while keeping the conversation purposeful, the coach also needs to keep the conversation focused on what the client is aware of, perceiving, thinking, and feeling, to expand the client's field of view.

To be good at this, a coach must have highly developed listening skills—listening for meaning, for the story, for the commitment in the story, for the values in the story, for the emotion, for the somatic messages, and, of course, for what is not being said. Such a tall order can only be achieved from a state of "being" that is evolved and quiet. The less noise inside the coach, the better the listening.

The kind of listening to which we are referring integrates boundary awareness and genuine curiosity. By boundary awareness, we mean that the coach stays separate while being connected to the client. The coach knows where his or her story starts and stops, and how the coach's story is *not* the client's experience. The client has his or her own experience for the coach to witness. The intent is to listen to clients' stories and manage our boundary awareness in service of clients. Are we able to grasp how their structural determinism shapes the array of possibilities that they are able to notice? The coach doesn't simply point out new or different possibilities by virtue of a different structural determinism and body of distinctions. Rather, the coach, through asking "powerful questions," evokes from the client "the opening of new eyes." Listening and evoking represent the key combination of doing and invite the client to explore what and how they notice. Later, the coach and the client will be able to see the client's story as a story and then determine options for restructuring the story.

We have often found the saying "Name, Claim, Reframe" to be very apropos in working with coaching clients. Assigning a "name" to the story helps clients see their story as a story. Many stories represent repeatable themes that show up in several domains of clients' lives. For example, the story name might be "That's my '*I have too much on my plate*' story," or "That's my '*going small when I could play big*' story." When the client and coach name the client's story, they also create the possibility that the client will claim the story as the client's creation. *The client is the author.* Once the client can recognize and claim authorship, then a new possibility becomes available: reframing. Reframing is learning to assemble the factual elements of the story into a new interpretation, one in which the clients reclaims the power of authorship and choice.

ON BECOMING A COACH: USING

The coach's craft extends beyond *being* and *doing*. The third element, equally significant, is *using*. Using as a concept refers to the tools, techniques, and frameworks that the coach employs in service of the client. We will devote a limited amount of time to the concept of using, as many of the applications that coaches use are addressed in subsequent chapters of this book.

Yet a few thoughts are valuable here. First, tools, techniques, and frameworks are good and useful only to the extent that they serve the client and expand the client's field of view, or lens, and range of action. We encourage coaches to be creative in applying these tools and not to be overreliant on any tools. Being creative with tools not only keeps the coach active in imagining how to help the client move in the desired direction, but it also mitigates a one-size-fits-all mentality. New coaches can fall into the trap of thinking that an exercise they love, such as a certain meditation exercise, is right for every client, or that every client needs to do a values exercise. However, this is not so. As coaches, meeting clients where they are builds a trusting relationship where much good work can be accomplished. Leaders are interested in accomplishing goals, and a coach must be focused on the best ways to do that.

Second, a coach whose listening skills are superb will be able to detect and creatively "use" frameworks from the client's own life and thereby develop experiments and practices that will fit the client's ability and desire to stretch. For instance, a stressed executive confided that years ago, creating music was his way of relaxing. The coach asked the client to imagine bringing music back into his life. She then asked whether he could commit to doing one activity a week that had to do with music, where he would be engaged with music, versus passively listening to it. What this assignment did was to reopen the client's love of composition and recording; six months later, the client handed the coach a self-published CD of his writing and playing. Relaxing back into music had a parallel consequence for the client at work. The client began to see more clearly. Stories that he had been wedded to about how the world at work should unfold started to lose their power. He started to see how stress had affected his thinking, and his every moment, and shifted his story about how to be engaged at work and how work should engage with him. The point here is that in a truly dynamic and alive coaching relationship, the coach is never "doing to"—and coaches, both new and seasoned, need to remember that applying tools to a coaching situation is more than using the same tools repeatedly. This is the art of coaching, using the craft in masterful ways.

Tools and frameworks represent a two-edged sword, offering both the possibility of expanding and limiting options. Most coaches and consultants are familiar with various personality instruments, from the MBTI®,[4] to the DISC®,[5] to Personalysis®,[6] to name a few. The distinctions from each of these represent useful and powerful descriptive frameworks for exploring individual differences. Yet many individuals operate as if their type defines who they are. They begin to explain their behavior (create a story) from the perspective of the type's rationale (i.e., "I don't participate in the meeting because I'm so introverted," or, "I am 'very red' when I am at my best, and so I can't really do planning"). The "type" itself becomes a story from which individuals choose options. Of course, this is limiting. The point here is to neither criticize any of these tools, as they are all brilliant and useful, nor discourage assessment tools in the practice of coaching. Rather, coaches need to be clear about their intentions when they use tools and frameworks, listen for the story the client may be creating, and keep working to keep the client from limiting thought patterns.

The coach's body of distinctions, when made explicit and used with awareness, is a set of tools that clients can benefit from. In leadership coaching, for example, the coach's distinctions about leadership become invaluable in helping the clients learn their own distinctions about leadership. Later chapters in this book point to distinctions that are used in leadership coaching.

The greater question in bringing tools into coaching involves "In service of what?" Coaching embraces many objectives, not the least of which is to help clients expand the array of choices available to them. It is imperative that coaches continually deploy tools and frameworks creatively in service of helping clients explore their choices, from a stance of curiosity.

In summary, coaches have an obligation to be in and stay in their own development. We have covered three broad ways of thinking about what it takes to *become a coach* and encourage all coaches, seasoned or not, to revisit their roots, their stories, their automatic actions, and the tools they are using. In the absence of such reflection, coaches run the risk of dousing their spark, creating unexamined habits and burning out. We take the process of "becoming" very seriously, and we ask coaches to periodically ask themselves these questions:

- What am I learning about myself?
- What story am I living in?
- How is that story empowering me or limiting me?
- What do I need to pay more attention to?
- What clients am I attracting?
- How does being in my own development help me serve my clients?
- Who am I in the process of becoming?

NOTES

1. Neil Stroul and Christine Wahl, "Being, Doing, Using: A Way to Understanding Coaching," *Choice* (Fall 2003), 43–45.

2. Gordon W. Allport, *Becoming: Basic Considerations for a Psychology of Personality* (New Haven, CT: Yale University Press, 1963).
3. Humberto Maturana and Francisco Varela, "Structural Determinism," *The Tree of Knowledge* (Boston: Shambhala Publications, 1987).
4. Myers-Briggs Type Indicator˙ (Consulting Psychologists Press), www.cpp.com.
5. DISC˙ Personality Profile, www.discprofile.com.
6. Personalysis˙ Questionnaire, www.personalysis.com.

CHAPTER 2

MAPPING THE TERRAIN: AN OVERVIEW OF PROFESSIONAL COACHING

WILLIAM J. COURVILLE

THE FIELD OF PROFESSIONAL COACHING IS an often misunderstood phenomenon. There is much debate and confusion about what coaching is and isn't, what it does and doesn't do, how it is similar and different from other interventions, and even how it is defined. This chapter provides an overview of the field. It traces the development of coaching from etiology to definition and explores the distinctions between different types of coaching and coaching and other similar interventions.

Professional coaching, a hybrid intervention melding Western therapeutic counseling and spiritual traditions, has recently emerged as a relatively new phenomenon in the fields of professional development and personal growth. As an emerging field, it has no theory or methodology that it can call its own; however, it borrows from three traditional academic fields: psychology, business management, and adult education (training) and development. Given its cross-disciplinary and cross-methodological underpinnings, it employs methodologies and techniques from transpersonal psychology, humanistic psychology, depth psychology, psychoanalysis, developmental psychology, cognitive behavioral psychology, and ancient wisdom traditions among others. Recently, it has begun to be linked to a fourth academic field of study: spirituality

Professional coaching, as a new therapeutic intervention, arose primarily out of the need to find meaning, values, and purpose that were perceived as missing in what were otherwise rich, full, material lives. The field emerged first with an application of the concepts of eastern religious practices to draw upon personal interior experiences to improve physical prowess and quickly developed into professional and psychological models for achieving success in different areas of personal and professional life. The result has been the development of many types of coaching distinguished by content, population, and expertise as well as a multiplicity of definitions of coaching. It has led to some confusion about how coaching as an intervention is distinct from other similar interventions, and some concerns have been expressed about the use of coaching as a back door method of providing therapy.

FOUNDATIONS OF PROFESSIONAL COACHING

Executive development—heretofore the domain of psychological assessments, behavioral psychology, and emotional competencies—has recently been opened up by the work of professional coaches who are comfortable in the worlds of humanistic and transpersonal psychology, depth psychology, psychoanalytic theory, management, and spirituality. They have derived models that have antecedents in both form and structure in traditions of spiritual direction, psychology, counseling, adult learning, and management theory.

Generally speaking, the literature coming out of the field of professional coaching has an applied focus, is practice oriented, and does not have a theoretical perspective. While this suggests that professional coaching, as a distinct intervention, is greatly undertheorized, it is not to say that it is without theories. The history of how the term "professional coaching" itself came into existence can be traced back to the development of coaching from its beginnings as a sports-based philosophy in the mid 1970s to the psychological model for personal and professional development that we know today. Different theories and models of professional coaching were created along the way and underlie the methodologies and techniques that are used by professional coaches worldwide.

TRAVELING THE COACHING ROUTE: FROM ETIOLOGY TO DEFINITION

There are some who would say that coaching could be traced back to Socrates and his Socratic method of teaching by inquiry (Bennett

2006). Socrates employed the fiction of "not knowing" in order to elicit ideas and theories from his students. Lewis Stern (Stern 2004) says that the word "coach" comes from the Hungarian village of Krocs where the covered carriage (*koczi*) was first developed to carry people from their point of departure to their destination with comfort. Whatever its origins, in our lifetime the term has been more often associated with sports coaching, academic coaching, and personal training (individual coaching for health and fitness) before gaining traction as a term associated with executive development and self-actualization.

It is unclear when the term "professional coaching" as we use it today came in use, but widespread acceptance of coaching for professional development began in the early 1990s as consulting firms proliferated. Most people agree that coaching began appearing sometime in the 1980s in the business world, where it described consulting for business managers and leaders. Between 1950 and 1979 organizational development (OD) professionals began using a blend of OD and psychological assessments in working with executives. Sometime between 1980 and 1990 standardized services began being built around 360-degree multi-tirater assessments accompanied by one-on-one feedback. From 1995 to the present, professional coaching schools and professional organizations for coaching, e.g., the International Coach Federation (ICF), proliferated (Kampa-Kokesch and Anderson 2001).

During this same period of time, the practice of professional coaching also took hold outside the business world and outside of the academic discipline of psychology. In fact, in tracking the historical development of professional coaching, executive coaching seems to be an outgrowth of professional and personal coaching, and not the other way around. It perhaps could be seen as a classic example of Maslow's hierarchy of needs playing out in a capitalistic society. Having satisfied all physical needs, people were searching for guidance in a move toward self-actualization.

RECENT HISTORY

In the 1980s, Thomas Leonard introduced coaching to a wider audience as a professional and personal intervention. Leonard, a financial planner, is credited with developing and introducing coaching as an intervention to help prosperous clients find meaning and value in what they were experiencing in comfortable but otherwise empty lives. Leonard, encouraged by the results of his work and the demand for his services, began training coaches in 1989. In the early 1990s he started Coach U, and in 1994 he established what would become the ICF.

Thus, he began the process of creating procedures and setting standards for what is known as professional coaching today (Capuzzi Simon 2003).

Today, the ICF estimates that there are about 47,500 professional coaches worldwide, the use of coaching by organizations around the globe has increased exponentially, and there is now a well-recognized industry offering a range of coaching certification programs as well as university graduate programs with a concentration in coaching.

About the same time that coaching as a profession was being introduced by Leonard into the personal and professional worlds, coaching as an organizational intervention was being introduced into the workplace by management consulting firms such as Personnel Decisions International (PDI) and the Center for Creative Leadership (CCL). According to Dr. Carol Dellamore, the director of the National Leadership Institute (NLI) at the University of Maryland University College, "the original focus of PDI, which began its operations in 1967, was helping organizations assess and select talent and was mostly concerned with job placement and career advice."(Personal Communication, 2007). Over the next three decades, PDI developed 360-degree feedback tools, personality assessments, executive coaching, and leadership development programs to link "the art and science of human behavior to business needs, providing both individuals and organizations with distinctive expertise in building leadership talent that provides a real competitive advantage" (Personnel Decisions International 2008). PDI was the first management consulting firm to offer a coaching program that was both structured and individually based (Kampa-Kokesch and Anderson 2001; Hellervik, Hazucha, and Schneider 1992). PDI's coaching approach is a process that involves gathering information to explore the difference between perceptions and abilities in four major areas: goals and values (what do you want to do?), abilities (what can you do?), perceptions (how do others see you?), and success factors (what do others expect from you?).

In 1970 the CCL was established to "advance the understanding, practice, and development of leadership for the benefit of society worldwide" (Center for Creative Leadership 2008, see http://www.ccl.org). Dr. Dellamore has worked with CCL since its inception. NLI is the network affiliate of CCL based in Washington, DC, and was the first satellite location providing CCL's programs outside of its headquarters in North Carolina. Dellamore says that CCL was founded by psychologists who came from a theoretical background and initially wanted to provide assessments for business leaders by using psychometric instruments. The idea of using psychometric analysis for business was seen as a very new and exciting option at the time, and psychologists were seen as the proper delivery system for presenting that feedback. The program was so successful that the demand for psychologists soon exceeded the supply, and eventually CCL programs expanded by using other professionals, all of whom worked under the supervision of a "chief assessor" who was a credentialed psychologist and acted in a supervisory role for the feedback givers. Even today, all the coaches who work in CCL programs work under the supervision of a chief assessor who is a credentialed psychologist.

In the mid-1970s, CCL expanded its services to provide a weeklong program for developing leaders that included support for behavioral change in addition to the feedback on the assessment instruments; the people providing that support were called "feedback coaches." In the mid-1980s, CCL expanded the role of the feedback givers and began using the term "executive coach" to describe their role in providing assessment, challenge, and support to aid the executive in bringing about a change in behavior. In its role as a developer of executive leaders, CCL has more recently begun providing one-on-one executive coaching as a stand-alone component and in 2007 began providing training for people interested in developing coaching skills. *Using your Executive Coach* by Wayne Hart and Karen Kirkland (Hart and Kirkland 2001) is published by CCL and provides guidelines for choosing and hiring a coach, and it also lays out the general parameters of the coaching process. Hart and Kirkland describe coaching as a private, personalized, one-on-one development program that can deliver significant improvements to a manager's leadership effectiveness particularly when used in conjunction with an assessment of the manager's strengths and development needs, challenging practices, and affirmative support.

While the corporate world was developing coaching in an organizational context, the profession, practice, and craft of professional and personal coaching continued to grow. The development of professional schools of thought dedicated to training coaches was growing to meet the increasing demand for these skilled professionals by individuals and organizations. These schools were based on the concepts developed by Timothy Gallwey and Sir John Whitmore and enlarged upon by others such as Laura Whitworth (Whitworth et al. 1998), Julio Olalla (Olalla 2001), Frederick Hudson (Hudson 1999), and James Flaherty (Flaherty 1999). These original schools were followed by programs at universities and eventually by the field of psychology itself with the work of Martin Seligman (Seligman and Csikszentmihalyi 2000).

Seligman, the father of the new field of positive psychology, partnered with a coach training school (MentorCoach) to apply his new approach to the field of professional coaching.

The Coaches Training Institute (CTI), another commercial coach training organization, was founded in 1992 by Laura Whitworth and Henry Kimsey-House. Whitworth says that their coactive coaching model takes a different stance from commercial coaching and mentoring because it involves the active and collaborative participation of both the coach and the client. It is a relationship between two equals where it is believed that the clients have the answers or can find the answers. Thus, Whitworth sets the stage for one of the most important distinctions for professional and personal coaching and makes an important contribution to the theory and practice of the field: it is client-centered and client-directed; the agenda comes from the client, not the coach. This assertion begins a debate within the field of the role of coach as advice giver or expert versus coach as facilitator. Whitworth adds two other distinctions that appear to distinguish professional coaching from other similar interventions: (1) coaching moves the client to action and (2) coaching takes place in a relational space that provides curiosity, listening, and intuition.

Julio Olalla, the founder of the Newfield Network, another coach training school, was one of the first to develop a philosophical framework for professional coaching. In an unpublished paper, "A New Discourse on Learning," Ollala lays the foundation of a coaching philosophy as he reflects on learning in relation to establishing a new grounding for coaching: not learning for learning's sake, but to live rich, full, satisfying lives. In order to elaborate on such a discourse of learning, Olalla turns to philosophy and its ontological, epistemological, and ethical perspectives for learning to form the basis of his coaching model and methodology. Thus, he grounds his coaching methodology in who we are and how we know. He adds to this his ethical perspective which gives direction to the who and the how. His goal is "to broaden the scope of our model of learning to encompass all four dimensions of being [language, society, emotions/body, and transcendence] and recover the building of connectivity and meaning" (Olalla 2001, 17).

One of the aspects of the Newfield approach, and a major contribution to the field of professional coaching, is the "power of language" that Olalla describes as "the ability to acquire distinctions for the sake of cognizing and making sense of our world and the ability to coordinate action via speech acts" (Olalla 2001, 10). Olalla showed that "language can frame opportunities, discourage innovation, or illuminate wasteful habits." In the Newfield approach, the language aspect is extremely significant and "has several components, including emotional benchmarking, body language, and verbal clues" (Eckberg 2001). The Newfield approach generally follows these steps: observation leads to action, which drives the results. "When systems disconnect and fail to achieve a desired result, leaders usually revert to another action, which can lead to more failure. Instead, they should start completely over at the observation stage" (Eckberg 2001). David Martin, a Newfield-trained coach says, "You need to look at the way you look at the world because if a coach doesn't challenge how someone looks at the world, they will continue to act in the same way" (Eckberg 2001). In short, if you want a different result, instead of changing the action, you change the way the observer sees the world, which will result in different actions and a change in results.

James Flaherty (Flaherty 1999) takes a phenomenological approach and adds to Olalla's philosophical discussion about coaching with his book *Coaching: Evoking Excellence in Others*. Flaherty draws from phenomenology, "a school of modern philosophy centered on the way phenomena actually show up in people's lives, as distinct from metaphysical schools of philosophy in which events and experiences are categorized by preexisting distinctions" (Flaherty 1999). That is to say, for the phenomenological approach there is no objective reality "out there"; the only reality is our experience of the event/object, not the object itself. Flaherty uses this phenomenological approach to provide a basis for his coaching theory and the foundation for his coach training school, New Ventures West. Flaherty says that coaching must account for behavior—because behavior leads to outcomes—and suggests that coaches do that "by understanding it [behavior] as what follows from the way the world is showing up for someone" (Flaherty 1999). Flaherty posits that there are two ways to do this: first, "by providing a new language that allows the client to make new observations" and, second, "by providing practices that allow the language introduced to become permanently part of the client's structure of interpretation" (Flaherty 1999). Flaherty grounds his theory of coaching in phenomenology and develops a model for coaching that proclaims that language and practices can change the structure of an individual's interpretation which, in turn, can lead to a change in behavior.

If Olalla and Flaherty attempted to ground coaching in a philosophical framework, it is fair to say that Seligman and his new positive psychology have been instrumental in grounding coaching in a psychological one. "The roots of coaching psychology...are related to the factors underpinning the emergence of the Positive Psychology movement" (Grant 2006). "There have been long-standing calls for psychology to broaden its relevance to society in ways that would help the general public to use psychology in a positive manner in their daily lives" (Miller 1969, in Grant 2006). Seligman heard that call clearly and took up the task of crafting a psychology that focuses on developing human strengths and competencies. In 1998, as president of the American Psychological Association (APA), he suggested that "psychology should turn toward understanding and building the human strengths to complement our emphasis on healing damage" and decided to teach an undergraduate seminar in positive psychology (Seligman 1999). He said, "I believe that a psychology of positive human functioning will arise that achieves a scientific understanding and effective interventions to build thriving individuals, families, and communities" (Seligman 1999). That class resulted in his first book on positive psychology called *Authentic Happiness* (Seligman 2002). Given that "positive psychology can be understood as 'the scientific study of optimal functioning, focusing on aspects of the human condition that lead to happiness, fulfillment, and flourishing' (Linley and Harrington 2005, 13)" (Grant 2006) and that this is one of the goals of professional coaching, "links between positive psychology and coaching psychology are clear" (Grant 2006).

Another leader in establishing training programs for professional coaches is Frederick Hudson (Hudson 1999). Hudson founded the Fielding Institute in 1973 to provide graduate programs for midcareer adults. He left Fielding in 1986 to establish the Hudson Institute of Santa Barbara as "a training ground where leaders and professionals can learn how to sustain resilience, future vision, and renewal within themselves and the environments in which they live and work" (Hudson 2008, 1). The Hudson Institute is a nondegree adult training center, combining personal, professional, and organizational renewal and grounded in adult development. Hudson appears to have been the first one to utilize a developmental approach to coaching as a model for understanding how we move through life and negotiate transition points. He used a development map to identify and work with adults during these transitions. Hudson is the author of *The Handbook of Coaching: A Comprehensive Resource Guide for Managers, Executives, Consultants, and Human Resource Professionals.*

In 2000, Chris Wahl (Wahl 2000, 2008) was invited by Georgetown University to design and develop a coaching program for the university's School of Continuing Studies. Seeing a gap and a need for a coaching program that would bridge coaching and OD, Chris took a different approach from the traditional models presented above where the program was centered around a particular theory and a particular leader. Instead of a central leader, she put together a diverse team of professionals who were fully versed in their own theories, thinking, and models (coaches trained by New Ventures West, Newfield, CTI, etc.) and who had thriving coaching practices in organizational contexts. Rather than rely on one particular theory, she designed and developed a program that was a blend of different styles and approaches to coaching based on universal principles, where people could learn from practitioners who used different approaches and styles and were successful in both OD and coaching. This group of faculty came together in the spirit of collaboration, not competition. They offered their best expertise and collaborated to create an incredible contribution to the field that blended coaching theory and organization development theory. The program continues to be a flagship program at Georgetown and has attracted a global audience.

The Georgetown Leadership Coaching program presents an eclectic blend of coaching theories and models, including adult development, organization development, sociology, somatics, behavioral sciences, and linguistics. The students are encouraged to develop their own models of coaching using these different styles, approaches, and techniques.

THE DEFINITION

So, what *is* this thing called "coaching"? We've seen how coaching as a profession has developed, how it draws from other disciplines and theories, but what does coaching do and what makes it distinctive from the other fields from which it draws its methodologies and techniques? I think it is useful to begin by presenting an overview of the multiplicity of definitions of coaching in order to give the reader a perspective of how difficult it is to define the term. With the term "coaching," one encounters a definition issue. In fact, one finds that there are almost as many definitions of coaching as there are people who coach.

Quite bluntly, the definition of coaching is not clear. Despite the fact that the definition of coaching has been the subject of much debate, it appears that coaching as a distinct field, practice, craft, profession, or domain remains ill-defined and with a variety of definitions, not unlike the Sufi tale of the blind men and the elephant. Each man who touched the elephant in different places described a different animal. To wit, "A number of authors have stated that executive coaching as a distinct intervention remains poorly defined (Brotman et al. 1998; Kilburg 1996b, 1996c, 2000; Tobias 1996)" (Kampa-Kokesch and

Anderson 2001). Anthony Grant maintains that "definitions of coaching vary considerably (Palmer and Whybrow 2005) and have been the subject of much debate (e.g. D'Abate, Eddy, and Tannenbaum 2003; Kilburg 1996; Mace 1950)" (Grant 2006). Given the above, it is not the purpose of this section to set out all of the definitions of coaching that exist or to try to come up with a definitive definition, but rather to present what might be seen as a representative sample of what one finds in the literature in order to see what the definitions have in common. For example, Shelley McNamara, a human resources manager at Proctor & Gamble, says, "Coaching is about asking questions that help people discover what they want out of life and how to go get it. It's offering them ways to create something new for themselves personally, for their organization, or for the business" (Capuzzi Simon 2003). Mary Ellen Brantley in her PhD dissertation "Executive Coaching and Deep Learning" describes coaching as "working individually with a leader using both the content of her work and the way she makes meaning of it to assist her in developing new perspectives, new ways of making meaning, and more effective ways of being in a leadership role so that the individual, the company, and the employees are benefited" (Brantley 2007). Patrick Williams who once practiced as a clinical psychologist and later founded the Institute for Life Coach Training, a coach-training program for therapists, says, "coaching is about 'futuring' people" (Capuzzi Simon 2003). On the basis of his reviews of the existing literature, Kilburg (1996c, 2000) proposed the following definition of executive coaching:

> A helping relationship formed between a client who has managerial authority and responsibility in an organization and a consultant who uses a wide variety of behavioral techniques and methods to help the client achieve a mutually identified set of goals to improve his or her professional performance and personal satisfaction and, consequently, to improve the effectiveness of the client's organization within a formally defined coaching agreement (Kilburg 2000, 67). (Kampa-Kokesch and Anderson 2001)

Kampa-Kokesch adds "that it [coaching] can be used for both developmental and remedial purposes, and it seems to occur in six stages: relationship building, assessment, feedback, planning, implementation, and evaluation and follow up and that these stages are consistent with other consultation models" (Kampa-Kokesch and Anderson 2001). It is "a highly confidential personal learning process that focuses not only on interpersonal issues, but also on intrapersonal ones (O'Brien 1997;

Witherspoon and White 1996a)" (Kampa-Kokesch and Anderson 2001).

Dearlove and Crainer say, "executive coaching may be seen as a combination of mentoring, professional development, and support offered through a one-on-one relationship between a coach and an executive" (Dearlove and Crainer 2003).

Allison Rossett (Rossett and Marino 2005), a professor of educational technology at San Diego State University, says, "coaching is about purposeful interactions between a coach and the person or persons being coached" (Rossett and Marino 2005). To Lewis Stern, "executive coaching (EC) is an important method that can be applied as part of an organizational consulting intervention. It entails a coach working one-on-one with executives to help them learn how to manage and lead and assist them to establish, structure, plan, and lead the executives' organization" (Stern 2004).

That the definition of coaching is still in flux is evident even if one looks only at the definition put forth by its official professional organization, the ICF. In an article published in 2001, Sheila Kampa-Kokesch quotes a definition taken from an ICF conference in 2000 as follows:

> Executive coaching is a facilitative one-to-one, mutually designed relationship between a professional coach and a key contributor who has a powerful position in the organization. This relationship occurs in areas of business, government, not-for-profit, and educational organizations where there are multiple stakeholders and organizational sponsorship for the coach or coaching group. The coaching is contracted for the benefit of a client who is accountable for highly complex decisions with [a] wide scope of impact on the organization and industry as a whole. The focus of the coaching is usually focused on organizational performance or development, but may also have a personal component as well. The results produced from this relationship are observable and measurable. (International Coaching Federation Conference 2000). (Kampa-Kokesch and Anderson 2001).

Compare that definition to the one John Bennett found on the ICF website in 2001. In an article in 2006, he quotes the 2001 ICF definition as follows:

> Coaches help people set better goals and then reach those goals; ask their clients to do more than they would have done on their

own; focus their clients better to more quickly produce results; [and,] provide the tools, support and structure to accomplish more (International Coach Federation 2001). (Bennett 2006)

And in a recent search of the ICF website in 2008, one finds the following definition:

Coaching is partnering with clients in a thought-provoking and creative process that inspires them to maximize their personal and professional potential. Professional coaches provide an ongoing partnership designed to help clients produce fulfilling results in their personal and professional lives. Coaches help people improve their performance and enhance the quality of their lives. Coaches are trained to listen, to observe and to customize their approach to individual client needs. They seek to elicit solutions and strategies from the client; they believe the client is naturally creative and resourceful. The coach's job is to provide support to enhance the skills, resources, and creativity that the client already has. (International Coach Federation 2008)

Teri-E Belf, author of *Coaching with Spirit* gives both her official and unofficial (functional) definitions of coaching. She says, "my official definition of coaching, derived from the British training I received in 1987, is an inquiry process of helping people master the ability to consistently obtain the results they want in all life areas with a sense of well-being," but her preferred definition of coaching is "when a client takes the initiative to create a space of unconditional acceptance or love (as well as a coach, a human being, can), then, for a time period of at least four months and for as long as the coaching partnership lasts, the client can just be who he or she truly is" (Belf 2002). James Flaherty in his book *Coaching: Evoking Excellence in Others* defines coaching as "a way of working with people that leaves them more competent and more fulfilled so that they are more able to contribute to their organizations and find meaning in what they are doing" (Flaherty 1999). For Flaherty, "coaching is a principle-shaped ontological stance and not a series of techniques" (Flaherty 1999). He adds that "one of the most powerful ways of understanding coaching is from the end" or from what coaching produces. "Whitmore adds the idea of 'unlocking a person's potential' (Whitmore 2003)" (Brantley 2007).

It appears that the definition of professional coaching is indeed not clearly articulated, that the definitions vary considerably, and that there continues to be much debate—even within the professional association that attempts to govern the field. "The difficulty of defining executive coaching may also be a result of the many different individuals and disciplines involved in providing executive coaching services" (Kampa-Kokesch and Anderson 2001). However, one does find some agreement:

> Central to most definitions are the assumptions of an absence of serious mental health problems in the client (Bluckert 2005), the notion that the client is resourceful (Berg and Szabo 2005), willing to engage in finding solutions (Hudson 1999), and that coaching is an outcome-focused activity which seeks to foster self-directed learning through collaborative goal setting, brainstorming, and action planning (Greene and Grant 2003). (Grant 2006)

"Coaching is thus collaborative, individualized, solution-focused, results-oriented, systematic, stretching, fosters self-directed learning, and should be evidence-based and incorporate ethical professional practice" (Grant 2006). In addition, one might add that coaching helps to give people a sense of well-being, is not only client-centered but also client-directed, is appreciative, is future-oriented, moves people to action, and involves one's search for meaning, values, and purpose.

Because of the multiplicity of definitions of the term I think it is often more useful to describe what coaching *does* (i.e., how one experiences coaching) rather than trying to define what it *is*. To get a sense of that, let's look at the different approaches to coaching and the different methodologies and how they are used.

APPROACHES TO PROFESSIONAL COACHING

THE MAIN PLAYERS IN THE DEVELOPMENT OF PROFESSIONAL COACHING MODELS

In addition to drawing from the psychological models of cognitive behavioral theory and Rogerian "person-centered theory," the field of professional coaching has developed its own models of coaching. Professional coaches, who are not psychologists, employ a range of theoretical perspectives that draw from the fields of sports, philosophy, adult learning, and ancient wisdom traditions.

The main players in the development of professional coaching were Timothy Gallwey (Gallwey 1974), Sir John Whitmore (Whitmore 2003), Julio Olalla (Olalla 2001), James Flaherty (Flaherty 1999), and Laura Whitworth, Henry Kimsey-House, and Phil Sandahl (Whitworth et al. 1998).

In many ways, psychologists are "late to the party" when it comes to professional coaching. The first model used by professional coaches, as distinct from coaches with a psychology or management background, was a model that came from the field of professional sports in the early 1970s. That model, developed by Timothy Gallwey, a professional tennis coach, encouraged people to look at their game from both an inner and outer perspective. Gallwey maintained that the inner perspective was as important as the outer game, and he developed a model to strengthen the inner game. His model borrowed from the perennial wisdom traditions, and his ideas echo some of those found in James Hillman's work in archetypal psychology. Gallwey's model replaces the coach as "expert" with the coach as "facilitator of learning" in order to help people develop their full potential (i.e., the acorn becomes the oak that is inherent in the acorn from the beginning). His model is encapsulated as "performance is equal to potential minus interference" or $P = P - I$. Gallwey's model was the first to suggest that the coach did not need to be a content expert but rather a facilitator and that coaching was applicable in areas outside of sports. It suggested that people had inside of themselves all that they needed to be successful and that all they needed was an objective observer to help them remove obstacles to growth.

The second professional coaching model was developed, implemented, and marketed by Sir John Whitmore. Whitmore too comes from the world of sports and business, and he took Gallwey's idea and expanded it to make it more useful for business. His model is very methodical and suggests step-by-step guidelines that one can follow to remove the obstacles that are interfering with successful performance. A coach needs first to explore what the client is hoping to achieve (goals); second, he or she needs to call the client to honesty by examining the reality associated with those goals (reality); third, the coach explores options and determines which of those are "live" or real options for the client (options); and finally, the coach discusses with the client which of those options s/he would like to explore and moves the client toward a commitment to one of those options in order to move the client forward (willing). His model is encapsulated as the GROW model and has become a standard coaching model utilized by many professionals as they begin their career as professional coaches in the business world. Because of its simplicity, it is often used as a tool to develop line managers into "coaches" for their direct reports. The

GROW model gives them a method to apply basic coaching techniques in their organizations.

The model developed by Olalla and taught in the Newfield professional coaching program moves from an archetypal and process view to an ontological view. The focus is on the observer and how the observer knows and learns. If one wants to change the results one is getting, then instead of focusing on changing the actions (behaviors) one would focus on changing the way the observer sees the world. If the observer sees differently or with more distinctions, the observer will change and that will change the actions, which will in turn change the results. The goal of the Newfield's model is to give people new distinctions (for example, emotions, moods, somatics) with which they can see the world.

James Flaherty developed another professional coaching model with a phenomenological view, and he based the New Ventures West coaching school on it. Flaherty's model is based on his theory that how we make meaning or how we structure our interpretation of the world determines to a large extent how we behave. His model helps the client understand the way he or she structures his or her interpretation of events and then helps him or her change that structure so that the client sees things differently. With a different interpretation, one develops a different structure that produces different actions that can bring about the different results. His approach uses two basic techniques for bringing about this alteration in interpretation: first, it provides new language that allows a client to make new observations; second, it offers practices that will make that new way of seeing permanent. His model could be depicted as follows: Behavior = Structure of Interpretation, and Structure of Interpretation = Language + Practices.

Laura Whitworth, Henry Kimsey-House, and Karen Kimsey-House developed what they call the "coactive coaching model" that comes from their experience working with clients and training coaches at the CTI. Their model draws from the above-mentioned theories of coaching, and while they offer no new insights or theories, they organize the skills, techniques, and practices of professional coaching in a way that makes it accessible to people who want to join the practice. Their model is based on what they call four cornerstones: "one, the client is naturally creative, resourceful, and whole; two, coactive coaching addresses the client's whole life; three, the agenda comes from the client; and four, the relationship is a designed alliance" (Whitworth et al. 1998, 3).

Dr. Neil Stroul (Stroul 2001), a psychologist on the faculty of Georgetown University's Leadership Coaching Program, has developed a leadership coaching model that is based on a narrative constructivist approach for developing authentic leadership. The premise of his model is that "we experience our self-continuity as a narrative that moves through time. In other words, it is a story. Because it is a story, because it is our story, we continually rework and edit the story so that it makes sense. The story is always a 'first-person' story, and in making sense of the story, we give our lives meaning" (Stroul 2001).

Stroul says, "the coach operates on the premise that clients are gifted people. The purpose of coaching is to work with clients to help them better understand the nature of their gifts. To the extent they write the story of their lives with their gifts as a major plot line, they will be more happy and more effective" (Stroul 2001).

In 2004, David Rock (Rock 2006 and 2009) developed a brain-based approach to coaching that attempts to apply new research in neuroscience and the physiology of the brain as a theoretical basis for coaching. His model is based on techniques and approaches that target the neural basis of issues such as self-awareness, status, certainty, autonomy, relationships, fairness, reflection, insights, and accountability. This effort to ground coaching more in the hard sciences could lead to a new direction in approaches to coaching. For example, an approach could emerge that uses a language that is more empirical and rational rather than subjective and emotional; this would be a language more palatable and accessible to the more rational business types.

SOME VARIATIONS OF PROFESSIONAL COACHING

Now that we've looked at the different approaches to coaching and have seen how they can be used, let's step back and take a look at the many types of coaching that populate this landscape of what we call "professional coaching" and see what makes them different and distinct from one another—or not.

"In the last 20 or so years, at the same time EC [executive coaching] evolved as a recognized practice or methodology, many other forms of coaching have also morphed into our organizational and personal lives" (Stern 2004). Carol Dellamore says that what differentiates different types of coaching are the [client] population, the content, and the [coach's] expertise in the specific field. Lewis Stern (Stern 2004) provides the following list of different types of coaching that supports what Dellamore says by demonstrating the distinctions among some current popular forms of coaching:

Personal or life coaching primarily focuses on an individual's personal goals, thinking, feeling, and action and on how an individual can change his or her life for greater personal effectiveness and satisfaction.

Career coaching primarily focuses on the individual's short- and long-range career objectives. It helps the client to decide on career directions and then plan, seek, or change them over the short or long term.

Performance coaching focuses on an employee's specific performance potential, job requirements, deficiencies, or derailers and on how to fill performance gaps and shape the job to optimize the individual's performance.

New assigned-leader coaching focuses on helping the leader to assimilate into a new role and successfully define and implement his or her new business charter along with key constituents and his or her team.

Relationship coaching focuses on specific relationships between individuals and helps form or change those relationships for greater productivity and satisfaction.

High-potential or developmental coaching helps employees with potential for greater responsibility to develop the skills and prepare for moving into new roles.

Coaching to provide feedback debriefing and development planning helps individuals understand and use their assessment results and 360-degree feedback in the context of their personal and professional history and their career and business objectives.

Targeted behavioral coaching aims to modify specific behavior or habits (e.g., intimidation, risk aversion, nonassertiveness) or develop new behaviors to allow an individual to be more effective in his or her current or future roles.

Legacy coaching helps the retiring or winding-down leader to identify the legacy he or she would like to leave behind and to take the appropriate actions to make that legacy become a reality.

Video coaching is defined by its method of using immediate video recording and playback to allow people to become more aware of how they come across to others and to shape their verbal and nonverbal communication to convey the intended messages and achieve the desired influence.

Team coaching, different from most of the other coaching methods, provides one or more coaches who specialize in team dynamics and effectiveness to work together with the leader and each member of a team. The team coach has an ongoing, helping relationship with both the team and the individual executive (Stern 2004).

One can see from this rather extensive list that almost any content, population, or expertise can form the basis for a coaching engagement. As the term has becomes increasingly popular, it seems to have become what Lucy Bregman (Bregman 2006) refers to as a "glow word"—that is, a word that we like to use because it makes us feel good when we do and yet a word whose definition remains elusive. We see the term "coaching" popping up more and more as a way to describe almost any kind of one-on-one helping relationship that wants to share in the new "glow" of the term coaching. "Want to drop a few pounds? Get a coach. Want to motivate employees? Get a coach. Want to monitor progress toward retirement? Get a coach. Want to become more creative, less dependent, or stop pulling your hair? Get a coach. Are you ready for a special date with a special person? That's right, get a coach. People with needs, many kinds of needs, are turning to coaches. Coaching is big for matters from the sublime to the ridiculous" (Rossett and Marino 2005). As the supply of coaches proliferates, coaching is quickly becoming an overprescribed and undifferentiated solution.

There is another perspective on what distinguishes different types of coaching. Otto Laske says that "the way in which the level of self is construed, both theoretically and practically, determines the telos adopted for the coaching and the kind of coaching that is actually done" (Laske 1999). That is, the way we are wired determines both the kind of coaching and the end or purpose (telos) of the coaching. Laske's notion of "the construction of self" and "telos" seems to better describe two other types of coaching not covered by Stern: leadership coaching and spiritual coaching.

LEADERSHIP COACHING

Peter Senge (Senge 1994) in his introduction to Joseph Jaworski's (Jaworski 1996) *Synchronicity: The Inner Path of Leadership* contrasts leadership books about what leaders do and how they operate with the book by Robert Greenleaf, *Servant Leadership*, that "invites people to consider a domain of leadership grounded in a state of being, not doing" (Jaworski 1996). Senge says, "leadership is about creating a domain in which human beings continually deepen their understanding of reality and become more capable of participating in the unfolding of the world. Ultimately, leadership is about creating new values" (Jaworski 1996). Kevin Cashman (Cashman 1998) echoes Jaworski and Senge. He says, "leadership is not simply something we do. It comes from somewhere inside us. Leadership is a process, an intimate expression of who we are. It is our being in action" (Cashman 1998). Bill George, a Harvard Business School professor and former CEO of Medtronic, says that "authentic leaders demonstrate a passion for their purpose, practice their values consistently, and lead with their hearts as well as their heads. They establish long-term relationships and have the self-discipline to get results. They know who they are" (George et al. 2007). And finally, celebrated leadership gurus such as Warren Bennis (Bennis 2003), Jim Collins (Collins 2001), and Stephen Covey (Covey 2004) agree that authenticity, willful humility, and purpose are fundamental for effective leadership.

In a 2007 Bill George, Peter Sims, Andrew McLean, and Diana Mayer conducted a study described as "the largest in-depth study of leadership development ever undertaken" (George et al. 2007). After interviewing 125 leaders, they concluded that there were no "universal characteristics, traits, skills, or styles that led to their leadership success." Instead, the authors learned that "their leadership emerged from their life stories. Consciously and subconsciously, they were testing themselves through real-world experiences and reframing their life stories to understand who they were at their core. In doing so, the subjects of the study discovered the purpose of their leadership and learned that being authentic made them more effective" (George et al. 2007). The authors describe three steps in the process that people used to become authentic leaders. "First, and most important, the leaders frame their life stories in ways that allow them to see themselves not as passive observers of their lives but rather as individuals who can develop self-awareness from their experiences." Second, they "act on that awareness by practicing their values and principles, sometimes at substantial risk to themselves." And third, "authentic leaders keep a strong support team around them, ensuring that they live integrated, grounded lives" (George et al. 2007). "The journey to authentic leadership begins with understanding the story of your life. Your life story provides the context for your experiences, and through it, you can find the inspiration to make an impact in the world" (George et al. 2007). "It is your personal narrative that matters, not the mere facts of your life" (George et al. 2007). Or, as James Hillman explains in *The Soul's Code*, when you read the story of your life backwards, it tells you more about who you are than the mere facts of the story.

Georgetown University has developed a certificate program for leadership coaching that uses a model based on the concept of story and how one can use story (narrative constructivism) to develop authenticity and values, discover meaning and purpose, and integrate and ground oneself in life. "Asked what empowered them to lead,...leaders consistently replied that they found their strength through transformative experiences. Those experiences enabled them to understand the deeper purpose of their leadership" (George et al. 2007). "Authentic leaders used these formative experiences to give meaning to their lives" (George et al. 2007). And, "As John Donahoe, president of eBay Marketplaces and former worldwide managing director of Bain, stressed, being authentic meant maintaining a sense of self no matter where you are" (George et al. 2007).

Leadership coaching involves working with a population of leaders—people who are leading in their own lives or leading corporations. As Kevin Cashman says, "Leaders lead from who they are; only the domains of influence are different" (Cashman 1998). This suggests that leadership coaching could be seen as a distinctive type of coaching not only as defined by Dellamore (content, population, experience) but also as defined by Laske (the way in which the level of self is construed and the telos adopted). One could usefully describe the content of leadership coaching as "essence" or "authenticity," the experience as a developed expertise in the therapeutic traditions of humanistic psychology and self-actualization or spirituality and perennial wisdom, and the population as people who are in leadership roles—either in their personal lives or organizations—thus satisfying Dellamore's conditions. One could also usefully describe leadership coaching as the development of levels of the self or levels of consciousness. The progressive development of higher levels of consciousness is synonymous with the development of what might usefully be called a "spiritual intelligence" or "existential intelligence," that is, the intelligence that human beings use to become self aware, make sense of their world, and construct meaning and values for themselves. The telos or purpose of leadership coaching is assisting people in their attempt to live integrated, grounded, connected (authentic) lives, a definition that also satisfies Laske's criteria.

Laske's criteria of what distinguishes types of coaching are important for two other reasons. One, because Laske's conditions establish the criteria for what might be a useful distinction between so-called transformational coaching and transactional coaching. Transactional coaching has as its primary focus changing behavior; transformational coaching has as its focus "changing character, identity, and one's deep assumptions about self and the world" (Hodgetts 2003). "In transactional coaching, the person learns to behave differently, but the self that learns basically stays the same at its core; the person's core identity and deep assumptions about self and the world are not worked with, not challenged, not identified directly" (Hodgetts 2003). In transactional coaching, the client might behave better, but the *person* does not change or develop; in transformational coaching, what changes is the client's "core identity, his or her sense of who he or she is, and his or her fundamental beliefs and assumptions about self and world" (Hodgetts 2003). Transformational coaching thus seems to align more closely with Laske's definition, which characterizes coaching by what constitutes the self and how one works with the levels of self. Secondly, Laske's definition more closely reflects the type of coaching that could be described as spiritual. Spiritual coaching can be seen as a type of coaching that focuses on the development of levels of consciousness, the sense of who a person is at his or her core, his or her fundamental beliefs and assumptions about who he or she is, why he or she exists, and what his or her purpose or "call" is. These characteristics of spiritual coaching are more closely aligned with Laske's definition, which characterizes types of coaching by the way they work with levels of self and by their teleology.

SPIRITUAL COACHING

There seem to be two ways of describing what is called "spiritual coaching": (1) coaching models that specifically and unabashedly utilize the language of spirituality in their methodology and practice and are unapologetic about referring to their work as "spiritual coaching," and (2) professional coaching models that employ methodologies, theories, and practices from perennial wisdom (spiritual) traditions and spiritual direction, take part in a discourse about spirituality that could be described as unconscious and implicit, and are teleologically based (i.e., defined in terms of a goal or purpose) that could be described as spiritual growth, such as self-actualization, purpose, or meaning.

Many coaches would agree that there is an element of spirituality to what they do, but few are comfortable calling it by that name. Frank Ball, the former codirector of the Leadership Coaching Certificate Program at Georgetown University's School of Continuing Studies says, "I've been saying for years that coaches are secular clergy." And Dearlove and Crainer say, "often the executive coach is a corporate father confessor" (Dearlove and Crainer 2003). Coaches have even been referred to as "the new high priests" (Conlin 2002).

In spite of the evidence of a spirituality discourse in the world of business, spirituality is often, like Harry Potter's Voldemort "that which must not be named." As one coach who uses a holistic approach to executive coaching explained to me, "it's like getting the camel's nose under the tent." She described her coaching as a "Trojan horse" used to get spirituality into organizations without calling it spirituality. Jim Loehr and Tony Schwartz (Loehr and Schwartz 2001) in an article for the *Harvard Business Review* describe a high-performance pyramid that builds from a base of physical capacity to a peak of spiritual capacity. They say,

> Most executives are wary of addressing the spiritual level of the performance pyramid in business settings, and understandably so. The word "spiritual" prompts conflicting emotions and doesn't seem immediately relevant to high performance. So let's be clear: by spiritual capacity, we simple mean the energy that is unleashed by tapping into one's deepest values and defining a strong sense of purpose. This capacity, we have found, serves as sustenance in the face of adversity and as a powerful source of motivation, focus, determination, and resilience. (Loehr and Schwartz 2001)

An explicit spirituality discourse in professional coaching would allow us to be clear about what spirituality is, how it operates within a coaching engagement, and how it affects the way coaches work. Like emotions—which we are uncomfortable discussing and often omit from our conversations—I would suggest that spirituality exists in coaching engagements whether it is acknowledged or not. A spirituality discourse would allow coaches to name what it is they are doing and see themselves as "spiritual counselors" able to tap into a dynamic process that has been shown to be a source of motivation, focus, determination, and resilience.

COACHING AND OTHER INTERVENTIONS

When I work with clients, I often hear them say some variation of, "this looks a lot like consulting, mentoring, training, and therapy, what's different"?

1. COACHING VERSUS THERAPY

Given the similarities in the content, setting, and vocabulary utilized in both psychotherapy and coaching, there appears to be a legitimate concern over whether there is indeed a distinction between the two. To clients, coaching can look a lot like therapy: two people working together one-on-one, private space, confidentiality, often dealing with emotions. In fact, "Tobias argued that coaching by psychologists is a mere repackaging of practices once done under the umbrella of consultation and counseling" (Kampa-Kokesch and Anderson 2001). So what is different?

Teri E-Belf says, "Coaching picks up where traditional therapy leaves off, moving people to integrate their therapeutic insights into practical everyday living" (Belf 2002), and "therapy takes bad things and chunks them smaller while coaching takes good things and chunks them bigger" (Belf 2002).

There is also a difference in the training. "Years of training can separate therapists and coaches. Therapists with PhDs may train for more than six years. Coaches need a minimum of 60 hours of training and 250 hours of coaching client experience for 'associate' certification; 'master' certification requires 200 hours of education and 2,500 hours of coaching experience" (Capuzzi Simon 2003). "But the major difference between coach and therapist is in the degree of active intervention" (Capuzzi Simon 2003).

Another important place where coaching and therapy differ is the status of the relationship. "The issue here is about the role of expert knowledge in coaching and how expert knowledge can be best utilized within the coaching relationship" (Grant 2006). "In essence, this issue is about striking the right balance between process facilitation and content or information delivery" (Grant 2006).

A further distinction is that in therapy, "the relationship is protected by an ethical and legal framework. The coaching relationship, on the other hand, functions as a collaborative business arrangement" (Capuzzi Simon 2003). And unlike therapy, "coaching doesn't look back" (Capuzzi Simon 2003). With coaching, we don't care why you are the way you are, but given who you are, what do you want to do about it and how can you be most effective?

Additionally, coaching does not deal with people who have mental disorders but rather coaches work with what they refer to as "'high-functioning' individuals who want their lives to be better in some way" (Capuzzi Simon 2003). That said, "It may be that some individuals seek coaching as a more socially acceptable form of therapy" (Grant 2006). Capuzzi says, "there are others, especially men, who would never consider psychotherapy but who would talk through problems with a seemingly less threatening, more positive coach" (Capuzzi Simon 2003), and "for people who are 'terrified of treatment,' says

Washington clinical psychologist and coach Lynn Friedman, coaching is a good thing. It allows them to get help in a way that doesn't make them feel bad" (Capuzzi Simon 2003, 2 F).

One could sum up the distinctions between coaching and therapy as follows: (1) coaching doesn't develop therapeutic insights, but rather might take therapeutic insights and integrate them into everyday life; (2) coaches are trained facilitators not trained therapists; (3) therapists actively intervene in patients' lives while coaches are guided by the client; (4) therapists have expert knowledge whereas coaches use the client's knowledge; (5) therapy is protected by a legal framework whereas coaching is a collaborative business arrangement ; (6) coaching is more about the future than the past; (7) coaches work with high-functioning individuals rather than people with mental disorders; (8) coaching is appreciative—focusing on what works rather than on what doesn't work.

All of these distinctions lead Grant to conclude, "Thus, rather than act as a coach, it makes more sense for a psychologist to actually be a coach, to develop coaching skills and psychological frameworks that go beyond existing clinical or counseling frameworks and applications" (Grant 2006). That of course, begs the question of "what are these 'coaching skills' that go beyond clinical or counseling frameworks?"

2. COACHING VERSUS TRAINING, CONSULTING, MENTORING

In addition to therapy, professional coaching is often confused with other interventions or practices such as consulting, mentoring, and training. Dearlove and Crainer say, "step back from the hyperbole, and executive coaching may be seen as a combination of mentoring, professional development, and support" (Dearlove and Crainer 2003). My personal observations, discussions with colleagues, and interviews with practitioners in the field of professional coaching have produced the following distinctions.

Training is an intervention that is designed based on generic skills or expectations for an organization, a group, or a position. It may or may not involve individual progress, has a short time frame, and uses required information to provide learning. **Coaching**, on the other hand, is individualized, tailored, customized to the individual, and it is based on data. It requires individual progress, on ongoing time frame and uses open-ended questions and reflection to promote learning.

Mentoring is a practice where advice is expected. It emphasizes organizational goals, usually occurs between a senior and junior person, and generally focuses on career development. **Coaching** requires questions rather than advice, balances individual and organizational goals, can occur between peers, and focuses on learning or development rather than on performance.

The focus of **consulting** is problem solving. It uses available data to diagnose problems and provide solutions. The consultant is the expert and accountable for success, and the emphasis is on group change or organizational change. As we have seen, the focus of **coaching** is to deepen learning and move the action forward. It uses data, but only to set goals, not to diagnose problems or provide solutions. In coaching, the client is the expert and is accountable for success, and coaching emphasizes personal change.

Common to all of the above interventions of therapy, consulting, training, and mentoring is that they are all expert-centered. The therapist is responsible for one's mental health; the consultant is in charge of diagnosing and solving the problem; the trainer's position is to impart specific skills or knowledge, and the mentor's role is to share experiences and give advice. One of the things that make coaching different is its focus. Coaching is client-centered and client-directed, and the responsibility for success rests with the client. Further, coaching is focused on learning and development rather than on performance, on the future rather than on the past, on strengths rather than on weaknesses, on movement toward action rather than on stasis, and on questions and reflection rather than on advice or problem solving. In addition, coaching is customized and tailored to the individual rather than to a methodology or theoretical stance, and its primary tools are questions rather than answers.

One of the basic tenets of professional coaching is that coaching helps clients see things differently. Each client has a story about what he or she is doing and why he or she is doing it. The primary skill utilized and developed by professional coaches that goes beyond existing clinical or counseling frameworks and applications is the ability—even in areas where they have little or no expertise—to lead the client with a few well-placed questions to focus on variables that are critical to his or her success and to bring clarity to his or her story. Often adjusting the lens through which the story is viewed can have a major impact on the options for action and hence on the outcome.

Earlier I posed a question about distinctive coaching skills that go beyond existing clinical or counseling frameworks and applications. I am not convinced that there are distinctive coaching skills; what is distinctive about coaching is the framework and process within which those skills, techniques, and methodologies borrowed from other disciplines are practiced and applied. The coach becomes a relational container, confessor, partner, facilitator, provocateur, confidant, challenger, truth-sayer, and supporter.

History suggests that Gallwey and Leonard introduced the phenomenon of professional coaching in North America in the mid-1970s and that it was focused on finding meaning, values, and purpose. With the entry of psychologists and management consultants into the field in the mid-1980s, the focus of coaching began to shift from meaning to means of production, from fulfillment to efficiency, from purpose to engagement, and from personal values to the bottom line. This is not the first time that psychology has appropriated language and experience from another domain, "psychologized" it, and utilized it in the service of business.

TOWARD A NEW UNDERSTANDING OF PROFESSIONAL COACHING

While the field of professional coaching is becoming increasingly popular and widespread due to its "glow," it is not without its detractors and its concerns. Not the least of these, from an academic viewpoint, is the fact that there has historically been a lack of published work to conceptualize and theorize this new field and thus a dearth of theoretical literature about it.

In addition to the fact that the field is undertheorized, Kampa-Kokesch identifies the following concerns regarding this new social phenomenon: "the absence of a clear and widely accepted (a) definition, (b) standard of practice, and (c) agreement as to the appropriate service providers" (Kampa-Kokesch and Anderson 2001). She argues correctly that "there is surprisingly little empirical research on the efficacy of executive coaching" (Kampa-Kokesch and Anderson 2001) and that there is "increased concern regarding the definition and standardization of executive coaching as well as who is most qualified to deliver such services (Brotman et al 1998; Filipczak 1998; Harris 1999; Kilburg 1996b, 1996c, and 1997; Saporito 1996; Tobias 1996)" (Kampa-Kokesch and Anderson 2001). While there have been many attempts—and some progress—on measuring the effectiveness or ROI for executive coaching since 2001, it still remains an open question as to whether a hard business case can be made to justify the investment in coaching for organizations and establish how—or even if—coaching is effective.

Another issue "involves the myriad backgrounds of executive coaches. Currently, professionals from business, teaching, law, and sports are claiming to be executive coaches (Brotman et al 1998; Kilburg

1996b). In part, this is a result of the increased demands for executive coaching [and its accompanying revenues], and, as such, there is concern over unqualified professionals making claims and threatening the legitimacy of executive coaching as a viable intervention (Harris 1999; Kilburg 2000)" (Kampa-Kokesch and Anderson 2001).

In an attempt to address these concerns, "guidelines for successful coaching have been proposed by various individuals (e.g., Kiel et al 1996), but to date no standards or guidelines have been widely adopted" (Kampa-Kokesch and Anderson 2001). Grant says that "because coaching is an industry and not a profession, there are no barriers to entry, no regulations, no government-sanctioned accreditation or qualification process and no clear authority to be a coach; anyone can call himself a 'master coach.' Worldwide there is a veritable industry offering a range of 'coach certification' programs" (Grant 2006).

Though it has not been for lack of effort, there is still no general agreement on what effective coaching is, and while there has been much work done on standards of practice, there is still no agreement on what coaches do and who is most qualified to deliver these services. Substantive research on what effective coaching is might give more clarity to who is most qualified to deliver this service as well as indicate the best path to the development of effective coaches.

Lastly, another of the underdeveloped areas of professional coaching is the discourse about spirituality that was the impetus for its emergence and about the role spirituality continues to play in professional coaching. As we have seen, most of the literature in professional journals and academic literature is centered on the theory, methodology, and practice of coaching from a psychological, philosophical, and adult development perspective. What is lacking in the field and the professional literature is a more robust discourse about the spiritual or religious aspects of professional coaching that were present at its origin and that still operate—implicitly or explicitly—at its core; a spirituality discourse that speaks to our search for meaning, purpose, values—our ultimate concern. This argument for a "spiritual or existential" intelligence and an examination of coaching as a means for developing that intelligence and of coaches as spiritual directors is a subject for another chapter.

BIBLIOGRAPHY

Belf, T. *Coaching with Spirit: Allowing Success to Emerge.* San Francisco: Jossey-Bass/Pfeiffer, 2002.

Bennett, J. L. "An Agenda for Coaching-Related Research: A Challenge for Researchers." *Consulting Psychology Journal: Practice and Research* 58, no. 4 (2006): 240–249.

Bennis, W. G. *On Becoming a Leader.* Cambridge, MA: Perseus, 2003.

Brantley, M. E. "Executive Coaching and Deep Learning." Ph.D. diss., Fielding Graduate University, 2007.

Bregman, L. "The Interpreter/Experiencer Split: Three Models in the Psychology of Religion." *Journal of the American Academy of Religion* 46, no. 2 (1978): 115–149.

Bregman, L. "Spirituality: A Glowing and Useful Term in Search of a Meaning." *Omega Journal of Death and Dying* 53, no. 1–2 (2006): 5–25.

Campbell Quick, J., and M. Macik-Frey. "Behind the Mask Coaching Through Deep Interpersonal Communication." *Consulting Psychology Journal: Practice and Research*, 56, no. 2 (2004): 67–74.

Capuzzi Simon, C. "A Coach for Team You." *Washington Post*, (2003), F1–F3.

Cashman, K. *Leadership from the Inside Out.* Minneapolis, MN: LeaderSource, 1998.

Center for creative leadership. Retrieved 1/20/2008, from http://www.ccl.org/leadership/about/quickFacts.aspx?pageId=654, 2008.

Cocivera, T., and S. Cronshaw. "Action Frame Theory as a Practical Framework for the Executive Coaching Process." *Consulting Psychology Journal: Practice and Research.Coaching* 56, no. 4 (2004): 234–245.

Collins, J. "Religion in the Workplace." *Business Week*, November 1, 1999.

Collins, J. "Level 5 Leadership." *Harvard Business Review*, 1, no. 13 (2001).

Collins, J. J. *Good to Great: Why Some Companies Make the Leap... and Others Don't.* New York: HarperBusiness, 2001.

Conlin, M. "CEO Coaches." *BusinessWeek*, November 11, 2002, 98–104.

Cook-Greuter, S. R. "Making the Case for a Developmental Perspective." *Industrial and Commercial Training* 36, no. 7 (2004): 275–281.

Covey, S. R. *The 7 Habits of Highly Effective People: Restoring the Character Ethic.* New York: Free Press, 2004.

D'Abate, C. P., E. R. Eddy, and S. I. Tannenbaum. "What's in a Name? A Literature-based Approach to Understanding Mentoring, Coaching, and Other Constructs that Describe Developmental Interactions." *Human Resource Development Review* 2, no. 4 (2003): 360–384.

Dearlove, D., and S. Crainer. 2003. "My Coach and I." *Business + Strategy* 31 (11/21/07).

Ducharme, M. J. "The Cognitive-Behavioural Approach to Executive Coaching." *Consulting Psychology Journal: Practice and Research* 56, no. 4 (2004): 214–224.

Eckberg, J. "Coaching Helps Firms Focus." *The Cincinnati Enquirer*, 2001, B7–B8.

Ennis, S., L. R. Stern, N. Yahanda, M. Vitti, J. Otto, and W. Hodgetts. "The Executive Coaching Handbook." Unpublished manuscript, 2003.

Field, D. "The Relationship Between Transformational Leadership and Spirituality in Business Leaders." Ph.D. diss., Regent University, 2004.

Fitzgerald, C. "Creating Workplaces that Integrate Reality and Vision, Mind and Heart: Why It's Important and Why It's So Hard." Unpublished manuscript, 1998.

Fitzgerald, C. "Coaching Senior Executives in Mid-life: When Conversation Becomes Transformative." *The Art and Practice of Coaching Leaders.*

(National Leadership Institute, University of Maryland University College, 1998).

Fitzgerald, C., and J. Berger, eds. *Executive Coaching: Practices & Perspectives*. Palo Alto, CA: Cavies-Black, 2002.

Flaherty, J. *Coaching: Evoking Excellence in Others*. Woburn, MA: Butterworth-Heinman, 1999.

Gallwey, T. W. *What Is the Inner Game?* Retrieved 1/17/08 from http://www.theinnergame.com/html/whatisInnerGame.html#, 2008.

Gallwey, T. W. *The Inner Game of Tennis*. New York: Random House, 1974.

Gallwey, T. W. *Inner Tennis: Playing the Game*. 1st ed. New York: Random House, 1976.

George, B., P. Sims, A. N. McLean, and D. Mayer. "Discovering Your Authentic Leadership." *Harvard Business Review* (February, 2007): 129–138.

Goldsmith, M., L. Lyons, and A. Freas. *Coaching for Leadership: How the World's Greatest Coaches Help Leaders Learn*. San Francisco, CA: Jossey-Bass/Pfeiffer, 2002.

Grant, A. M. "A Personal Perspective on Professional Coaching and the Development of Coaching Psychology." *International Coaching Psychology Review* 1, no. 1 (2006): 12–22.

Hart, E. W., and K. Kirkland. *Using Your Executive Coach*. Greensboro, NC: Center for Creative Leadership, 2001.

Hillman, J. *The Soul's Code : In Search of Character and Calling*. New York: Warner Books, 1997.

Hodgetts, W. 2003. *The Deeper Work of Executive Coaching*. Conference Board Conference: Coaching for Business Results, New York, 2–5.

Hudson, F. *The Hudson Institute of Santa Barbara*. Retrieved 3/17/2008 from http://www.hudsoninstitute.com/pages/about.asp, 2008.

Hudson, F. M. *The Handbook of Coaching: A Comprehensive Resource Guide for Managers, Executives, Consultants, and Human Resource Professionals*. San Francisco: Jossey-Bass Publishers, 1999.

International Coach Federation. *FAQs About Coaching*. Retrieved 1/17/08 from http://www.coachfederation.org/aboutcoaching/about.html, 2001.

International Coach Federation. Retrieved 1/20/08 from http://www.coachfederation.org/ICF/For+Coaching+Clients/What+is+a+Coach/, 2008.

Jaworski, J. *Synchronicity: The Inner Path of Leadership*. San Francisco: Berrett-Koehler, 1996.

Judge, W. Q., and J. Cowell. "The Brave New World of Executive Coaching." *Business Horizons* 40, no. 4 (1997): 71–77.

Kampa-Kokesch, S., and M. Z. Anderson. "Executive Coaching: A Comprehensive Review of the Literature." *Consulting Psychology Journal: Practice and Research* 53, no. 4 (2001): 205–228.

Kilburg, R. R. "Executive Coaching [Special Issue]." *Consulting Psychology Journal: Practice and Research* 48, no. 2 (1996).

Kilburg, R. R. *Executive Coaching: Developing Managerial Wisdom in a World of Chaos*. Washington, DC: American Psychological Association, 2000.

Kilburg, R. R. "Trudging Toward Dodoville: Conceptual Approaches and Case Studies in Executive Coaching." *Consulting Psychology Journal:*

Practice and Research. Special Issue: Trudging Toward Dodoville, Part 1: Conceptual Approaches in Executive Coaching 56, no. 4 (2004): 203–213.

Kilburg, R. R. "When Shadows Fall: Using Psychodynamic Approaches in Executive Coaching." *Consulting Psychology Journal: Practice and Research. Special Issue: Trudging Toward Dodoville, Part 1: Conceptual Approaches in Executive Coaching* 56, no. 4 (2004): 246–268.

Laske, O. E. An Integrated Model of Developmental Coaching. *Consulting Psychology Journal: Practice and Research* 51, no. 3 (1999): 139–159.

Loehr, J., and T. Schwartz. "The Making of a Corporate Athlete." *Harvard Business Review* (January, 2001): 120–128.

Maslow, A. H. *Towards a Psychology of Being.* New York: Wiley, 1968.

Olalla, J. A. "A New Discourse on Learning." Unpublished Manuscript, 2001.

O'Neill, M. L. *Executive Coaching with Backbone and Heart: A Systems Approach to Engaging Leaders with Their Challenges.* San Francisco: Jossey-Bass, 2007.

Passmore, J. "An Integrative Model for Executive Coaching." *Consulting Psychology Journal: Practice and Research* 59, no. 1 (2007): 68–78.

Peltier, B. *The Psychology of Executive Coaching: Theory and Application.* New York: Brunner-Routledge, 2001.

Personnel Decisions International. Retrieved 1/20/2008 from http://www.personneldecisions.com/press/mediakit.asp, 2008.

Quick, J. C., and M. Macik-Frey. "Behind the Mask: Coaching Through Deep Interpersonal Communication." *Consulting Psychology Journal: Practice and Research* 56, no. 2 (2004): 67–74.

Rock, D., and J. Schwartz. *The Neuroscience of Leadership.* Retrieved 11/1/2007 from http://www.strategy-business.com/press/freearticle/06207, 2006.

Rock, D. *Quiet Leadership.* New York: HarperCollins, 2006.

Rock, D. *Coaching with the Brain in Mind: Foundations for Practice.* Hoboken, NY: John Wiley, 2009.

Rogers, C. R. *Client-Centered Therapy.* Boston: Houghton-Mifflin, 1951.

Rossett, A., and G. Marino. "If Coaching is Good, then E-coaching is…." *T+D* (November, 2005): 46–49.

Rotenberg, C. T. "Psychodynamic Psychotherapy and Executive Coaching: Overlapping Paradigms." *Journal of the American Academy of Psychoanalysis* 28, no. 4 (2000): 653–662.

Sarbin, T. R. 1998. *Believed-in Imaginings: A Narrative Approach.* Washington, DC: American Psychological Association, 1998.

Schumacher, E. *The "ZEN" of Tennis….* Retrieved 4/3 2008 from http://www1.epinions.com/book-review-270A-109DE406-3991FABD-prod1, 2000.

Seligman, M. E. "Teaching Positive Psychology." *APA Monitor Online* 30 (7), retrieved 1/19/2008 from http://www.apa.org/monitor/julaug99/speaking.html, 1999.

Seligman, M. E., and M. Csikszentmihalyi. "Positive Psychology: An Introduction." *American Psychologist* 55, no. 1 (2000): 5–14.

Seligman, M. E. "Positive Psychology, Positive Prevention, and Positive Therapy." In *Handbook of Positive Psychology*, edited by C. R. Snyder and S. J. Lopez, 3–9. New York: Oxford University Press, 2001.

Seligman, Martin E. P. *Authentic Happiness: Using the New Positive Psychology to Realize Your Potential for Lasting Fulfillment*. New York: Free Press, 2002.

Senge, P. M. *The Fifth Discipline Fieldbook: Strategies and Tools for Building a Learning Organization*. New York: Currency Doubleday, 1994.

Sherin, J., and L. Caiger. "Rational-Emotive Behavior Therapy: A Behavioral Change Model for Executive Coaching?" *Consulting Psychology Journal: Practice and Research* 56 (2004): 225–233.

Sherman, S., and A. Freas. "The Wild West of Executive Coaching." *Harvard Business Review* 82, no. 11 (2004): 82–90.

Skiffington, S., and P. Zeus. *Behavioural Coaching*. Sydney: McGraw-Hill, 2003.

Stern, L. R. "Executive Coaching: A Working Definition." *Consulting Psychology Journal: Practice and Research* 56, no. 3 (2004): 154–162.

Stroul, N. A. "Coaching: A Conceptual Framework." Unpublished Manuscript, 2001.

Stroul, N. A., and M. O'Brien. "Coaching: The Provocative Proposition." Unpublished Manuscript, 2007.

Tobias, L. L. "Coaching Executives." *Consulting Psychology Journal: Practice and Research* 48, no. 87 (1996): 95.

Wahl, C. and B. Braham. *Be Your Own Coach*. Menlo Park, CA: Crisp Publications, 2009.

Wahl, C., C. Scriber, and B. Bloomfield, eds. *On Becoming a Leadership Coach: A Holistic Approach to Coaching Excellence*. New York: Palgrave Macmillan, 2008.

Whitmore, J. *Coaching for Performance: Growing People, Performance. and Purpose*. 3rd ed. Yarmouth: Nicholas Brealey, 2003.

Whitworth, L., K. Kimsey-House, H. Kimsey-House, and P. Sandahl. *Co-active Coaching: New Skills for Coaching People Toward Success in Work and Life*. Palo Alto, CA: Davies-Black Publishing, 1998.

Wilber, K. *Eye to Eye*. New York: Anchor Books, 1983.

CHAPTER 3

SACRED SPACE: WHERE POSSIBILITIES ABOUND AND CHANGE IS ENGENDERED

JULIE K. SHOWS AND CLARICE SCRIBER

Early morning—at dawn—I find my rhythm, my mind quiets, and I am completely at peace. The house is quiet. I am connected with spirit, known to myself and the universe. It is a time full of grace, a time when I am connected to my center and open to what is calling me. My dreams whisper to me. The answers to the questions I pose are revealed. I trust what I hear. This is for me sacred space. (Clarice Scriber)

At the start of another day, I focus my mind on the stillness and feeling of calmness. I push away my thoughts of things to do and obligations to others—this is a sacred time that is mine alone. I breathe deeply and release the worries and concerns. I breathe deeply and connect to the wisdom of my spirit. It is in this space that I can pause and set my intentions for the day, reflect on what is important to me, and connect to what inspires me. From this sacred space, I start my day with a feeling of purpose and presence. I am ready for another day. (Julie K. Shows)

WE BEGIN THIS CHAPTER WITH THE PREMISE that each human being has a wellspring of innate intelligence from which deep qualities like presence, wisdom, common sense, resiliency, and peace of mind emerge. To access that innate intelligence, we coaches learn to create a space for ourselves and for the leaders we coach. We call this *sacred space*.

The coaching hour provides the opportunity so that men and women who are called to "do" can learn to "be." It's a space where leaders reconnect with their values, shift into possibility, and explore future options. As leadership coaches, we cocreate *sacred space* with leaders to help them fashion strategies that bring positive action in service to the organizations they lead. It allows our clients to leave ego out of the conversation and to connect with their greater wisdom and authenticity. It is the space for conversations about learning and growth, intentions and desires, and values and purpose. From this space, leaders can move forward with clarity of intention, foresight, and balance.

How does the practice of creating sacred space influence our ability to be masterful leadership coaches? What qualities allow the coach to be present—to listen with the "third ear," intuitively and deeply, for what is spoken and not said? How do coaches facilitate moments of grace in which leaders learn and grow?

QUALITIES THAT EMBODY SACRED SPACE

We had our own ideas and, at the same time, we wondered what other leadership coaches believe about creating sacred space. With that question in mind, we distributed an online survey to 100 coaches. Those coaches were selected for gender diversity, variety in training venues, number of years of experience, and geographical differences. We received a 50 percent response rate from the survey. Subsequently, we followed up with interviews of twenty coaches to gain additional insight into the question of sacred space.

We began by identifying attributes that we believe coaches embody when they create sacred space (table 3.1). We asked coaches to select the top five qualities that a leadership coach should embody to create sacred space. In a companion survey, we asked the same questions of coaching clients to see if what coaches think and experience matches what clients observe and experience. Although not quantitatively valid, the survey and follow-up interviews yielded rich data culled from the experience of the coach respondents and clients.

The coach respondents selected and thereby validated the qualities that we deem most important to the coaching relationship.

Table 3.1 Leadership coaching survey: Qualities

Please select the top five qualities a leadership coach should embody to create sacred space. Then, rank your selections in order of importance with 1 being the most important and 5 being the least important.

1.	Ability to connect
2.	Commitment to others
3.	Confidence
4.	Congruence
5.	Comfortable
6.	Equanimity
7.	Grace
8.	Heart
9.	Humor
10.	Intelligence
11.	Inspiration
12.	Motivation
13.	Openness
14.	Political savvy
15.	Presence
16.	Self-awareness
17.	Spirit
18.	Trust
19.	Warmth
20.	Wisdom

If there are other qualities that you believe are important to a leadership coach, please list them:

_____

_____

_____

_____

_____

_____

The qualities both the coach respondents and we selected were as follows:

- Ability to connect
- Trust
- Presence
- Self-awareness
- Wisdom

ABILITY TO CONNECT

"The essence of communication is connection."[1] The ability to connect was the quality most identified by coaches and leaders alike. What makes that quality so important? For the coach and the client, it is the catalyst for the genesis of the partnership, and it recurs throughout the course of the alliance. It is not static; it deepens as trust grows.

This ability is fed by the leaders who reveal themselves, warts and all, as the coach reciprocates with regard and respect and compassion. Both leader and coach become more open and thereby vulnerable.

The coach is open to the client; the leader feels safe to disclose, to try on new behaviors, to wade and perhaps later plunge into uncharted water, to be courageous in the face of uncertainty. There is a dance—an exchange of energy—as the client and coach garner trust to challenge, to hold accountability for new actions. During this exchange, it becomes even more likely leaders will "act" into the future they imagine.

> If you don't connect, then the coachees are less likely to open up when they don't feel the connection. When people do connect, [there is] more of a free flow of dialogue, said a manager in a global law firm who worked with her coach for a year.[2]

Therefore, how the connection is established sets the tone for the coaching relationship. As in many relationships, a decision to work together occurs quickly. Is the coach someone who makes it easy to engage? Can leaders see themselves in partnership with their coaches? Is the coach able to create the space for discernment to occur—for them both to choose to relate and to form a relationship?

TRUST

If the ability to connect is the catalyst to forming the relationship, then trust is the glue that cements the coaching alliance. Trust is what allows the clients to be truthful and to fully reveal their challenges, concerns, dreams, and strengths. In other words, they can be vulnerable and not be judged. Trust is a two-way street, a complementary process.

The coach enters the coaching alliance with the premise that the client is whole and competent, and the coach helps to establish trust by partnering with the client to create the parameters for the coaching engagement.

In large organizations, the coaching hour may be the only place a leader can fully reveal what it is like to sit in the leadership seat or to be held accountable by someone whose purpose is to hold an agenda. In this setting, the leader-clients are able to root for themselves and to act as their best selves for personal change and growth as individuals and as leaders. One consultant (who is also trained as a coach) we interviewed put it this way:

> For any work relationship, a level of trust between people that is comparable to the level of vulnerability and power that people have over one another [must] be very high for the coach. If it's a good coaching relationship, the clients will share information that puts them in a very vulnerable situation. If they don't open up, that [lack] will hurt the coaching relationship.[3]

To that end, contracting around confidentiality is a crucial element. A frank discussion of the terms of confidentiality—what the coach won't and what the coach is obliged to reveal can help make the process trustworthy and transparent. Throughout the engagement, the coach holds the client's agenda, listens deeply, and fosters both reflection and self-examination. As time elapses, both the client and coach can move into that sacred space comfortably with each other and can trust the process.

PRESENCE

Presence is the quality that affects the coach's capacity to hold the space. It is the essence of the individual, and presence manifests itself both physically and spiritually. It is the embodiment of the individual.

In the context of coaching, we view this presence as a positive force, as the ability to manifest compelling energy that is confident without being cocky and is open without crossing boundaries. Spirit abounds. It contributes to the chemistry of coaching.

The coach's presence helps us to attract the clients for whom we can contribute. Presence fosters credibility with the leader. When the coach is congruent, centered, relaxed, and fully aware of herself and is in tune with the client and the environs, the clients are freer to access their own willingness and intuition.

The coaches' presence (i.e., their way of being) can engender positive energy that is conducive to openings for new possibilities.

Presence also supports the connection that the coach makes with the leader. For all of us, when we are in tune with our values, our beliefs, and ourselves, it shows. And it allows us to engage confidently, welcomingly, empathically, and powerfully.

> The coach's full presence needs to be there, observed a coach. "[That presence] is to provide a big enough container to take everything in." [The client] needs to know that there's a spine there, not just a friendly, nice, empathetic energy, but one that can question, push back—a clear gravitas to the coach.[4]

SELF-AWARENESS

Now we come to the quality of self-awareness. The self-aware coaches do the internal work to understand their boundaries, triggers, gifts, and limitations. In this way, the coaches are able to enter the coaching space authentically and confidently.

How do we increase self-awareness and thereby enhance the safety of the coaching alliance? Very simply, it is by following many of the tenets we propose for our clients. Consistent self-care—the day-to-day activities that engender health and well-being; self-observations and practices that encourage reflection; willingness to examine our successes and our mistakes, and the ability to learn from them are factors that foster self-awareness. Beyond these basic practices, we find coaches regularly include many other activities in their daily routines to support their work. These range from yoga to morning poetry readings. Later in this chapter, we address in more detail the practices coaches use to get themselves into shape mentally, physically, and spiritually that in turn foster greater self-awareness.

We want to point out that self-awareness alone does not lead to action. From careful self-observation, we learn what we want to change as we show up and behave differently. Self-awareness is a catalyst for new thinking, new possibilities, new behaviors, and new outcomes.

WISDOM

The fifth quality or characteristic that our respondents identified was wisdom. The word *wisdom* means more than knowledge. It is accessing the wisdom of a greater intelligence, the wisdom of the ages. It is using all the senses to listen. It is cognitive—and more. Wisdom embraces the domains of body, emotion, and spirit. It is being able to tap into an inner knowing for both the client and the coach. Such wisdom is possible only through the creation of sacred space that is built on connection, self-awareness, trust, and presence. The access to wisdom is the internal process for a coach and a leader; the external process comes from inquiry. By asking questions from a place of curiosity and by being in service to the highest potential of our clients, we coaches allow the leaders to connect to their own authenticity. Then the insights and answers will emerge.

The wise coach knows when to be silent; when to challenge; when to observe as the client moves into space and behavior that might derail; and when to intervene with humor, a story, a poem, or a practice. Coaches who call on their wisdom will tap into their knowledge of human nature, organizations, and the universe. In this sense, wisdom is bigger than both coach and client. It is capturing and practicing lessons of time immemorial. It is best used to know ourselves as coaches in service to client-leaders who join with us in their own development to become more humane, more competent leaders.

Does the coach create sacred space with every client? Absolutely not! We all have our off days—coach and leader alike. There are times when we are distracted and when the client is distracted or when conditions are too hectic to engage. There are times when the coach is grabbed by the leader's story and loses perspective. Occasionally, trust erodes. When such conditions show up—on either side of the relationship—we maintain that it is the coach who is called on to return to center and to seek discernment around the commitment to the relationship. If the client disengages, we coaches should seek to understand why and should endeavor to re-enroll. When we as coaches are harried, we should return to the practices that generate the capacity for creating sacred space.

WAYS FOR COACHES TO GET IN SHAPE

This discussion leads us to the second part of the chapter: how does the coach get in shape for creating sacred space?

In our brief online survey, we asked leadership coaches about the practices they engage in to support their work. The list ranged from walking, journaling, meditating, practicing yoga, and praying—the more popular practices—to weight lifting, horseback riding, and practicing Reiki (table 3.2).

A common thread among all coaches who talked with us was that they engaged in those practices not only to create their own sacred space but also as a method of getting in condition to coach. If we believe that as coaches our work is about our own growth, then the practices that allow us to create our own sacred space so that we can access our own

Table 3.2   Leadership coaching survey: Practices

Please check all of the practices in which you regularly engage (at least 3 times per week) and include the number of hours each week you engage in those practices.

Practice

1.	Journaling
2.	Sitting meditation (30 minutes or more)
3.	Yoga
4.	Stopping
5.	Prayer
6.	Tai Chi
7.	Aikido
8.	Poetry or inspirational readings
9.	Walking (30 minutes or more)
10.	Running
11.	Visualization

What other practices do you regularly commit to (i.e., massage, Rolfing, Reiki), and how often do you engage in those practices?

_____

_____

_____

_____

_____

_____

wisdom will become one of the foundations of our work. If as coaches we can create our own sacred space, then we can genuinely invite our clients to create that space for themselves.

It takes discipline to maintain such practices, and life gets in the way. As coaches and humans, we face the challenges of leading busy lives, being tired, or having too many commitments and daily interruptions—just as our clients do. It is also by creating the discipline to do those practices that we can understand the struggle that our clients go through in their busy lives as they try to create new ways of doing things. We can more consistently stay grounded and be present with our clients as they walk their journey when we have taken the time to be centered in our own day.

The most popular practices mentioned by the coaches interviewed were these:

- Praying
- Walking
- Reading poetry or inspirational writings
- Journaling
- Stopping

PRAYING

Prayer—a conversation with a greater wisdom—was named as the number one practice that coaches engaged in as a daily practice. Prayer is used as a practice for centering, as a time for reflection, and as a time for gratitude. Prayer is the connection between the sacred and the present moment.

WALKING

Used as exercise, as a way of being in nature, or as a meditation, walking was the next practice that coaches mentioned. Taking the time to be connected with nature regularly and walking as a moving meditation provide a structure for pausing in our lives and connecting to our own sacred space.

READING POETRY OR INSPIRATIONAL WRITINGS

Both poetry and inspirational readings can be used in reflective practices, as well as being offered to the leaders we coach. Starting a meditation period with a poem often sparks new learning or observations about one's self and gives food for thought for journaling or self-observation.

JOURNALING

As we record our inner thoughts and use reflective learning, journaling lends itself to slowing down. It allows us to speak from our hearts, to connect to the joy of learning, and the wonder of being a beginner. It gives us a place to be ourselves without the fear of judgment. It allows us to solve problems and to clear our mind for the day so that we can be present with our clients and ourselves.

STOPPING

By taking time out from our busy schedules as we stop or pause, that respite helps us to come back to ourselves, to rediscover day in and day out our sacred space. We stop, recover, and reconnect to our inner sense of ourselves. At Georgetown University, an important component of the leadership coach training program is for our students to take on a new practice in a domain where they want to build capacity, as well as learn a practice that allows them to stop and to pause from the busyness of the day. We ask students to write in a journal so they enhance their self-awareness. For some students, the journal is a welcome developmental tool that allows them to learn about themselves and to discover entrenched beliefs that hinder growth. For others, journaling is a tedious practice and is difficult to begin, much less maintain. That revelation in itself provides a conversation for the coach and the leader in the hour of sacred coaching space. Laura Divine and Joanne Hunt speak about such a stop in their article titled "The Power of Pause":

> There are certain words associated with pausing that we do not hold as positive within our culture. Words such as delay, hesitate, or doubt give us some insight into how pausing can be held as something that delays action, forward movement, or success. Pausing can be interpreted as a lack of decisiveness or a sense of being unsure. As coaches, we need to take into consideration both what frightens people about slowing down...as well as how our culture holds this construct. Together these two forces create resistance in our ability to value and build this competency as an individual or as a society.[5]

By experiencing the resistance as well as the joy of pausing and reflective learning, the coaches will better use those practices in their own lives before introducing them to the clients they serve. We want to emphasize, as well, that pausing or finding sacred time in one's routine is an important concept not only for the coach, but also for leaders, many of whom rarely come up for air during the grueling work day. When practiced consistently, the pause is generative and refreshing.

When we interviewed coaches, we learned that what seems to matter most is the consistency of the practice. Like the leaders who have competing commitments, our respondents acknowledged the challenge of keeping the intention and commitment of practice. How did those coaches bring consistency into the relentless demands of day-to-day living? For most, it required another rigor: scheduling the time. When they put the practice on their calendar, they found it easier to stick to their commitment. One coach we surveyed said, "When I get too busy with clients, secular space gets in the way. Being unfocused, my own resistance gets in the way of connecting, [of] being congruent."[6]

The coach-respondent also remarked, "Practices are patterns of attitude and habits. [Because] we experience and understand it, [we're] in the position to help others to create patterns for the way they want to be."[7]

Jim Loehr and Tony Schwartz more fully describe this practice of brief periods of stopping for renewal and its applicability for leaders in their article, "The Making of the Corporate Athlete,"[8] which appears in the January 2001 issue of the *Harvard Business Review*. In their research, Schwartz and Loehr found that world-class athletes and top executives engage in a cycle of work and renewal to foster excellent performance over time. By incorporating downtime in a busy day and thereby managing their energy, the authors posit that top leaders will reap multiple benefits.

So again, as we coaches build in the practice of stopping, we want to ask leaders how they can schedule time to walk, to write in a journal, simply to breathe, to go to a gym, to eat lunch regularly, or to attend a yoga class. We should ask this question: what will leaders do to fulfill their intentions to themselves and to build a capacity for future "right" action (as they define it)?

CONCLUSION

As coaches, we do the following:

- Connect to build and sustain relationship.
- Engender trust to allow the client's truth to emerge.
- Self-observe and take on practices to generate self-awareness.
- Demonstrate presence that is open, grounded, and optimistic.
- Access wisdom to serve the client's agenda for a more effective and generative leadership stance.

To be sure, other ingredients can help the coach facilitate a safe, supportive environment, but we feel the ones we've discussed in this article are integral. By practicing those tenets, coaches create environments of self-examination and of learning for future success. By introducing leaders to the practice of creating time for reflecting; by accessing their wisdom and their capacity for growth and action; and by using the tools of self-care—be it through prayer, meditation, exercise, or pauses—coaches can more fully engage and hold a *sacred space* for the leaders whom we coach.

NOTES

1. Richard Strozzi-Heckler, *Being Human at Work: Bringing Somatic Intelligence into Your Professional Life* (Berkeley, CA: North Atlantic Books, 2003).
2. Jacqueline Wilson Cranford, in discussion with Clarice Scriber, May 9, 2005.
3. Beatriz Boccalandro, in discussion with Clarice Scriber, May 13, 2005.
4. Ibid.
5. Joanne Hunt and Laura Divine, "The Power of Pause," Integral Institute of Canada, 2002.
6. Zayd Abdul-Karim, in discussion with Clarice Scriber, March 17, 2005.
7. Ibid.
8. Loehr, Jim and Tony Schwartz, "The Making of the Corporate Athlete," *Harvard Business Review*, January 2001.

CHAPTER 4

CULTURES IN COACHING

KAREN CURNOW

HAVE YOU EVER HAD MOMENTS in your coaching when you hit a roadblock that absolutely stumped you? Where you "missed" your client in some fundamental way? Where you suddenly realized that your client thinks in a very different way than you do? Most coaches have had experiences like this.

Over years of training coaches, I have seen many who are skilled listeners, who ask powerful questions, who offer observations to provoke awareness, and who generally demonstrate solid coaching competencies but are still blind to the cultural influences right in front of them. This blindness can, and often does, limit both trust and the depth of coaching conversations.

We can look to our clients to show us when we are caught in our cultural blindness. If we're lucky, it will be obvious. Our client may look confused or actually say something about the disconnect he or she is experiencing with us. Most of the time, the reaction is more subtle and indirect than that. We may see our clients resisting a conversation they said they wanted to have. They may also respond "politely" (and superficially) to our unintentionally culturally ignorant comments or questions.

While these reactions could happen for multiple reasons, it is possible that we are operating from the assumption that our clients are like us when they are not. We could be blind to a difference that matters to them. We're not talking about a difference of opinion; we're talking about a different way of seeing, thinking, believing, acting, and valuing. The cost of being ignorant of those differences is the clients' diminished trust in the coach's ability to really understand and support them, which is likely to result in shallow coaching.

We all have our moments of cultural blindness, but with intentional focus and practice, we can lessen how often we fall into this blindness and learn how to move away from ethnocentric thinking that can trap our clients and us.

In this chapter, we will look at how culture is constantly playing in the background for us and our clients, how it affects coaching, and how we can use aspects of culture to deepen our clients' learning.

WHAT IS CULTURE AND WHY DOES IT MATTER?

Culture is the way we have been taught to see and engage with the world. Each of us is multi-cultured, reflecting not only our country culture, but also our regional, family, religious, ethnic, generational, organizational, and other cultures. Even if we choose to operate differently than we were taught, we are nonetheless influenced by that acculturation. When coaching, we are always reaching across these different cultural backgrounds. We are *always* coaching across cultures.

As mentioned above, including an awareness of cultures as part of your coaching can help build trust while deepening your coaching impact. Ignoring the relevance of culture runs the risk of keeping your coaching and your client in too small a frame, since your client is not the only source of his or her actions, challenges, and viewpoints. Deliberately spotlighting the cultural influences in your client's life helps prevent the self-defeating tendency of clients to think that "it's all my fault" and keeps the coaching realistic and future-focused. While we might imagine that our clients' thoughts and actions are based on their own conscious choices, in fact larger cultural forces are always influencing every individual we coach.

That said, we have to be careful not to devolve into stereotyping. Stereotyping occurs when we oversimplify, assuming that people will behave and think in a certain way *because* of their membership in a particular group. This rigid view does not acknowledge the individual shifts that come with living a full life. Cultural awareness is also not to be used as an excuse or justification for a way of being, but as one way to understand the larger forces that may be influencing your client.

For example, I worked with a client who was convinced that something was wrong with him (that he was a "case" to be fixed). He had received feedback about his tendency to speak very directly without attention to the impact of his words and was struggling to be less blunt. When we looked at where he had learned to be so direct, he could see more clearly that his bluntness made perfect sense, given his family and national heritage, his past professional experiences, and his new, foreign location. This awareness removed the sting of self-doubt that had actually paralyzed his learning. Acknowledging the cultural influences opened up the possibility for change.

Recognizing the larger influences in a person's life helps provide context, compassion, and connection. Without this cultural recognition, the coach is doomed to coach from a disconnected perspective. When we understand that cultures strongly influence our clients in ways they perhaps cannot see, we open possibilities for change, learning, and effective action that are more generative.

Recognizing our own cultural conditioning is also imperative for coaches. Our cultures are reflected in our internal responses and external comments, in how we are "present" with our clients (whether we are in person, on the computer, or on the phone), in the coaching model that we use, and in the kinds of questions we can imagine. In an August 2012 interview, Julio Olalla (founder and president of Newfield Network and a pioneer in transformational learning) suggests, "So many have lost the capacity to see that your thinking is not your thinking. It is *our* thinking.... Although there will be modifications here and there, the way US Americans ask questions is typically different and more utilitarian than the way Venezuelans do, and New Yorkers' questions are different from Californians' questions." Just like our clients, we as coaches have simply accepted and privileged without question certain ways of being as a result of our cultural history. If we don't recognize our own cultural norms, we will be unable to leverage them when working with clients, where the contrast in cultures can sometimes open up new perspectives.

While coaches don't have to become experts in every culture, it can be helpful to learn about the cultures that have influenced your client. This might include learning about a person's history, heritage, or geographical roots. It may also include learning more about the visible and invisible norms in your client's organizational culture. If a coach works with a leader without understanding the pressures and tendencies inherent in his or her company culture, the coach could potentially suggest practices and actions to the client that are not sustainable within that culture.

If the coach ignores the impact and importance of culture for coach and client, the client may not feel fully seen and the coach may misread the client's real issues.

CULTURE AS AN ICEBERG

In his seminal book, *Beyond Culture* (1976), Edward T. Hall proposes that culture is like an iceberg, with the tip above the surface representing the small part of culture that you can see (external elements of culture) and a much larger part below the surface representing what you cannot see (internal elements).

External elements of culture are those that are often explicitly learned, conscious, and more easily changed. They include characteristics such as dress, language, behaviors (for example, how close one stands to others or how direct one is in giving feedback), operational codes of conduct for work, religious or holiday rituals, gestures, and preferred aesthetics, among others.

Internal elements of culture are those that are implicitly learned, often unconscious, and therefore not as easily changed. They include aspects such as education, values, beliefs (organizational, religious, and political, for example), history, work ethic, and concepts of leadership, fairness, and beauty.

The connection between internal and external elements of culture is clear: internal or invisible aspects of culture (beliefs, values, etc.) help manifest the visible, external facets and surface behaviors that serve as cultural markers.

Now imagine that both coach and client come together with their "icebergs," each making assumptions, drawing conclusions, and speaking based on their visible and invisible cultural norms. But where do icebergs hit first when they collide? Below the surface. In coaching, this cultural collision may create discomfort or a tug-of-war feeling in the coaching conversation. Why? Because values or beliefs collide below the surface—well before anything shows up in behaviors above the surface. Considering these uncomfortable moments as possibly resulting from cultural differences can help the coach recognize what is happening and enable a shift in approach.

WAKING UP FROM ETHNOCENTRIC THINKING: THE ETHNORELATIVE COACH

To be more culturally astute, the coach needs to make a shift from an *ethnocentric* to an *ethnorelative* perspective. Ethnorelativism means seeing the legitimacy and value of multiple cultures, while ethnocentrism is the belief in the inherent superiority of one's own culture. For coaches, this distinction is critical. In Coaching: An Ethnorelative, Not Just Global, Profession, Liora Rosen explains that an ethnorelative point of view requires coaches to accept the existence of culturally different ways of thinking and operating, expand their own worldview to understand and be understood across cultural boundaries, and act in culturally relevant ways to shift smoothly between cultures (Rosen 2011).

In the book *Coaching Across Cultures*, Philippe Rosinski adds that in ethnorelativism, "you perceive cultural differences as inevitable, and you acknowledge that your worldview is not central to everyone's reality. Yet you don't feel threatened, but instead become curious and eager to learn about differences....Importantly, you do it without giving up your own integrity. You become more flexible without changing who you are" (Rosinski 2003).

Some may argue that there is no need for ethnorelativism since we are becoming more homogeneous as technology connects all parts of the globe. But evidence exists that shows this is not in fact true. In his July 2010 TEDGlobal TEDTalk, *"Listening to Global Voices,"* Ethan Zuckerman (cofounder of Global Voices and researcher at Harvard's Berkman Center for Internet and Society) suggests that we think everyone is coming together in some "imaginary cosmopolitanism," but the reality is we still spend most of our time tweeting and blogging within our own cultural group, communicating with people who are like us (Zuckerman 2010). We think we are all becoming one global culture, but we're not. If we as coaches think that everyone thinks the way we do as a result of today's technologically connected world, we are kidding ourselves and are almost sure to fall prey to ethnocentric blindness.

STRATEGIES FOR USING CULTURE IN COACHING

Use the iceberg model. Once we create an ethnorelative context, we can then use specific strategies to bring culture into our coaching. The iceberg model provides a simple structure that allows us to work intentionally with both internal and external elements of culture. We can directly observe our clients' behaviors and characteristics "above the surface." We can also work below the surface as we get our clients to consider their motivations and values—then support them above the surface as they put into practice those values they care about most deeply.

Sometimes, simply pointing out or asking about aspects of culture can make what was invisible to our client visible, since it can be hard to see one's own cultural norms. Commenting on this phenomenon, Olalla said, "As I have coached in the United States over the years, people have often asked me, 'How did you see that?' The logic in the US culture was that I was brilliant for noticing a tendency. In reality, I was simply making observations that Americans couldn't make because I am a very different cultural observer. I was able to see things that many people within their own culture could not."[1]

In my own practice, I remember working with a client years ago who laughed each time we touched on a sensitive topic that was difficult for her. When I shared with her my observation of this behavior, she revealed that that was how she had been taught to deal with challenges—both in her family and in her company (where people were expected to always be in an optimistic mood). These messages about literally "laughing off" difficulties came from two cultural sources and had a strong grip on her. In our coaching, she was able to acknowledge her "teachers," choose the way she wanted to operate going forward, and begin the process of developing new skills and approaches based on her expanded awareness. Being aware of this cultural norm allowed her to break free from a patterned response.

At times, we are aware that we are blind in some way but are unsure how. We can't name it. The iceberg model can provide some topics for exploration. For example, to better understand the concerns that our clients bring to coaching, we can ask them about the milestones in their company's history that affected them, the core values they find most important, or the role of education and learning in their lives.

Finally, we can use this model as a way to open a direct conversation about culture. By simply sharing this model with our clients, we can ask them to teach us about themselves so that we can serve them more completely.

In addition to using the iceberg model as a way to better understand your clients and the cultures that have helped form them, you can also use the following cross-cultural skills and approaches in your coaching.

Clarify that there are multiple cultures present—in the client and in the coach—and acknowledge with your client the impact that may have on the coaching.

Don't assume—ask. Rather than assuming that your clients would operate in the same way you would, ask questions to get to know their cultural influences. Who are their heroes? What values do they cherish most deeply? What is their relationship with time? With nature? What does failure mean?

Do your homework. Research your client's cultures. In addition to asking our clients, we can learn about our clients' cultures in many ways, such as doing text and publication research, reading books, watching movies from or about their traditions, or speaking with others from that culture.

Acknowledge that some cultural concepts will be difficult to "get." Since we can't be all things to all people, we will have moments when we just can't seem to understand an aspect of our client's culture. Admitting this and trusting the foundation of cultural awareness and acceptance you have built with your client will be important in these moments.

Observe, observe, observe. Notice your clients' behaviors. What is always on your client's radar? What is never noticed? Your observations may provide you with evidence of your client's cultural focuses, preferences, and blind spots. Offering an alternative perspective through your cultural lens may expand what your clients can see—including what options they can see for responding effectively to the situation they are in.

Be aware of nonverbal messages you are giving and receiving (including gestures, facial expressions, body postures, and vocal expressions). Some of these nonverbal signals are universal, while others are culturally bound. The research of Susana Bloch (on breathing, posture, and facial expressions), Paul Ekman (on facial microexpressions), and others highlights universal nonverbal signals, particularly for such basic emotions as anger, sadness, fear, surprise, disgust, joy, and tenderness.

There are also some nonverbal messages that are specific to a culture. Ignoring the cultural aspects of nonverbal cues can lead to misinterpretations that can limit a leader's and a coach's effectiveness. For example, a manager I worked with was consistently frustrated by one of her staff member's insubordinate, defiant behaviors. When giving her reasons for her assessment, the manager claimed insubordination whenever she delegated anything to her, although the employee did complete the assigned tasks. Probing further, we discovered that the actual behavior was not in the staff member's words at all (she never actually said "no" to her boss), but in her nonverbal action of shaking her head when she accepted a new task. Come to find out, the staff member was from a part of India where this shaking of the head is quite a normal way of showing agreement, and the manager was from the United States, where the same nonverbal message indicates disagreement. Understanding this simple cultural difference changed everything for the manager and helped her let go of the resentment and frustration that had been building for many months.

Culturally linked nonverbals can also be found in vocal cadence, projection, inflection, and tone. When one client I coached seemed to always speak with a harsh tone, I found myself wondering why he was so angry all the time. (This reaction showcased my own cultural assessment that his tone was "harsh" and that that meant he was angry.) My assessments and my coaching shifted when I realized that the normal intonation and pacing of his native language was monotone, fast, and abrupt. Although his English was quite good, he had held onto the vocal norms of his native language. Recognizing this enabled me as his coach to release my culturally bound interpretations of his vocal habits and then serve him more effectively.

Live a day in their shoes. Ask your clients to walk you through a typical day, with a focus on the impact of their cultures (racial, family, country, organizational). Listen deeply for how their cultures influence their thinking and therefore their actions. Ask them to "translate" both verbal and nonverbal messages that you don't understand.

Assess the important cultural tendencies. Invite your clients to assess their cultural tendencies using the following cultural dichotomies. Where would you assess yourself? What might the differences suggest for your coaching?

Individualism_____	Collectivism
Equality_____	Status
Informality_____	Formality
Future Orientation_____	Heritage/Past
Time as a resource_____	Timelessness
Achievement_____	Fate
Direct/Assertiveness_____	Indirect

Other differences important to your client?

_____

Be aware of additional challenges expatriate leaders face. Internationally mobile leaders will experience a cultural and emotional adaptation process in each new location where they are assigned. They will need multicultural competencies when working internationally, as they face the added demands of leading multicultural and possibly geographically dispersed teams in addition to their other leadership responsibilities. Coaches who support these international leaders need to be aware of these demands and become culturally literate not just about the country in question but also about the nature of international living.

SUMMARY

Today's coaches are always coaching across cultures. Being blind to this fact can limit our learning and our coaching. Maintaining an ethnorelative perspective and using approaches that acknowledge internal and external aspects of culture raise the competence and impact of leadership coaches.

When we consider culture, our built-in multiculturalism, and cultural influences on our thoughts and actions, we see through a new lens that can increase awareness for both coach and client. With awareness, our clients can step into their leadership more powerfully—and we as coaches can better see our clients, meet them where they are, and serve them most effectively.

NOTE

1. Julio Olalla, personal interview conducted by Karen Curnow, August 10, 2012.

BIBLIOGRAPHY

Bloch, Susana. *Alba of Emotions*. 3d ed. Uqbar, 2008.

Ekman, Paul. *Emotions Revealed: Recognizing Faces and Feelings to Improve Communication and Emotional Life*. 2d ed. New York: Owl Books, 2007.

Hall, Edward T. *Beyond Culture*. New York: Anchor Books, (1977) 1989.

Rosen, Liora. "Coaching: An Ethnorelative, Not Just Global, Profession." *Coaching World* (e-zine). October 2011. www.coachfederation.org/articles.

Rosinski, Philippe. *Coaching Across Cultures*. Yarmouth, Maine: Intercultural Press, 2003.

Zuckerman, Ethan. TEDGlobal TEDTalk, "Listening to Global Voices," (Ethan Zuckerman, cofounder of Global Voices and researcher at Harvard's Berkman Center for Internet and Society), July 2010.

CHAPTER 5

EASTERN INFLUENCE ON COACHING

RANDY CHITTUM

THIS CHAPTER IS NOT MEANT TO BE a scholarly treatment of the topic, but instead an effort to build awareness that coaching principles, philosophy, and practice are heavily influenced by, or at least related to, the diverse notion of "Eastern thinking." It is my hope that it may inspire further thinking and exploration on the part of the reader.

Writing requires linearity and reductionism, both of which are at least partly contradictory to the philosophy of Eastern thought. Know that all the parts are connected to all the other parts. There is a line in *The Tao* that essentially says, "He who speaks of the Tao, knows not the Tao." That which is most important may be well beyond the words we use to express it. It is with this full awareness that we forge ahead!

For this writing, I have reduced Eastern thinking into its parts, as suggested in Table 5.1, which is a somewhat generalized and simplified version.

BEING

The first, and perhaps most, significant way in which Eastern thought appears to influence or be aligned with coaching is in the domain of "being versus doing." Eastern thought takes the position that we are more than our actions, more than what we do. What matters most is who we are in the process of being, and in some cases, becoming. What we do is merely the reflection of who we are being.

Table 5.1 Eastern/Western thinking

Eastern thinking	Western thinking
I am who I am	I am what I do
I am connected	I am isolated
Nonattachment	Attached to beliefs and possessions
Wholeness	Parts
Lightness	Seriousness
Journey	Destination
Simplicity	Complexity
Mindful and Present	Distracted

Coaches similarly believe that the leverage in creating sustainable change is in changing the person, not the behavior. The behavior is an extension or symptom of who we are. Who we are is the core. As you might suspect, questions such as those that follow are deep, personal, and rewarding. A willingness to delve deeply into questions like these is one door into the sustainable and transformative change that most coaches seek.

Consider, who am I? When you sift away the roles, the history, the descriptors, who am I? If I am not my job, and not my relationships, then who am I? If I am not my body, then who am I? Who am I beyond personality, desires, and dreams? There are those who believe that a life's work is involved in answering and subsequently dealing with the implications of those answers. I believe that this is a conversation that coaches can and should have with leaders. Certainly not all leaders are interested or ready for this, but on average I think we sell many of our leaders short in this regard. I find that many of the leaders I coach are craving purpose and greater understanding. I am not shy about introducing questions in an attempt to get closer to the core. In an attempt to enter this domain I might ask questions like these. What do you imagine your enduring legacy to be? Who are you at your core and what do you stand for in the world? What matters to you? I have pondered, considered, meditated, and discussed such questions for more than 20 years and they still provide me new awareness and possibility.

I once had a teacher who told me that I could choose to either follow conventional wisdom and "don't just sit there, do something," or follow another path expressed in "don't just do something, sit there." Eastern thinking values the promise of stillness, whether manifested through meditation or truly simply doing nothing. One of my favorite Zen sayings expresses this—"sitting here quietly doing nothing, spring comes and the grass grows by itself." Many leaders are caught in a cycle of "deliverables" and doing. More rarely seen is the person who takes the time to be still, or pause. That person reaps the reward of a calm mind and presence, enlightened perspective, and lightness. Ample research points to the significance of our physical presence in leadership, the importance of healthy perspective, and the relationship of daily stress to our effectiveness and creativity. We have quickly forgotten the lessons of "sharpen your saw." It is not uncommon for a coach to work with leaders to help them practice pausing as a way to stay more centered. I have asked leaders to develop a practice of being quiet (internally and externally) for a few minutes several times a day. I have asked leaders to learn and practice basic breathing and meditation exercises. I have asked leaders to participate in a yoga class that I offer for leaders who I think are ready to benefit from a program. I have asked leaders to take a walk for 15 minutes each workday and practice noticing. Any activity request is obviously specific to the leader and his/her needs and abilities. The significant point I think is to risk where appropriate to invite leaders into this domain of experience.

CONNECTION AND WHOLENESS

Another way in which Eastern thought and coaching are aligned is in the significance of dealing with the whole as more than the sum of its parts. Simply stated, Eastern thought has maintained its focus on understanding the universe in its entirety where the Western approach has been to use science to break it into its parts in an attempt to understand it. It is fascinating to note that through the understandings afforded us from quantum physics and other "new sciences," that both schools of thought appear now to be arriving at the same place. This sense of wholeness extends beyond the "I." As the earlier quote so beautifully expresses, the wholeness extends to the universe. In this way, we are universally whole. In practical terms, leaders who can see beyond the needs of their team or department represent a form of wholeness. Leaders who can see beyond the needs of their organization to the greater needs of the community represent at a higher level. In a personal way, leaders who understand that they are connected to others through an invisible web are likely to be more thoughtful in how they behave and therefore how they impact others.

Being part of a whole raises issues of self that are present in both Eastern thinking as well as coaching. The "self" is, in most Eastern thinking, an illusion—but one in which we dearly believe. The "self" is home to the ego and pride, to name a few inhabitants.

Coaches are often faced with the challenge of working with leaders who think that if she can just learn how to present more powerfully, or be more assertive, or listen more, then all will be well. Particularly in high-pressure business environments, our mostly successful clients are taught to identify and then solve problems.

Coaching, with its emphasis on sustainable change and development, will likely push beyond the limits of the "parts" approach identified earlier. Instead, the coach will be interested in the entire experience of the client who wants to be more assertive. What belief systems does she hold that interfere with her performance? How does she explain things to herself? What emotions does she carry before and during an opportunity to be more assertive? What "shows up" in her body in terms of stress, and how does she hold her body to enable or interfere with her desired goal of more assertive behavior? Finally, what skills or information might be missing that would enable her? In short, the coach is interested in the whole person.

Another way in which coaches coach the whole person is that we may not be exclusively focused on the person at work. We understand and honor that she is more than an employee or a leader. Who is she as a person and how does that support or challenge her in achieving her stated goal?

One of the most commonly expressed interests for leaders in coaching is in achieving balance. For many, the world of work has taken a disproportionate place in our lives. We have neglected our families, our health, our communities, and our spirits for too long. Those being coached often come with this awareness but with little understanding of how to make changes. Eastern thinkers have had a lot to say about balance. Perhaps the most insightful antidote to an unbalanced life is presence. The notion of "being where you are" is profound and challenging for most of us. The simple act of attending and "not-doing" can be a significant life challenge. Similarly powerful is the notion of being wholehearted in our lives. To do everything wholeheartedly is another path to presence and balance.

In general, I believe that the leaders I have encountered over the past twenty years prove the point. The leaders I have known who are most powerful exhibit the qualities of wholeheartedness, balance, wholeness, and an understanding of their connection to others. The leaders I have known who are least powerful do not often demonstrate those same qualities. One person always stands out to me. He is a very senior executive in a large company. This company is the market leader in its industry. If you were to ask 100 people in this company, who is the best pure leader in the company, at least 90 would come back with his name. What is the source of this influence? He is completely present when he is with you. He separates from his desk, phone, computer,

Blackberry, and so on and actually makes you feel as if you matter to him. He is vigorous and wholehearted. He demonstrates outstanding and consistent energy. In part his energy level is a result of a balanced and healthy life, but it is also a result of uncompromising belief in the importance of the purpose. I have heard him talk compellingly about the importance of going home and then being home to hundreds of his leaders. He is compelling in this case because he believes it. Finally, I notice how simply he lives by a set of self-authored principles. You rarely have to guess how he might respond to something because you so clearly know where he stands.

ATTACHMENT

Letting go is often a fertile area for coaches and is one of the most profound ideas to come from Eastern thinking. Our inability to let go is the source of enormous suffering for many. Think about all the things to which you are attached—relationships, work, friends, possessions, status, pride, ideas, and opinions? The list is unending. The rise in popularity of emotional intelligence has put this issue into the conversation in some organizations. As a coach, I find that the source of suffering is very often an attachment. Beyond needless suffering, the consequence of attachment is limited possibility. Coaches then, are often in the conversation that creates the possibility of "letting go." As you might imagine, it is an area that is fraught with fear and uncertainty.

Similarly, one of the biggest attachments I see is to my sense of who I am. Sometimes, a coach is working to get a client to let go of their attachment to their very identity. Few things are more frightening than truly "reinventing" oneself as reinvention requires a letting go of "who you were" to become "who you wish to be." The ability to consciously choose who to be is the pinnacle of living a masterful and purposeful life—precisely because the risk of letting go seems so high.

The attachment to sense of self is arguably in part a developmental issue and therefore not everyone is developmentally ready to discuss concepts like true self-authoring. For those leaders who are ready, their coach has to also be ready and ideally have begun the journey. This is another of those areas where the coach would benefit from having a coach.

Related to letting go is the concept of acceptance. Acceptance is different from settling or giving up. Acceptance comes in that graceful space where one is able to release oneself from the hold of emotion that is limiting them. In the world of leaders, acceptance often comes after a huge effort to change or achieve something. After the effort, there can be a place where the client accepts whatever outcome awaits. I find that leaders often struggle to be unattached to outcomes. A degree of attachment to outcomes can serve a leader, up to a point. It eventually becomes unhealthy for the leader who can never let go of the outcome.

LIGHTNESS

What naturally flows from a sense of acceptance and letting go? I believe a sense of perspective and lightness. In this case, think of lightness as playfulness, not taking yourself or events so seriously. You can imagine that the person able to do this is more likely to be adept at acceptance. It is possible that the universe is absurd and unpredictable. The desire to feel a sense of control over it, or even over oneself, is a potential source of suffering. The master has figured this out and learned to laugh and let go.

How does this present in coaching? The leaders I work with are often rooted in the desire for the control mentioned earlier. They crave a linear, rational model that allows for planning and predictable outcomes. They may be unable to change course, even though they tout the benefits and even the necessity of change. The desire for control generates suffering and, I would argue, lost productivity. It is the leader with perspective, who holds plans lightly, who is most beloved and effective. President Dwight D. Eisenhower was quoted as saying, "[S]trategic plans are worthless. Strategic planning is invaluable."[1] This implies the truth in the notion that the product of planning and work should be held lightly and, furthermore, that the benefit in this work is the connections and the process.

JOURNEY

Those even tangentially aware of "Eastern thought" are likely familiar with quotes such as the one mentioned earlier. The notion that the journey matters as much or more than the destination has found its way into the popular Western lexicon. Unfortunately, popular awareness has not necessarily led to popular adoption. Organizations, with their relentless focus on achieving specific outcomes are seemingly more focused than ever on the destination over the journey. The journey is forgotten in pursuit of the next objective. One of the ways I get leaders to pay attention to this is to ask questions about learning. For example, at the end of this project what would you like to know better about yourself? As you engage in this work, what opportunities do you see along the way for you to practice new ways of being or behaving?

Tim Gallwey[2] is noted for saying that coaches need merely to help their clients pay close attention to the teacher, experience. Experience is the teacher, and as we learned in grade school, learning involves paying close attention to the teacher. It is notable that the experience is the journey. Perhaps the art of coaching is simply to help clients make meaning from their experiences, leading to new ways of being. The meaning making, or learning, requires at least some attention be paid to the experience or journey.

SIMPLICITY

Perhaps more than any other single word, Eastern thought might be known for its emphasis on keeping things simple. Simple is believed to be profound. Simple is believed to be elegant. Simple is a more accurate representation of that which is true. I see clients every day who are overwhelmed by the complexity in their lives, particularly at work. We have come to believe that we need all manner of technology and infrastructure to manage our complex lives. For some it is even a badge of honor. Yet, the most commonly taught strategy in organizations today might be—do what you are good at and focus on a few critical objectives. This is an organizational version of—keep it simple.

I have come to believe that it is our complexity that keeps us safe. Simplicity is dangerous, too close to the truth, leaving nowhere to hide. In some ways, it goes back to the "who am I" question. Without the complexity, the self-importance, who am I? If I am fearful of that question and its possible answers, I may be well served by keeping my life complex.

MINDFULNESS

Similar to the expression "be here now," mindfulness suggests an ongoing awareness of both internal processes (emotional, cognitive, and physical) as well as environmental factors. It is a form of "active noticing," without doing. It often takes the form of meditation, though the master is mindful at all times. It is "non-doing" in action. It deals with the possibility that *this* is it. Everything real is contained in this moment and if I am not present to it, I am missing not just this moment but everything.

In coaching, this is evident in many ways. The most pedestrian is that all of us live distracted lives. Living in either the future (possibilities, planning) or the past (assessments, emotions), but so rarely in the present. Put this in the category of simple and not easy. Mindfulness is to be cultivated and the more desire one has for it, the more elusive it may be.

Leaders often express the desire to have something we are currently calling "executive presence." I fear that we have substituted the expression for charisma, and consequently we have little understanding of what it actually means. In the context of mindfulness and presence, executive presence would start with sharing the same moment with others. To share in that moment I have to be present in it. However, the sources of interference to being present and mindful are too numerous to list. There is great power for coaches who are able to have this conversation with their clients.

CONCLUSION

The reader is reminded that this chapter was not intended to be a full discussion of "Eastern thought" and in fact that the very term "Eastern thought" borders on slighting in its simplicity. However, the similarities between coaching and Eastern thought are too obvious to be ignored. It is my hope that by shining a feeble light on the relationship, we will be better able to consider the distinctions and possibilities that exist.

NOTES

1. John T. Woolley and Gerhard Peters, "The American Presidency Project," President Dwight D. Eisenhower, remarks at the National Defense Executive Reserve Conference, November 14, 1957 (Santa Barbara: University of California, Gerhard Peters Database), http://www.presidency.ucsb.edu/ws/?pid=10951 (accessed November 13, 2007).
2. *Tim Gallwey*, "The Inner Game: Learning to Get Out of Your Own Way" (presentation, annual conference of International Coach Federation, Orlando, FL, 1999).

CHAPTER 6

THE CASE FOR CULTIVATING PRESENT-MOMENT SELF-AWARENESS IN LEADERS AND COACHES

STEVE HELLER

ASK MOST COACHES WHAT OUR WORK IS ABOUT, what it is that we do, and you will likely get some variation of the following: we assist our clients in getting from where they are today to where they want to be. Whether the coaching objective is concrete or more vague, whether the challenge is tactical or aspirational, whether the goal is a solution to a problem, the overcoming of some obstacle, or addresses some element of personal transformation, we generally see our work as being about helping our client find his or her way from some point A to some point B. And, while there is truth to such a characterization, and while the work on this level is important and useful and necessary, I maintain that there is always something much more fundamental going on in an effective coaching relationship.

And what is going on is this: The greatest strategy, the most powerful intention, the most profound new way of being will be for naught without the client's ability to catch himself or herself in the moment, to recognize that this moment, right now, presents an opportunity to employ that new strategy, to deliver on that stated intention, to show up in that new way. That is, our work, no matter what else it might seem to be about, is always fundamentally about helping our clients develop their capacity for self-awareness in the present moment. Clients' ability to be both in the action and look at themselves acting, to be both subject to the given circumstances and able to examine those circumstances and their relationship with them as object, determines whether the new behavior will be exercised or the old, habitual response is launched automatically. Nothing new happens without sufficient present-moment self-awareness to realize that "here comes the trigger; this is one of those moments for which my coaching has prepared me to be on the lookout; now's the time to exercise my new behavior."

In this chapter, we examine the paramount importance of the role that present-moment self-awareness plays for both leaders and coaches. We look at its role in two ways for each of the two players. For just as the coaching engagement itself can be seen as having both the more visible, exterior agenda (getting from point A to point B) and a crucial, though generally less noticeable, interior agenda (the strengthening of the capacity necessary to embody new intentions), so the disciplines of leadership and coaching themselves also each have exterior and interior agendas. We can think of these two agendas as the "doing" agenda and the "being" agenda (or, as Doug Silsbee so aptly refers to them, the "project" and the "curriculum"). In each of these *disciplines*, present-moment self-awareness plays an important role in both of these *agendas*.

DOING LEADERSHIP: THE EXTERIOR AGENDA OF THE LEADER

In their seminal 2002 book *Leadership on the Line: Staying Alive Through the Dangers of Leading*, Ronald Heifetz and Marty Linsky argue that perhaps the most critical competency for a leader is the ability to move back and forth between the dance floor and the balcony, between the role of participant and that of observer,

> making interventions, observing their impact in real time, and then returning to the action. The goal is to come as close as you can to being in both places simultaneously, as if you had one eye looking from the dance floor and one eye looking down from the balcony, watching all the action, including your own. This is a critical point: When you observe from the balcony you must see yourself as well as the other participants. Perhaps this is the hardest task of all—to see yourself objectively.

Oscillating between these two roles is essential to success in meeting the expectation that leaders ensure that the organization both does things right and does the right things. Managing this polarity requires that the leader be not only a dispassionate observer of the system, but also a dispassionate observer of him/herself and his/her role in that system—that is, the leader must demonstrate present-moment self-awareness.

BEING A LEADER: THE INTERIOR AGENDA OF THE LEADER

Given the leader's exterior agenda, one can conclude that a most critical element of a leader's personal development, therefore, involves finding ways of strengthening the ability to step back from the action and observe with a broader perspective in mind. Cultivating the "being of a leader," then, means cultivating the capacity to observe with present-moment self-awareness. Being a leader might be said to be most fundamentally about the way in which one pays attention.

Les Fehmi and Jim Robbins, in *The Open-Focus Brain: Harnessing the Power of Attention to Heal Mind and Body*, identify four very different types of attention and propose that we can train ourselves to be aware of how we are attending and be intentional about which style of attention we choose to employ in any given situation. This versatility in the domain of attention may just be the "secret sauce" of exceptional leadership and the single most important item on the interior agenda of the leader's development.

Consider the case of Alice (I'll call her), a senior vice president at a large trade association in Washington, DC. Alice struggled with what she saw as a serious gap between her expectations of her staff and their performance. She was not getting the results that she wanted on even seemingly straightforward follow-up actions discussed during her weekly staff meetings. By directing her attention to her own behavior in these meetings, Alice came to notice the degree to which she was taking for granted that people understood what she wanted done, and that she was, in fact, failing to be explicit and clear about what she was asking of them. Her personal work then focused on staying present to her own expectations, in real time, noticing when she had something that she wanted someone to pursue, and maintaining the presence of mind to remember to make certain that all of the elements of an effective request were being explicitly expressed. The impact, as she later described it, was enormous. The shift in her attention to the quality of her requests dramatically improved the nature of her relationships with her staff and the overall performance of the team.

In another example, Robert (again, not his actual name), a senior scientist and internationally known leader in his highly technical field, struggled with his frequent inability to maintain his composure and patience when dealing with the demands of his children upon his return home after a long day in the lab. Through work that focused on building his awareness of his state of mind when entering the house and on noticing the relationship between that state of mind and the quality of his subsequent interaction with his children, Robert developed a practice of sitting in his car in the driveway for several minutes of breathing-focused mindfulness meditation before going inside. He reported a gradual but steady decrease in the frequency of incidents of impatience and a noticeable improvement in the quality of his relationship with his kids.

IMPLICATIONS FOR THE LEADER

A leader then, should look for ways, both in the fulfilling of his/her responsibilities to the organization and in his/her personal development efforts, to continually exercise and strengthen the muscle of present-moment self-awareness.

Potential questions for the leader to consider:

- What structures might I put into place to cause me to periodically interrupt what I'm doing and ask myself: Am I, at this moment, on the dance floor or on the balcony, and might I benefit from considering the other perspective?
- How might I build some sort of pause practice into my routine (meditation, yoga, martial arts, other mindfulness practices)?
- To what extent might daily journaling about what I have noticed with regard to my own present-moment self-awareness heighten my powers of attention?
- How might I engage in activities (e.g., artistic endeavors, physical activities, spiritual practices) that trigger the flow state for me (that sense of peak experience involving challenge, intense concentration, and full engagement)?
- How might I explicitly engage my coach in helping me formulate an approach toward strengthening my capacity for present-moment self-awareness?

DOING COACHING:
THE EXTERIOR AGENDA OF THE COACH

One can easily argue that nearly every one of the eleven ICF (International Coach Federation) coaching core competencies stands on a foundation of present-moment self-awareness. Doing coaching effectively means accessing the appropriate tools at the appropriate moments while staying fully present in the conversation. It means letting go of attachment to outcomes and staying firmly rooted in curiosity. It means striking just the right balance between the art and the science of the work so as to invite the client into the flow, creating the space for the client's best work to emerge. It means finding that sweet spot between providing enough challenge (but not *too* much) and enough support (but not *too* much), so that the client can stretch and develop. All of this requires that the coach be simultaneously in the conversation (on the dance floor) and looking *at* the conversation (from the balcony). In a very real sense, the coach models this very capacity through the doing of coaching.

Furthermore, if, as is proposed above, the work of the leader requires that he/she continually develop his/her capacity for present-moment self-awareness, then the coach must challenge the client in ways intended to do just that. The coach's competencies (deep listening, powerful questions, creating awareness, etc.) are focused on helping the client see through new eyes, that is to say, become more reflective and self-aware. Indeed, the self-observations, practices, inquiries, exercises, and structures of support that the coach and client cocreate are, above all else, tools to strengthen that muscle.

BEING A COACH: THE INTERIOR AGENDA OF THE COACH

By now, the parallels between leader and coach are clear. As with the leader, the coach's exterior work demands present-moment self-awareness. As with the leader, the coach's instrument is self. Therefore, the coach must continually engage in the interior work necessary to sustain the ways of being that enable him/her to do the exterior work of the effective coach described above. Obviously, fundamental to that way of being is that very same muscle of awareness. Clearly, if the coach is to model the capacity for present-moment self-awareness through the way in which the coach does coaching, then the coach needs to show up with that capacity.

Like leadership, then, coaching is most fundamentally about the way in which one pays attention. The coach's personal development practices, therefore, need to place a strong emphasis on the ongoing development of the muscle of attention, the muscle of present-moment self-awareness.

In the years since I personally began focusing with intention on developing my own capacity for present-moment self-awareness and in the slightly more than one year that I have been engaged in a daily sitting meditation practice, I have noticed the following about myself and my coaching:

- I seem to be more able to be both *in* the coaching conversation and looking *at* it, which provides me with a much broader range of options to access in the moment, a much richer palette of possibilities from which to draw.
- I am more likely to be mindful of my client's capacity for present-moment self-awareness and to bring more conscious intention to the process of developing suitable "assignments" for the client to consider undertaking.
- I believe I am less judgmental, seeing things less through the lens of black or white, operating less from an either/or perspective.
- I am more likely to preface my observations with qualifiers such as "in my opinion," "it's my belief that," "what I notice about my own reaction is."
- I am living more fully into the daily mantra upon which I stumbled many years ago, namely, "what am I willing to be wrong about today?"

IMPLICATIONS FOR THE COACH

In a very fundamental way, then, the essence of the coach's ongoing personal developmental work must center on the strengthening of the muscle of present-moment self-awareness. Coaches can accumulate tools and techniques, certifications and credentials, instruments and frameworks—clearly, the learning opportunities are unending—but unless the coach can show up for the session and be fully present to the client in every moment of the conversation, be engaged in a way that allows him/her to be both in the dance and on the balcony, then the most powerful of tools will be, at best, a disconnected distraction. The coach must *meet* the client to enable this connection, and that puts a demand on the coach to show up in shape to coach. Present-moment self-awareness is the key to showing up in this way.

Potential questions for the coach to consider:

- What structures might I put into place to cause me to periodically check in with myself to consider whether I am, in this moment, operating from the perspective of the dance floor or the balcony?

- How might my current pause practice (assuming that I have one) be strengthened or made more impactful?
- To what extent might I leverage journaling to help me strengthen my own muscle of present-moment self-awareness?
- What are the activities that trigger the flow state for me? What might I do to increase the opportunity to experience this state more frequently?
- To what extent are the assignments that I offer my coaching clients explicitly designed to assist my clients in exercising the capacity for present-moment self-awareness? Consider, for example, the power of having a client recount a past peak performance experience *in the present tense* as one means of embodying the experience of being fully in the moment.

CONCLUSION

The journey of developing the ability to observe oneself in the moment can be viewed as a process of shrinking the amount of time that it takes us to notice what is happening to us and how we respond. By focusing my attention on my ability to observe myself, I will, over time, move from "As I look back on what happened in that meeting last week, I can now see how my behavior...." to realizing upon walking out of a meeting, "Oh no, I just did it again!" to noticing in the moment, "Ooh, I just got triggered!" and, finally, to thinking, "Here comes the trigger. I can be at choice with respect to how I respond."

As we have seen, this capacity is central to the disciplines of doing leadership and being a leader and of doing coaching and being a coach. We can and must be intentional about developing and strengthening this capacity in ourselves if we are to be optimally effective in our chosen role. The goal is, in the simple but elegant words of the title of Baba Ram Dass's 1971 book on spirituality, yoga, and meditation, to "Be Here Now."

BIBLIOGRAPHY

Chödrön, Pema. *When Things Fall Apart: Heart Advice For Difficult Times.* Boston, MA: Shambhala Publications, 1997.

Dass, Ram. *Remember, Be Here Now.* San Cristobal, NM: Lama Foundation, 1971.

Fehmi, Les and Jim Robbins. *The Open-Focus Brain: Harnessing the Power of Attention to Heal Mind and Body.* Boston, MA: Trumpeter Books, 2007.

George, Bill, Peter Sims, Andrew N. McLean, and Diana Mayer. "Discovering Your Authentic Leadership," *Harvard Business Review* 85, no. 2 (February 2007): 129–138.

Heifetz, Ronald, and Marty Linsky. *Leadership on the Line: Staying Alive Through the Dangers of Leading.* Boston, MA: Harvard Business School Publishing, 2002.

Heller, Stuart, and David Sheppard Surrenda. *Retooling on the Run: Real Change for Leaders with No Time.* Berkeley, CA: Frog Books, 1995.

Kapleau, Roshi Philip. *The Three Pillars of Zen: Teaching, Practice and Enlightenment.* New York, NY: Anchor Books, 1989.

Silsbee, Doug. *Presence-Based Coaching: Cultivating Self-Generative Leaders Through Mind, Body, and Heart.* San Francisco, CA: Jossey-Bass, 2008.

Tan, Chade-Meng. *Search Inside Yourself: The Unexpected Path to Achieving Success, Happiness (and World Peace).* New York, NY: HarperCollins, 2012.

CHAPTER 7

EMBODYING CHANGE

ROSELYN KAY

AS COACHES, WE HELP LEADERS MAKE the changes they seek in order to enhance their leadership, use their talents, and grow their potential. Making the change is one thing; embodying it is another. In our coaching role, we are uniquely positioned to awaken consciousness by shining a light on the body, a rich source of information. The body is a crucial participant in change. It holds history in its cells, and experience and emotions in its muscles. No significant sustainable change happens without it. As a coach, I see the impact of engaging the body is significantly greater than working with story and language alone.

JOURNEY TO EMBODIMENT

We all know about habits. We talk about them often and make resolutions or commitments to change them—and then rarely do. I discovered through my Somatic Coach™ training program at the Strozzi Institute that my habits kept me from embodying positive change. When feeling vulnerable I contracted muscles around my diaphragm, forming an arch backward, creating distance between me and others. This limited my ability to learn and kept me from tapping colleagues for help. This habit lived at a level of consciousness only accessible through the body, a domain I had ignored for a long time.

During a workshop, Richard Strozzi-Heckler, of the Strozzi Institute, said, "Allow your bones to hold you up rather than muscles." I immediately felt my muscles let go of tension. Bones and muscles work in tandem, but when we contract muscles in stress or fear, our breathing, our energy, our listening, and our ability to get into action are affected. My diaphragm muscles tensed when I was afraid or vulnerable, especially when challenged, and this resulted in my moving away from people into negative self-talk. More, the message sent by my body was incongruent with what I was saying. It said, "Move away." My body, unable to lie, gave me away. It reflected my fear and desire to retreat. I couldn't reframe or choose another way. Instead, I moved away to try to figure it out on my own, unwilling to show the vulnerability.

My body in control moved me away from positivity, away from being open, generous, and ready for change. However, upon realizing I could make another choice, I committed to retrain my body to support the changes necessary for growth. After several months of practice, I did it automatically. When I was about to move away out of fear of being vulnerable, I shifted in the moment, dropped my breath deeper into my diaphragm, and relaxed the muscles around the rib cage. I made a connection with the person with whom I felt vulnerable. I could feel my body solidly in the presence I wanted to keep—a positive, strength-based, connected leader ready for possibility.

THE HABIT MACHINE

Change is challenging. Even when we are happy about change, it's difficult to embody something new. Not only do our muscles remember as they gain practice, but our brain develops neural pathways, like ruts made by tires in mud. The muscle memory and neural pathways pull us back to familiar habits, especially when we are under stress. Many leaders will try the practices offered by you or cocreated with you, and despite their best efforts, they will find themselves back in the worn saddle of old habits.

They will speak a commitment to the new way they'll try, and some will even succeed in building this congruence quickly. Others will struggle to engage in activities that will help them embody the leader they want to be. Their habit machines, well oiled for today, are sometimes rusty for tomorrow. There is comfort in habits; they are structures we develop to get through our days, and they are the last things we change. It's uncomfortable; there is risk.

Paying attention to the structure of the body, the alignment of muscles and bones, and inviting the client to make shifts in structure or movement can reveal a narrative that is holding the body back from action. A new narrative that is framed in what is desired along with structural changes to the body can produce action toward a new habit.

The autonomic nervous system, the reactor for fight or flight, triggers our forward or reverse movement when we face discomfort. The fight/flight/freeze response affects our presence and how other people experience us. It feeds our old habits.

Changing is not easy or simple. Once something is part of our repertoire, embodying a new habit doesn't result from the intention to change. It results from actually shifting the way we talk, the language we use, the shape we are, and how we physically engage in action. It's practicing what we preach that builds the competency to be the change we want to be.

KELLY'S STORY

Kelly is transitioning to a new role as a coach. She wants to be a coach who is present for her clients and lives in the moment. As she spoke her commitment, I noticed Kelly's head was facing up. She wasn't making eye contact. It was hard to feel connected to her.

She was invited to take a deep breath and allow her chin to come down slightly and share her commitment again. Her flight response kicked in with a statement, "I can't." With encouragement, she stayed in the new space, allowing the energy to run through her rather than contract. She spoke her commitment again from this place—chin down more, engaged more in her body, and her commitment was delivered with an authenticity easy to connect with. Kelly made a choice to practice noticing when her chin was high, bringing it back into alignment and working to reframe her story, the inner talk that drew her away from connection. Here is what she learned:

> I had previously no awareness that I kept my chin up. I realized I did this because I am very often looking to the next horizon, to what I need to do next, to where I need to be next, to what is expected of me next.
>
> As a result, I am not here with the person in front of me. It was a terrible realization. It made me sick and sad that I had spent so much of my life looking out and beyond, instead of directly facing what is in front of me in the moment. But then I used the UUN (Up Until Now) approach and made a conscious decision to change.
>
> Now, when I notice that my chin is up, I adjust it down. It's so relaxing. I am no longer worrying about what is coming next. All I have to do is right in front of me, and it's usually a very doable task. I don't need to worry that I will lose track of my long-term goals. That is a hardwired strength in me that does

not need more nurturing. Instead, I have this wonderful, simple tool that is always with me and immediately brings me back and makes me remember my beautiful life—the one that's right here in front of me. (Client interview)

As we coach, we help clients identify the inner dialogue supporting their strengths and the dialogue that doesn't. We can help them see what they can't see—the embodied habits in alignment or misalignment with what they care about. We also have to be willing to be conscious of our own habits, those embodied habits that keep us from being the coach we want to be in service to our clients. When we embody what we espouse, we have an easier time helping others do the same.

ELEVATING CONSCIOUSNESS THROUGH THE BODY

Coaching somatically, we are working with the whole self. We are focused on how emotions, thoughts and behaviors are reflected through the body—its musculature, energy flows—and we look for distinct movements that indicate something different than what is reflected through words. Clients are often unaware of the sensations in the body that produce physical contractions associated with fight, flight, freeze responses. When these are brought to awareness, there is surprise. Sometimes a narrative emerges to explain what is happening, providing for a rich conversation about how this narrative shapes the future.

A quick example of how the body plays its role:

1. Think of a time when you felt fully alive and excited and doing something meaningful. When was it? Where were you? As you reflect on this story, notice the shape of your body. What is your structure? How are you sitting? What sensations do you notice? What mood is evoked in you?
2. Now think of a time when things didn't go so well: a time when you felt fear, concern or were upset. What is the shape of your body as you recall this story? What are the thoughts evoked? What mood is stirred?
3. Go back to your fully alive story. Notice the shift in the body. Notice the sensations. What's different? Which of these shapes is likely to bring you to make a new choice or a commitment to act?

Becoming conscious of how our body is structured to support current thoughts and actions makes it possible for us to restructure the body, reframe thoughts, and gain confidence to take new action.

MINDSET AND BODYSET

As you begin your journey to be a successful coach, mindset and bodyset become tools for you to use. Mindset is structure we hold in our mind to make sense of the world. I use the term "bodyset" for the way our body is structured through years of response to fear, joy, and excitement and the way it's framed to create our experience. It shows up in our shape, for example, the chin up, the shoulders tight, or constantly shifting eyes. The structure of both mind and body influences the way we know and the way we behave. Leaders conscious of their bodyset, as Kelly's story shows, can open the door to their ability to reframe how they are shaped and better respond to today to create a better future.

MARYANNE'S STORY

Mindset and bodyset exploration is a powerful combination as is shown by Maryanne's story. Looking at Maryanne, you'd assess her as a bright, beautiful woman, a strong and capable business leader. However, she wasn't living as confidently as she appeared. Life had thrown her some hurdles: an ill husband and two daughters to nurture largely on her own. She had disowned parts of herself to maintain control of things.

- She was unaware of her practice of pulling her arms tightly to her chest as if to protect her heart and holding her legs close together, all contracted in a way that limited her ability to fully express her strength. The impact was a life lived and business driven by necessity rather than purpose. Her confidence regarding change was impacted.
- She wanted to feel the confidence, not just look it. We began with her sharing about her life and work. It was clear there were sparks of light there. Her face lit up when she spoke about her daughters and about establishing her business. Yet, her arms or upper body didn't move much. So, Maryanne was asked to stand with legs slightly apart and arms relaxed and open. This movement upset her structure (bodyset). Emotion seeped out as memories surfaced, and she experienced them in her body. As she became familiar with her body once again, new options emerged. She noticed sensations appearing in her arms, jaw, and hands. She was invited to breathe deeper, then deeper still. Emotions stirred. She realized that the contractions of her muscles held her back and dragged her confidence down.

- She made a commitment to being open, strong and confident. When it was clear she was solid, her voice, body, everything became aligned. When asked how her body felt, she said, "Like a tree."
- Maryanne developed a series of practices, including meditation, deep breathing, holding her arms more freely at her sides, noticing the language she used and reframing it as needed to help her embody her confidence. When asked recently what has helped her embody her new confidence, she replied, "Practicing my tree stance when I notice my confidence fade, daily meditation, a new awareness of language, reframing old stories and noticing when I am connected to my commitment."

HELPING CLIENTS EMBODY CHANGE

The most important ingredient to embodying change is to be really clear about why it is *important. No matter how desirable the change seems, we are not always willing participants in the embodiment process.* We start and we stop when we become aware life will have to change or when we realize that comfortable habits, our current situation, where we live, or the job must go. Fear jumps in, and we stop the practice.

CONSCIOUSNESS ABOUT CHOICE

Many times clients will say they have no choice, despite their increased consciousness. This may be true, and it may be the fear of giving up something that competes with the desire to be a strong, present leader. Or a deeper commitment to the status quo may be at work. Clients profoundly want to take the step into the new business or move to the new city, but they are unwilling to make the choices that manifest the dream because old structures have to die or be changed. Once the realization hits, they back up, slow down, and lose the sense of choice.

Remembering what we care about, what we want, and why we want it can invigorate practice. Embodiment of change takes time; it's not an overnight sensation.

Sometimes the choices involved aren't ours; that's when a leader needs resilience to deal with the challenges of change. The body is a vital resource. Our full presence, centered and grounded, provides a great resource for bouncing back into choice and dealing with setbacks.

CHOICE FOR COMMITMENT AND EMBODIMENT

How do we get into practice? What does it take to be fully committed to change? How do we know we are in a commitment to change?

Throughout the coaching engagement, clients will move between choice and commitment. It's a rocky road. The more clearly they feel the importance of the change deep in the body, the more likely the choice will sustain a commitment. Guiding your clients to a clear commitment includes getting the body, words, and voice aligned.

Here's a practice to offer:

1. Work with your client to clarify the choice he or she wants to make. Ask the client to put it in the frame of a commitment, using "I am committing to..."

2. Invite the client to stand in front of you. Help align his or her body by guiding the client to have feet flat on the floor, knees slightly flexed, hips even, and pelvis relaxed. Then work with the client to bring shoulders down, take a deep breath, drop energy into the center of the body, relax the jaw muscles, soften the eyes, relax the muscles around the forehead, and level out the chin.

3. Help the client set up his or her own body from feet to head. Ask the client what he or she notices in terms of sensations, muscle contractions, energy, or aliveness in the body.

4. Have your client state his or her commitment and notice what shifts occur in the body. As a coach, what assessments are you making? Ask the client what he or she notices or what's different. Ask for permission to share your assessment.

5. Ask powerful questions to help the client deepen the discovery and gain more clarity about what is important about this commitment.

6. When there is clear alignment, voice, body, and language are congruent. Ask the client, "What did you have to do with your physical body to align it with your commitment?" Or ask, "What did you have to do with your body to strengthen your commitment?" By speaking it, the client will find it easier to remember what to do physically to return to this state when, as easily happens, he or she gets off course.

Practice makes perfect. Energy follows where we put our attention. To achieve embodiment, the commitment must lie at the very foundation of what we want. We need clarity. When we have a commitment to get thin for the reunion, the wedding, or the job, it's usually for the short term and focused on the superficial. We diet, lose weight, the event happens, and habits and weight return. To achieve sustained change, we need our attention on our commitment with awareness of its importance.

Embodying change requires a willingness to step into murky water, wade through emotions, restructure the body and reframe narratives. It's hard work for the client and equally challenging for the coach. A new coach may find this deeper work is discomforting because it evokes strong emotions. Develop your capacity to breathe deeply, recognize your own triggers for stress and fear, and practice reshaping your body and reframing your story. The deeper you go in understanding your own body shaping, the more masterful you become at helping your client achieve sustained change.

SUMMARY

As coaches, we are privileged to work with leaders who want to be effective, resourceful, resilient, and lead in ways that compel engagement and results. Our gift to them is our ability to see what they can't see. We can encourage a level of consciousness that opens the door to choices serving the future they desire to create and hold them to their commitments to practice being exactly who they want to be. The body is a terrible thing to waste. By our learning how to work with bodyset and mindset, our own and our clients', we can be extraordinary partners with leaders on the journey to change.

BIBLIOGRAPHY

Hanna, T. *Somatics: Reawakening The Mind's Control of Movement, Flexibility, and Health.* Cambridge, MA: Perseus Books Group, 1988.

Kapuro, R., R. Hanson, and J. Oschman. *Awakening Somatic Intelligence: The Art and Practice of Embodied Mindfulness.* Berkeley, CA: North Atlantic Books, 2012.

Palmer, W. *The Intuitive Body: Discovering the Wisdom of Conscious Embodiment and Aikido.* Berkeley, CA: Blue Snake Books, 2008.

Siegel, D. *Mindsight: The New Science of Personal Transformation.* New York, NY: Bantam Books, 2011.

Silsbee, D. *Presence-Based Coaching: Cultivating Self-Generative Leaders Through Mind, Body, and Heart.* San Francisco, CA: Jossey-Bass, 2008.

Strozzi-Heckler, R. *Leadership Dojo: Build Your Foundation as an Exemplary Leader.* Berkeley, CA: Frog Books/North Atlantic Books, 2007.

Strozzi-Heckler, R. *Anatomy of Change: A Way to Move through Life's Transitions,* 2d ed. Berkeley, CA: North Atlantic Books, 1993.

PART II

DOING

PART II

DOING

CHAPTER 8

THE COACHING RELATIONSHIP: A MIRROR INTO THE SELF

KELLY LEWIS

MIRRORS CAN BE EFFECTIVE TOOLS for self-development. They give you a choice to see (or not) what is being reflected back to you. When I accept what I see in the mirror, I grow into a better version of myself. This is also true of what I call my inner mirror. This is the mirror in which I see the part of me that is sitting just below the surface, patiently waiting for my attention, the mirror in which I see reflected my relationship with my coaching clients. Like the mirror that reflects my physical image, this mirror allows me to interpret the reflection as I choose. Sometimes I will see an inspired coach, sometimes a harsh critic. The fact is, the mirror doesn't criticize, judge, exaggerate, or minimize light or shadow. I do that. The mirror, whether external or internal, creates an opportunity for me to accept or reject who I am at this very moment. It can facilitate or hinder my process of becoming, a process that I find essential for personal and professional development.

As Warren Bennis, a pioneer of the contemporary field of leadership, once said, "Becoming a leader is synonymous with becoming yourself. It is precisely that simple, and it is also that difficult."[1] I believe the same is true of becoming a leadership coach. It requires a wholehearted commitment to be in a continuous state of development—a condition that the best coaches foster not only in their clients but also in themselves.

The easier and more straightforward part of becoming a leadership coach is acquiring and applying "book knowledge"—the newest skills, the cutting-edge frameworks, the latest scientific research, the innovative 360-degree assessments—what is discussed in subsequent chapters as what we "do" as coaches. The more tumultuous and challenging part is discovering and integrating self-knowledge—who we "be" as coaches, which comes from our willingness to constantly look in our inner mirrors and claim ownership of what is reflected back.

Much of my self-knowledge comes from looking in that inner mirror and observing myself in my relationship with clients. As discussed in chapter 11 ("Whose Story Is This, Anyway?"), it is a pretty sure bet that, as leadership coaches, we will encounter clients with situations, issues, hopes, and fears similar to our own. These similarities may inspire or intrigue us, or they may make us feel uncomfortable or at risk. Whether these initial reactions are mildly electric or highly charged, they are invitations to view the coaching relationship in that inner mirror and acquire the self-knowledge that will make us better coaches. As coaches, we understand that if we don't claim our own light and sit with our own shadows, we significantly impact our ability to help our clients claim their own light and shadows. I question whether we can give our clients what we haven't experienced ourselves.

We are all familiar with the International Coach Federation competency, "Establishing Trust and Intimacy with the Client." We know what to do to establish a safe, supportive environment that facilitates a relationship between coach and client. What would it take to create a safe, supportive environment for us? Could looking at the coaching relationship as a mirror that reveals the self help us develop the same level of understanding, care, and compassion for ourselves? How might that level of intimacy allow us to become better coaches? For me, just being able to see, hold, and sit with my own "stuff" expands my ability to see, hold, and sit with the clients' "stuff."

My hope in this chapter is that both new and veteran coaches will accept the invitation to view the coach-client relationship as a source of self-knowledge, looking at both positive and negative aspects and being as open, courageous, and vulnerable in that exploration as we ask our clients to be every day. Perhaps sharing my personal experience with this practice will facilitate your process of becoming. I recommend that, if possible, we discuss this practice and our own discoveries with our coaches as part of our ongoing self-development.

ACCEPTING THE INVITATION

One important quality in acquiring self-knowledge is recognizing and accepting the invitation to look inside and see what the mirror wants to reveal. I like to think of this as intimacy with myself, or "*into me I see*," as one of my coaches once said. Typically, the coaching relationship mirror shows me pieces of myself that I have disassociated from or covered up or that perhaps hold the threat of judgment. Like the mirror that reflects my physical appearance, my inner mirror offers beauty or blemishes—and sometimes both at the same time—to recognize and claim.

REFLECTION #1

> I am many months into a coaching relationship with a 60-something, senior-level, government executive. His boss and peers consider him a "passionate technical expert, who is strong in his decisiveness and intuition and needs to work on being more inclusive, less critical, and listening more to others." I have come to know the man in that description and the person just below the surface, a deeply caring, tender-hearted person, who craves transferring something of value to the next generation and who wants more joy in his life. On this particular day, my phone rings at 4 p.m. and the voice on the other end sounds deflated and sad. As he speaks, it becomes evident that what is actually uppermost for my client is hurt and disappointment, and our work that day focuses on control or the lack of it. Dave recently experienced a loss in his life and is struggling with colleagues not supporting him in the way he expects to be supported—an expectation that is hidden from them. About halfway through the conversation, when I ask him, "How giving are you willing to be?" He says, "I can't give of myself *now*, when others didn't give to me when I needed it." It is clear we have touched a tender spot, so I "check in" with him. We keep going, and I offer this reframe: "You can choose to give of yourself, and you always have the choice not to. What is your choice?"

Two weeks to the day after that coaching session, I woke up with a vivid image from a dream. I found it strange, as I usually don't remember my dreams, but that morning I distinctly recalled that in my dream I was a warrior with a steel shield. I had no clue what this meant until later that morning when I looked at my calendar and saw that I had a coaching session with Dave. I was shocked. As though the early morning fog was lifting, I began to recognize the invitation to look into my inner mirror, an invitation I had been rejecting for some time. I pulled out my journal and began reflecting on a session with my coach that had occurred several months earlier. At that time I was working with a Strozzi-trained coach, so part of the coaching looked at the domain of the body.[2] During one of our sessions, she made this observation: "Kelly, it feels like you have a shield protecting your entire torso. I push with my fingers, and there is no give. It feels like armor." I recall saying, "I just work out a lot. I just have a really strong upper body." Aaahhhhh...I think that might have been me declining the initial invitation. No better time than the present to change my response and accept what wanted to be revealed. So...I was a warrior with a shield, because...? Maybe because, like Dave, I felt my heart was so sensitive and hurt that I had to defend and protect it. And while that shield had done just that—protected me and kept the hurtful things out—it had also kept locked in the love and joy I wanted to give and locked out the love and joy I wished to receive.

SEEING (MYSELF) AND BEING SEEN

Looking in our inner mirror can be challenging and at times unpleasant. Using this practice to build self-knowledge and claim more of our selves usually comes with some resistance and calls for courage, another quality I have found essential on the path of becoming. Fear appears to be my resistance of choice. A teacher of mine once said to me, "Kelly, fear is nothing but **F**alse **E**vidence that **A**ppears **R**eal, and the antidote for fear is to **F**ace **E**verything **A**nd **R**elease."

REFLECTION #2

A high-energy, empathetic consultant with a love of problem solving is on the other end of the telephone. Cara and I have been working to discover what she wants professionally and personally, to name her contribution to the world, and perhaps most importantly, to enable her to value herself and her contribution. Our work on this particular day is to find a way to generate and sustain her energy. At first, her voice is steady and her breathing is easy as we begin exploring what refreshes her and what depletes her. Then, in a split second, her speech quickens and her breathing becomes shallow as she blurts out, "People who complain about a problem when they don't need to be complaining, and I can't love and serve them. They deplete me." This is a big discovery for her. And she knows exactly what comes next— some exploration about what other actions are available to her when people are unable to receive her love and service.

Two days after that coaching session, I noticed myself highly frustrated in an interaction with a colleague. It was the usual dance I had experienced working with this person, and it was beginning to get exhausting. After he left, I heard myself say, "He just doesn't get it. He is so closed. What do you do when you feel like you can't be yourself?" Then I let out a big chuckle and said, "Thank you for the invitation, Cara." That evening I did some journaling on an odd question my first coach had offered me, "Who am I being that they are responding this way?" As I journaled, I discovered a frightened little girl who if truly seen and heard would not be accepted. I wanted to be sure that if I shared myself—my unique contribution—it would be welcomed and accepted. I discovered that when I perceive the stakes to be low or the relationship temporary, it is easier for me to reveal myself and perhaps be rejected. But in those relationships where I have more to lose—as with my colleague—I put on my shield, share less of my contribution and of myself. I wondered to myself, "What would happen if I choose to share, to give of myself, without any guarantee that what I was giving would be received?" That day I began to know inside my bones what Dr. Brené Brown writes about so insightfully:

> The root of the word courage is *cor*—the Latin word for heart.... Courage originally meant "To speak one's mind by telling all one's heart."...Today, courage is synonymous with being heroic or performing brave deeds. Heroics and bravery are important, but I think we've lost touch with the idea that speaking honestly and openly about who we [are] and about our experiences (good and bad) is the ultimate act of courage. Heroics are often about putting your life on the line. Courage is about putting your vulnerability on the line.... For me, practicing courage means telling my story with all of my heart. It means being honest about who I am, what I believe, and how I feel. It doesn't come easy for me—I have a tendency to self-protect—but it really is about practicing authenticity and letting myself be seen.[3]

LISTENING WITH MY HEART

The last quality of my practice of looking in the mirror is listening with my heart to the truehearted, integrated voice that is the source of my own inner wisdom. Distinguishing this voice from my analytical, inquisitive voice has been an important step in my development process. Both voices are genuinely curious, but my analytical voice has a need to understand first and to embrace second, while my truehearted voice is willing to embrace first and then to trust that it will understand when the time is right. Greater discernment of these two voices is coming with practice, and it is allowing me to claim new parts of myself and to let go of parts that no longer serve me. Discernment is creating a deeper connection with my true self. And when I am connected to this self, I understand where I end and where my clients begin. I am clear about what I have in common with my clients and how we are different. I can be fully present with and for them—*their* stories, *their* truth, *their* fears, and *their* hopes.

REFLECTION #3

A warmhearted, deeply feeling communications executive sits before me. She is determined to make the world a better place—for herself, for her son, and for humanity. She is a new leadership coach emerging from a transformational experience, and she is investing in her continued development. She desires to bring more of her authentic self to every encounter, and for her, this means becoming comfortable with owning her gifts, sharing her voice, and being visible. On this particular day, she is sharing what has happened since our last coaching session. She has hit the highlights, and then she says, "This isn't really important, but there is a quick story that I want to tell you." As she nears the end, she takes a big breath and says, "I took ownership of the mistake. I responded in a professional way and got it taken care of." I ask, "What else needs to be said?" Thirty seconds of silence later, Mary says, "I am angry that this person didn't trust me enough to come to me, and I am hurt by his unnecessarily harsh words." In that moment, she finds her voice and discovers what it feels like to solve the problem and fully express her self.

Following that coaching conversation with Mary, my truehearted voice spoke to me over three consecutive days during my yoga practice. As always, it offered me the opportunity to listen with the ears of my heart. Finally, on the third day, I listened and I saw more deeply into the woman who was looking back at me in the mirror, the woman who until then had been afraid to stand out because she always wanted to belong. On that day, like Mary, I found the courage to claim the freedom to fully express myself. I chose to create my own life by my own rules, to let go of the baggage that was no longer mine to carry. And I didn't need to understand what was happening; instead, I embraced it and watched a fuller expression of the Lord of the Dance pose emerge.[4]

SUMMARY

My inner mirror reveals the reciprocal nature of the coach-client relationship. Just as my clients learn from me, I learn from them. My relationship with them supports and educates me on my journey to becoming a great leadership coach—and to becoming myself.

This way of becoming is deeply challenging but also deeply rewarding. It requires a wholehearted commitment to be in a constant, and perhaps never-ending, state of development. It means accepting the invitation to look, having the courage to see and be seen, and listening with my heart. It calls for my patience, resilience, trust, and willingness to live into a fuller, truer, bigger expression of who I am. It allows me to acknowledge the parts of me sitting just below the surface and to discover the limitless depth of what is there. It feeds my spirit and affords me the freedom to be in greater service to myself and therefore to my clients.

I am grateful that I have made this practice of looking deeply a part of my everyday life and hope that others will consider doing the same on their path to becoming a great leadership coach—and to becoming themselves.

NOTES

1. Warren Bennis, *On Becoming a Leader* (New York: Basic Books, 2009), xxxvii.
2. Richard Strozzi-Heckler is the founder of the Strozzi work and president of Strozzi Institute. A nationally known speaker, coach, and consultant on leadership and mastery, he has spent four decades researching, developing, and teaching the practical application of Somatics (the unity of language, action, emotions, and meaning).
3. Brené Brown, *The Gift of Imperfection* (Center City: Hazelden, 2010), 12.
4. Lord of the Dance pose, or Natarajasana in Sanskrit, is a representation of Shiva, the presiding deity of yoga, who rules over transformation. Learning this pose requires patience, persistence, and resolve. In its full expression, the pose demands balance, presence, strength, and flexibility and offers the chance to become the lord of your own inner dance. See Kofi Busia, "Cosmic Dancer," *Yoga Journal*, Practice: Master Class: 1, available at http://www.yogajournal.com/practice/2305.

CHAPTER 9

G.R.A.C.E. AT WORK: STRONG RELATIONSHIPS FOR POWERFUL RESULTS

ERIC DE NIJS

COACHING IS, BY ITS VERY NATURE, a relationship. Many have labeled it a partnership, others call it an alliance. However you choose to describe it, it is still a relationship, and that relationship is at the heart and soul of coaching. The coaching relationship's vitality, balance, and strength are what determine a client's success.

Webster's Dictionary defines relationship as "a state of affairs existing between those having relations or dealings." What is most important to understand, however, is not the definition, but the condition of the relationship. *Webster's* definition **implies a relationship** between those "having relations or dealings." But in our warp-speed world we tend to remove the relationship from the interactions. People and organizations may have dealings together, but the art, science, and practice of relationships has been abandoned. It is critical that the coach never let this happen, but rather consciously work to establish meaningful coaching and leadership relationships.

Developing relationships is the single most critical success element for any leadership or coaching model. Coaches who develop powerful, purposeful, and productive relationships with their clients are more likely to inspire greater productivity, growth, innovation, and overall performance. Without a powerful relationship, when the coach and client have only those "relations or dealings" rather than a relationship, coaching is flat, unproductive, and ultimately wasted. The essence of successful and productive coaching conversation is a powerful relationship.

Because conversation is fast becoming a dying art, many people are unsure of themselves and their ability to develop these powerful and productive relationships. This article introduces a simple model that is easy to remember and follow, yet powerful in its results. It is a model of human dynamics that not only enables a coach to build the best relationships for client success, but also serves as an effective leadership guide for clients to follow. This model is not a list of competencies or skills. It is about the behavior of relationships. The profession of coaching has a great body of academic learning, including volumes on appropriate competencies, skills, and behaviors. All of that learning, each skill, competency, or behavior, can effectively be placed in one or more of the categories of this relationship model. The purpose of this model is to provide an easy and effective methodology, an "attitude alignment" model, for powerful relationships that yield productive and useful results for the client.

G.R.A.C.E. AT WORK: A NEW MODEL FOR POWERFUL, PURPOSEFUL, PRODUCTIVE RELATIONSHIPS

Powerful relationships are based on goodwill and a mutual commitment to a shared purpose that provides affirmation, inspiration, and personal transformation. These relationships emerge only through the presence and practice of five key components whose initials form the acronym **G.R.A.C.E.** These are **Goodwill, Results, Authenticity, Connectivity,** and **Empowerment** (figure 9.1).

"G.R.A.C.E. at work" was originally designed as a leadership model for application in the business environment, based on what is known to yield results, as a human interaction model. Coaches are leaders who have a powerful effect on the lives of their clients, often leaders themselves. This model provides a solid framework and structure around which the coaching relationship is built, maintained, and balanced. The model is easy to remember and can also serve clients who lead others. The five elements of G.R.A.C.E. are blended in combination and equal balance. All five must be present in the relationship to guarantee results. A basic premise of G.R.A.C.E is that any result you achieve in life comes by way of a conversation and a relationship; the conversation is about managing expectations and agreements, and the relationship is about intentionally seeking to transform the ordinary relationship into an extraordinary one. For example, sometimes coaches need to leverage the goodwill they've built with the client and tell the client something he or she does not want to hear even when it goes counter to their desire. Only by exercising G.R.A.C.E. can you and others experience an extraordinary relationship.

GOODWILL: IT ALL BEGINS HERE

Goodwill involves assuming positive intent, suspending judgment, looking out for the other person's best interest, giving without conditions, offering forgiveness, being at peace with what is, and providing support and safety in times of risk and failure. It's about making things all right regardless of what is happening in the relationship. All this begins with goodwill. The leader creates a "safe place" for working relationships to flourish, where people work together to achieve similar and collaborative goals.

Goodwill doesn't mean ignoring the effects of poor decisions. It means creating the conditions so both parties know each is looking out for the other's best interest. Sometimes expressing goodwill might involve giving without condition or extending forgiveness. Sometimes it can mean simply being at peace with what is. Goodwill is closely linked to trust and creates the psychological safety net that encourages people to take the risks associated with breakthrough performance.

In the coaching relationship, however, all the goals will focus on the client, not the coach. This differs from the standard leadership relationship where both parties have goals and objectives, and the goodwill is based on achieving those mutually acknowledged goals. This is most often not true in the coaching relationship. The nature of coaching demands that the coach holds the client's best interests as his or her own. Hopefully, both coach and client, however, approach the relationship basing their actions and words on mutual goodwill.

Figure 9.1 G.R.A.C.E. at Work: Playing in a bigger space

RESULTS: FORMULA FOR PURPOSE

There are actually *two* "R"s in this component: Reason and Results. This element of G.R.A.C.E. refers to the reason for being in a relationship, which ultimately yields results. It focuses on the ability of both parties to create meaning and value together and points to a shared sense of purpose.

Obviously, there must be a relationship of some sort to put goodwill to work. The working relationship between the coach and client is the *reason* for being together. And that reason is always to share a purpose and generate *results* and value for both parties.

Effective coaches help their clients identify their purpose and passion. G.R.A.C.E. helps answer the questions: "What's my reason for being?" and "Why are we in this relationship?" Long after leaving an organization or exiting a relationship, people realize that success isn't just about the numbers. It's about making a contribution by doing the things they love to do—things that are meaningful. Research conducted by the Corporate Leadership Council's Learning and Development Roundtable found that "by changing the way employees think about themselves, their jobs, and their organizations, managers have another means of obtaining dramatic improvements in the performance of their employees" (Corporate Leadership Council 2003, 20). Effective coaches and leaders recognize this desire as a powerful motivator for people, and they leverage it to create commitment to the vision and purpose of the organization or of the client.

AUTHENTICITY: ESSENTIAL REALITY

Authenticity is being real with yourself and others, choosing how you wish to relate to others, declaring what your stand is, holding yourself accountable for your actions, rewarding yourself appropriately, being open and vulnerable, openly communicating needs, desires, moods, attitudes, values, and feelings—even about the other person. Being real—and being all that you can be—is essential to any relationship, but especially to one with expectations for authentic results. Open and uncompromising standards, positive attitudes, and the desire to be exactly who you are, is the heart of a fruitful relationship. Authenticity keeps all relationships balanced and healthy. Each person must first identify, then "own up" to his or her own reality. Successful relationships thrive when both parties are exactly who they say they are, say exactly what they mean, and apply the same standards to self and others.

Great leadership and great coaching begin by knowing and leveraging strengths and weaknesses. Self-awareness in coaches and leaders represents a huge opportunity to create consistency between the walk and the talk and provides a measure of transparency to others that fosters trust in a relationship.

CONNECTIVITY: COCREATED VALUE

Connectivity means finding ways to identify with, affirm, and encourage the other person, understanding how the other person feels, what is important to him or her, sharing assumptions and beliefs, identifying and realizing differences in intention and impact on others, and the genuine desire to associate with and relate to others. When goodwill, a reason for being in relationship, and authenticity combine, they advance the relationship to the place of real connectivity. From a coaching perspective, connectivity is about empathizing with the client and finding ways to help clients achieve their goals.

It is the coach's responsibility to create connection through careful and deliberate observance and understanding of the client's most effective methods of engagement. Coaches connect with clients and essentially "team up" for shared results. When coach and client connect, through shared motives, values, goals, and understanding—and through effective engagement practices—the resulting bond can yield powerful results. The safe place of G.R.A.C.E. easily affords this vital connectivity.

EMPOWERMENT: ENABLING SUCCESS

Empowerment is helping others overcome obstacles, develop new skills, establish a safe environment in which to succeed (for self and others), create catalysts for change, see potential and possibilities, be open to possibilities, allow time for testing and learning, and see the larger whole but remain aware of its components. Empowerment is about enabling clients to achieve their own success, not doing it for them. It is about creating a "nutrient-rich" environment for free, unfettered growth.

It is essential that the coach maintain the critical balance of challenge and support, sufficiently motivating others to take risks, see new things and do new things, while still holding the client accountable. A good coach must create a dynamic tension, a balance, that motivates the client to advance his or her skills. For example, the coach must also provide a safe place of challenge and support. In this way, the coach creates and maintains this same balance between advocacy and inquiry, between task and relationship.

Coaches and clients need to cocreate the boundaries for empowerment, learning, and responsibility. Trust also plays a vital role in empowerment and begins with a common understanding of expectations and mutual commitments to goals, roles, and consequences.

PROVEN AND POWERFUL CHECKLIST

Accountability is something most people find difficult. But it is essential for the coach. A great coach systematically reviews his or her performance, always seeking areas for improvement. He or she is constantly learning, constantly checking, constantly improving. The following is a checklist that captures the main concepts of the G.R.A.C.E. at Work model, presented in a manner that allows coaches to monitor and realign their relationship-building behaviors, while at the same time building those same skills in their clients. A coach who practices G.R.A.C.E. at Work will build the kind of relationship that delivers results for clients. A client who learns and practices G.R.A.C.E. at Work will see results in the organization as well as in the individuals he or she leads; quite often, this is what the coaching is all about in the first place: becoming a more effective leader.

IT'S NOT ABOUT ME

This is not a popular sentiment today, but it is essential for the GRACE-full coach. Clients' success sometimes demands sacrifice. And that requires doing what's best for the client as opposed to pushing toward the coach's bias, perceptions of success for the client, or personal goals. In the game of baseball, a sacrifice fly or bunt may result in a player sacrificing his personal performance statistics to advance the team. Similarly, a sacrifice in a powerful relationship may mean that a person gives up his or her agenda, his or her need to be "right," or the need to be first. This is the meaning of goodwill and evidence of the capacity to coach and lead with G.R.A.C.E. It is also an attribute that, when successfully modeled, can be learned by others.

LEADING AND COACHING WITH GRACE

An interaction model for coaching relationships that facilitates trust and transparency is needed to guide performance and productivity and

G.R.A.C.E. at Work Questions Checklist

	Coach's Personal Checklist	Coaching (and Modeling) to Client Checklist
Goodwill	1. How am I approaching the coaching relationship with goodwill and positive intent for my client?	1. In what way is my client approaching his or her relationships with goodwill and positive intent? What does that look like?
	2. How do I suspend any judgment I may tend to make regarding this client?	2. How is my client holding onto judgments and prejudices, and would he or she be able to suspend/release them to move on?
	3. How am I truly interested in, and looking out for, my client's best interest?	3. How is my client interested in others, developing them, and mentoring them?
	4. How am I giving to him/her, without condition?	4. How or to what extent is my client giving without condition?
	5. How do I and will I freely extend forgiveness as needed?	5. How is my client able to freely extend forgiveness if needed, or is he or she harboring unforgiveness, or a grudge or living in past wrongs?
	6. How am I able to be "at peace with what is" in the relationship?	6. To what extent does my client know contentment in the moment, or is he or she at unrest? How do I help my client find peace with what is, yet still set appropriate goals?
	7. How have I created an environment of trust and safety for my client?	7. How trustful is my client of me and others? How is he or she able to create an environment of trust with others?
Results	1. What do I know of my client's dreams and goals? Can I describe what he or she thinks success looks like?	1. How does my client know what he or she is looking for? How will my client be able to recognize when his or her goals are achieved?
	2. How well am I fully understanding and embracing the purpose of this relationship—the intended results?	2. What does my client understand the purpose of this coaching relationship is, and how has he or she clearly stated the intended results? How can my client transfer this ability to identify intention and shared value to other relationships?
	3. In what ways am I being in service to the client?	3. How is my client able to support the intentions, purpose, and goals of others without imposing his or her own values, goals, or intentions?
	4. In what ways will I be genuinely pleased for my client when he or she achieves the success desired?	4. How well is my client able to be genuinely pleased with success in others?
	5. What have I identified, what and do I understand, to be the intended and unintended consequences of the stated results?	5. How has my client fully explored, identified, and accepted the intended and unintended consequences of his or her desired results?

Figure 9.2 G.R.A.C.E.: Full coaching checklist

G.R.A.C.E. at Work Questions Checklist

Coach's Personal Checklist	Coaching (and Modeling) to Client Checklist
6. What have I identified as my own purpose and passion, and is this coaching relationship built within that passion?	6. How can my client identify his or her purpose and passion? How can he or she help others to do the same?
7. How have I helped this client to establish a solid plan to achieve the intended and stated results?	7. To what extent does my client have a plan to achieve results? Does he or she know how to measure progress? Is he or she able to do this for others?

Authenticity

Coach's Personal Checklist	Coaching (and Modeling) to Client Checklist
1. How can I be real and authentic with this client? How well can I describe and articulate my values?	1. In what ways is my client real and authentic with me? With others? How is he or she able to articulate personal values and vision?
2. How do I keep myself accountable to "walk my talk," and how well do I honestly engage this client and keep him or her accountable?	2. How well is my client willing to engage on an authentic level and willing to be helped to "walk the talk" in this relationship? How well is this person able to do this with others and self?
3. How can I openly communicate needs, desires, moods, attitudes, values, and feelings with this client and with others?	3. How does my client openly communicate needs, desires, moods, attitudes, values, and feelings with me? Others?
4. How well am I able to have open and uncompromising standards, positive attitudes, and a deep desire to be exactly who I am with this client?	4. In what ways does my client have uncompromising standards, positive attitudes, and a deep desire to be exactly who he or she is?
5. How do I know what my strengths and weaknesses are, and am I able to leverage them, especially is this coaching relationship?	5. How well does my client know his or her strengths and weaknesses (areas of challenge), and is he or she able to leverage them in all relationships?
6. How am I "transparent" in this relationship?	6. How is my client "transparent" in all his or her relationships?
7. To what extent am I exactly who I say I am? How do I say exactly what I mean?	7. Does my client appear to be exactly who he or she says? Does this person say what he or she means? Does my client use the same standards for self and others?
1. How am I able to identify with, affirm, and encourage my client?	1. How is my client able to identify with, affirm, and encourage others?
2. What do I understand about how my client feels?	2. How does my client understand how others feel and what is important to them? How does he or she empathize with others?

Connectivity	3. To what extent do I have a genuine desire to connect and associate (relate) with this person?	3. In what ways does my client have a genuine desire to connect with others?
	4. How have I enabled my client to connect with me?	4. How has my client enabled others to connect with him or her?
	5. How have I put my own aspirations aside to be sensitive and of service to my client's needs?	5. How can my client put his or her aspirations aside to be sensitive and of service to the needs of others?
	6. How am I able to understand, empathize with my client's situation, and appreciate the impact this situation has on her or his mood, attitudes, identity, ego, and vision for success?	6. How is my client able to understand the situations of others and to appreciate how these situations impact the moods, attitudes, identities, egos, and vision of others?
	7. How can I honestly support and share my client's motives, values, goals, and desired results from this relationship?	7. How does my client honestly support and share the motives, values, goals, and desired results of others in relationship with him or her? How does he or she put the needs of others first in order to establish solid, productive connections with others?
Empowerment	1. How well am I able to help my client overcome obstacles, develop new skills, and create catalysts for change?	1. How is my client able to overcome obstacles and develop new skills? How is this person able to create catalysts for change in others as well?
	2. How am I able to help this client be open to possibilities and potential?	2. How is my client open to possibilities and potential? How is he or she able to help others in this regard?
	3. How can I help my client be aware of all components but still see the larger "whole"?	3. How is my client able to see the details and the whole picture, keeping perspective on both? How is he or she able to help others doing this?
	4. How am I able to create the right balance between challenge and support for this client?	4. How does my client know and understand the difference between challenge and support in his or her current relationships?
	5. In what ways am I equipped to assist this client in developing new skills or advancing toward his or her goals?	5. How self-sufficient is my client in terms of acquiring adequate resources for expected growth? How well is he or she able to provide that to stimulate and assist growth in others?
	6. How am I able to help my client tap into his or her own passion or purpose?	6. In what ways does my client understand working from passion, and how well is he or she able to discover and enable it in others?
	7. In what ways do I need to grow or reframe my perspective in order to be most effective for my client?	7. How is my client able to take the time necessary for testing and learning in both self and others? How is he or she able to recognize reality?

Figure 9.2 Continued

ultimate success for the client. Purposeful, productive, and powerful relationships can form the basis for achieving breakthrough performance and building the capacity for future growth. G.R.A.C.E. at work can provide greater opportunities to build relationships and facilitate performance. Coaches and clients are authentic, achieve a special kind of chemistry for growth, empower each other, and extend good will. It is the creation of a safe place for people to perform—within stated boundaries—without fear of failure. Figure 9.2 is a checklist that captures the main concepts of the G.R.A.C.E. at Work model.

The concepts behind the word "grace" lend themselves to this model well. *Grace* generally brings to mind two ideas. One, simply put, is unmerited favor. In other words, we are treated much better than we deserve. The other is a certain poise or elegance in movement. Both of these ideas contribute to leading and coaching with grace. G.R.A.C.E.-full coaching assumes goodwill, which will many times translate into unmerited favor. In a state of G.R.A.C.E., energy is abundant and performance effortless. Obstacles are anticipated, but with the expectation that they will be overcome. Failure is seen as an opportunity to learn. This does not imply that this kind of relationship is free of pain or even easy. It requires effort, commitment, and *grace*. But the anticipation and realization of success supersedes pain and difficulty.

Coaching and leading with G.R.A.C.E. encourages people to learn new things and express themselves authentically in a safe environment. G.R.A.C.E. encourages commitment, not compliance, because G.R.A.C.E. assumes that development and high performance occur most effectively in the context of a purposeful relationship. This relationship is based on goodwill and a mutual commitment to a shared purpose that provides affirmation, inspiration, and personal transformation. Without G.R.A.C.E., what remains is a series of transactional interactions that neither satisfies nor inspires, and it does not advance your clients to the success they seek. Are you insuring the success of your clients by building G.R.A.C.E.-full relationships?

BIBLIOGRAPHY

Corporate Leadership Council. 2003. "Engaging Managers as Agents of Employee Development: A Quantitative Analysis of Manager-Led Development Strategies," 20.

CHAPTER 10

USING STORY IN COACHING

MARGARET ECHOLS, KAREN GRAVENSTINE, AND SANDY MOBLEY

STORIES OF OUR BECOMING

Since ancient times, we humans have told stories to make meaning and sense of our lives. The Hindu *Mahabharata*, Homer's epics, the Greek tragedies, the Bible, Shakespeare, Aesop's Fables, the Grimm Brothers' Fairy tales, the "sacred bundle stories" of Native American Indians, and the country and western ballads of Nashville are all powerful and amazing stories that inspire wonder and awe. In these stories, facts are mostly irrelevant. What matters is the underlying message they mean to convey—the values, passions, concerns, hopes, and dreams of the ones who tell them.

In her book, *Corporate Legends & Lore*, Peg Neuhauser writes, "the stories of our own life are a personal treasure. They are your personal sacred bundle. Those sacred bundle stories represent the best of who you are, as well as the wisdom that you have accumulated over the years of your life."[1] Listen to another's sacred bundle stories and you listen to his heart. Hear another's legend and you witness the hero within. Attend to the ballads one sings about her life and you learn the recurring refrains by which she defines herself. Stand as witness to his fables and fairy tales and you enter into the core values, principles, and morals that guide his life.

"We all tell stories about who we are, where we come from, and where we are going. These personal myths in turn shape who we become and what we believe."[2] Stories told time and time again give us a glimpse into the spirit and soul of a tribe, a nation, a people, an organization, and an individual being. The myths, legends, ballads, parables, and fables we tell about ourselves reveal our essence. In the Native American Indian culture, the role of the "story teller" is to share the most important stories of the tribe so they continue from generation to generation. We are the keeper of our own stories, telling over and over again those that define who we are—those that reveal our spirit—our soul, both as individuals and as communities.

Sometimes we keep telling our stories as though they are irrefutable facts, unquestionable and unchangeable. We often live our lives as if the stories we hold about ourselves are real. When that happens we can get stuck in our past, seeing no possibility for the future. Scientists studying brain activity found that people remembering a situation have identical brain activity as those imagining a situation. Their hypothesis is that people mentally cannot distinguish between a real and imagined situation. If people are remembering, imagining, or anticipating a negative experience, it shapes how they view the world. And so is their world shaped when they hold a positive experience.[3] This is powerful for coaching. Coaching provides an editor's role in our story. It helps others to "detect the story line in their own lives...opening up a hidden world of self-discovery and meaning."[4] Coaching invites the insertion of new chapters. It creates the opportunity to write new, unimaginable endings. It allows the possibility to change the moral of the story and the outcome of the fairy tale.

"Storytelling is fundamental to the human search for meaning whether we tell tales of the creation of the earth or of our early choices."[5] These are the stories of our becoming.

STORIES FOR PERSONAL TRANSFORMATION

I asked Jean, my client, to tell me the story of her life, the momentous moments, and the people who have influenced/shaped her into the person she is today. She shared the highlights, both painful and joyful then said, I had never thought about how my life sounds when I talk about it as a complete picture. I heard my perceptions, my beliefs, the undercurrent of pain and dissatisfaction...and fear. Is this the story of my life? It's bleak—all black and gray. I want a better, happier story—I want bright colors, I want a hopeful mood, I want courage. How do I get there? How do I change how I view myself and my world—how do I change my story? (see figure 10.1)

Who are we? Who do we think we are? How have our life experiences shaped our bodies, our emotions, our beliefs—our way of seeing, and being in, the world? What is our story, our narratives, regarding the sum total of our experiences? It is how those experiences are felt, defined, reflected upon, and talked about that become our set of beliefs. These beliefs can severely cripple our ability to take action, or strengthen and embolden us to extraordinary feats. Our stories, and what we focus on, become our reality.

THE COACH'S ROLE

Stories are essential to our capacity to truly understand each other, our world, and ourselves. Physicians who fail to listen to their patients' stories may fail to provide the correct treatment, despite knowing all the relevant medical facts. *Narrative medicine programs* are emerging—evidence of the increased focus on training doctors to listen to the stories and learn to better "read" their patients. Coaches, also, must listen deeply to their clients' narratives. We must listen beneath the words, beneath the facts, to understand the lens through which the client is viewing the world, and the effects of that view.

In the earlier example, Jean told her story to her coach. With other clients, the coach may have them write their *up until now* story to capture a picture of their life up to the present. During the first month of coaching, the coach also gave Jean some self-observation exercises to help gain even further clarity on how she is seeing her world. One exercise, for example, was the following:

- Notice things you are doing well, your successes.
- Notice the challenges you are facing and what you are doing about them.
- Write what you are noticing in a journal. Keep a daily record.

During the first few weeks, Jean observed many problems/challenges and very few successes. It was clear to both coach and client that Jean's attention and energy were centered on her missteps and daily challenges.

The coach gave Jean the assignment of writing her *best self* (her most powerful, authentic self) story. She asked Jean to write about how she wanted to show up as her best self in her work, in her relationships,

SCAN

toward an understanding of who we are
and, ultimately, transformation to the person we can become.

Story > Commitment > Authentic self > New story and action

Figure 10.1 A model for using story in coaching: SCAN

and in her whole life. When they discussed this afterward, Jean was excited. She saw that she was already exhibiting some elements of her best self, yet never noticing. She saw that some of the challenges that loomed as mountains in her mind were not so large at all—she had been investing them with the power to paralyze her. Over time, she began to gain insight and see possibilities for herself not seen before. Through subsequent coaching sessions, Jean's energy and increasing belief in herself propelled her forward. She grappled with her "gremlins" and continued to shift her mental habit from focusing on problems to receiving solutions. She set her sights high and took bold action on goals she had identified. And little by little, day by day, Jean's life shifted from shades of gray, black and white to a full spectrum of vibrant color.

In the previous abbreviated story, we fleshed out Jean's "story" of her way of seeing the world up until now. We then explored Jean's real *commitment* to change. What does she want? What will that get her? How will she know?

Through coaching Jean gained increasing awareness of her *authentic* and *best self*. We uncovered layers of beliefs and experiences that had given rise to her gremlins of doubts, fears, and judgments. She began to advance to higher levels of learning, self-awareness, and emotional intelligence. Jean identified her *new story* as her best self and, through continued practice and feedback, started to live the story she had created.

STORIES FOR ORGANIZATIONAL CHANGE

How does an organization build, teach, and reinforce its culture? Most organizations have mission and values statements—does anyone read them? If they do read them, do they remember them or behave according to the values? What people remember are the organizational stories, and these stories describe what has meaning to the people.

For example, when two EDS employees were held hostage in a heavily guarded prison in Iran in 1979 and political negotiations broke down, EDS chairman, Ross Perot, took matters into his own hands. He handpicked a team of volunteers from his organization to go in and rescue the employees.[6] What a powerful message that conveyed about EDS taking care of its people.

Consider the leaders of Enron or WorldCom who put the organization in jeopardy and risked employees' retirement plans for their own gain. They sent a very different message to their workforce.

When people tell newcomers to an organization about the company, they tell the stories of risks taken, mistakes made, successes, and what happened to the people who won and lost. This tells the new employees what behavior is rewarded and punished far better than value statements or employee manuals.

Just as people can use story telling for transformation, so can organizations. How many organizations have come back from difficulties because people had confidence in their leadership and the leaders were able to create a vision that the workforce believed in? Think about the rebuilding of Chrysler and the new vision or story Lee Iacocca told the workforce and their debtors to make them believe and help Chrysler come back. Moreover, Iacocca didn't tell that story only once. He made hundreds of presentations reinforcing the pride of the workforce, the preeminence of Chrysler engineering, and the strong possibility of a successful outcome.[7] Could he have succeeded without a compelling story? We don't think so.

An organizational mini-story may be its tag line or vision statement. Some examples are: GE—"We bring good things to life" or Nike—"Just do it." These visions tell employees much more about the company than employee manuals.

"START WITH STORY" COACHING EXERCISES FOR YOUR CLIENT

HERO'S JOURNEY

- One way to use storytelling for transformation is in helping people tell their story of what they want to create. Using Joseph Campbell's model of the hero's journey,[8] begin by asking people what they are called to do or what vision they want to bring about. Then ask them to reflect on both their fears (monsters) and their resources for support. As they tell the story from startup to struggles to success they embolden themselves and engage others in the possibilities.

USE OF METAPHORS

- A metaphor is a mini-story. Symbolic representations bring power and deeper meaning to transformation. The coach might

ask, "If you were a flower, how would you describe yourself?"
The client might see herself as a shade plant, a toad lily. Yet, she
is a tall, fun-loving person who is working in a serious, harsh
organization characterized by overwork and lack of personal
connection. The coach might tell the client that she sees her as a
sunflower—growing taller and bolder as she got more sunshine.
Holding this image would allow her to look for organizational
possibilities for more fun and connection (sun) and supportive
leadership.

- In a career development workshop, one coach asked people to
  give her metaphors for their careers.
  - One person said he steps into an elevator and pushes the
    button for the penthouse but never gets there because other
    people push his buttons and derail his assent.
  - Another person said his career was like being a racecar driver.
    He goes around and around at high speed, but there is never
    a finish line.
  - With metaphors, you can help people see possibilities for
    change. In the first example, the coach asked, "How can you
    enlist others in helping you reach your destination?" In the
    second example she asked, "What are your own milestones for
    success that will tell you that you have completed the race?"

RECALL AND RESHAPE THE STORY

- We have clients make a list of significant turning points in their
  lives, and then list these events as chapters in a book, adding
  some narrative description.
  - Then they choose one of these turning points and describe
    what changed for them after this event (i.e., outlook, emotions,
    actions, and values).
  - Finally they identify any patterns in these events as they scan
    the whole story.
- We may ask a client to tell or write about a peak experience in
  his or her life, and to write about a painful experience. In these
  narratives people often realize the growth or shifts that came
  from these episodes.
- We ask clients to write their obituaries—"How you would like
  to be remembered?"
- Another story starter: "You are on the cover of Fortune magazine
  in five years—write the story." This exercise and the one preceding
  open clients to more possibilities for their lives. Clients begin to

realize they still have things they want to accomplish. And so they begin to create their new stories.

- This is a good targeted exercise: "Describe a conflict you had recently with a colleague. Write the story from your point of view. Now write the story from your colleague's point of view."

A CLOSING EXERCISE FOR COACHES, THEIR CLIENTS, THEIR FRIENDS, AND THEIR FAMILIES

TELLING YOUR SACRED BUNDLE STORIES

A "sacred bundle" is a symbolic collection of items—mementoes that capture the essence of who you are—your heart and soul.[9] Spend some time over the next two weeks reflecting on your life—what you value, key characteristics that describe you, your watershed experiences, the heroes and mentors who helped to form you, significant events, major disappointments, failures, or crisis—the most important things that contribute to your identity.

For each of these things find a small, symbolic, physical object that will help you remember and tell your story. Put these together in a "sacred bundle"—a basket, a precious box—someplace where you can keep them all together. Share your stories with a committed listener—someone who can help you see not only how these items describe your past history, but also support you in generating the future you want to create for yourself.

This same exercise can be done with groups—families, businesses, places of worship—with each person in the group bringing an item and telling the story that contributes to the creation of the group's "sacred bundle."

One of us, Karen Gravenstine, tells this story to illustrate, "My family created a sacred bundle as a gift for my parents for their fiftieth wedding anniversary. Each of us kids, ten in all, brought several items that reflected for us the essence of our family. We carried them to my parents' home as part of the celebration. As we each presented the object for the sacred bundle—a lovely basket my parents kept in a special place from that day on—we told the story related to it. Stories of church; reading; learning; service; vacation; singing; special foods; siblings who had died; neighbors and relatives. Some things we hadn't discussed for years! The grandchildren and the sons and daughters-in-law were in awe as they heard some family stories for the first time. They were initiated into, and we were reminded of, the essence of who we are as a family. My parents were touched by the power of the stories we told, the best of who we are as a family—the legacy they helped to create."

CONCLUSION

We are surrounded by our stories and the stories of others. These stories, as we have described in this chapter, have power and life. We can use them to achieve greater connection. We can revise them to achieve greater success. We invite you to use stories as a tool in your coaching practice. Recalling, telling, and revising stories can stimulate dramatic transformations for individuals and organizations. So...what's your story?

NOTES

1. Peg C. Neuhauser, *Corporate Legends & Lore: The Power of Storytelling as a Management Tool* (New York: McGraw-Hill, 1993), 68.
2. Sam Keen and Anne Valley-Fox, *Your Mythic Journey: Finding Meaning in Your Life through Writing and Storytelling* (Los Angeles: Tarcher/Putnam, 1989), David L. Miller, back cover comment.
3. B. Gonsalves, P.J. Reber, D.R. Gitelman, T.B. Parrish, M. Mesulam, and K.A. Paller, "Neural Evidence That Vivid Imagining Can Lead to False Remembering," *Psychological Science 15* (2004): 655–660.
4. See note 2 above.
5. Mary Catherine Bateson, *Composing a Life* (New York: Penguin Books, 1990), 34.
6. *Famous Texans*, "H. Ross Perot," http://www.famoustexans.com/rossperot.htm (accessed November 12, 2007).
7. Ari Weinberg, "The Dollar-A-Year Man," *Forbes*, May 8, 2002, http://www.forbes.com/2002/05/08/0508iacocca.html (accessed November 12, 2007).
8. Joseph Campbell, *The Power of Myth* (New York: Doubleday, 1998), 14.
9. See note 1 above, 41–48.

CHAPTER 11

WHOSE STORY IS THIS, ANYWAY? IDENTIFICATION WITH CLIENTS IN LEADERSHIP COACHING

DAVE SNAPP

My client Robert is a middle manager who is having trouble stepping up to the next level of leadership. After six weeks of coaching, it feels like we are closing in on his key issues: his ambition and his flight from ambition, his abundance of choices and his fear of committing to a single game plan, his sense of an inherent conflict between his career and his family life.

Then it hits me—this is just what is showing up in my life. This guy is *me!*

I'm excited because I know these issues, and I can be of help. But from somewhere inside comes a warning, "You haven't been paying enough attention to these issues for yourself. How can you expect to coach Robert? And whose story is this, anyway?"

IT IS ALMOST INEVITABLE THAT, as leadership coaches, we will encounter clients with situations and issues apparently similar to our own. These similarities may intrigue and stimulate us, or they may feel disquieting and uncomfortable.

Whether these initial reactions are positive or negative, they are signals we should pay attention to. Identification with a client's situation or issue may produce empathy and insight that can be helpful to the client, but it can cause significant problems.

Why can identification become problematic? When a client's situation provokes a response in us, it suggests that an active issue of our own is being stimulated. Using the analogy of electrical current, we can say that the issue is "charged" or "carries a charge." We can imagine a whole spectrum of reaction, ranging from "neutral" to "highly charged." The stronger the reaction, the greater the charge. And, often, the greater the charge, the more active, deep, or fundamental the issue is for us, and the more difficult it may be for us to see clearly and be helpful to our client. Alternatively, the more likely it is that we are responding to our own story instead of our client's.[1]

This is why the way in which coaches manage issues of identification can make the difference between masterful work with our clients and mediocre—even harmful—work.

This chapter explores the dynamics of identification in leadership coaching:

- Why does identification occur?
- How can we tell when identification is charged for us?
- How does identification affect our ability to coach leaders effectively?
- What can we do to coach effectively and ethically in such situations?

WHY DOES IDENTIFICATION OCCUR?

Judy learns that her client received a critical evaluation at work. Having had a similar experience, she identifies with the client situation and assumes she knows "how it is." In Judy's own case, the critical evaluation was devastating. She is anxious to support her client and probes for evidence of disappointment and sadness.

It's a common occurrence. A client describes a situation. The coach identifies with that situation, in one way or another assuming similarity where it may not exist.

Why does this happen? To some extent, it's unavoidable. One way humans try to make sense of the world is to classify incoming data about people and situations as "like me/mine" or "different than me/mine." Finding similarity provides reassurance that we can recognize and understand what is happening around us. For a coach, this may satisfy a need to understand or "know what to do."

HOW CAN WE TELL WHEN IDENTIFICATION IS CHARGED FOR US?

When identification occurs, we as coaches will often be aware of it. What may be harder is to assess whether this identification is charged for us in some way and may as a result present a challenge to our coaching. Fortunately, there are often warning signs that some degree of charged identification may be occurring. Some of these warning signs are

- An emotional response disproportionate to the situation, either positive or negative
- Pain, trauma, or discomfort in the body
- A strong desire to solve the client's problem or give advice
- A sense of being stuck, blocked, or at a total loss as to what to do
- A feeling of being in the client's story
- A persistent feeling that the coaching isn't working, whether the client agrees or not[2]

These clues may or may not indicate that the coach is "identifying" with the client's story. But they are often good signs that the coach is being "hooked" in some way and needs to take steps to figure out what is going on.

HOW DOES IDENTIFICATION AFFECT OUR ABILITY TO COACH LEADERS EFFECTIVELY?

Identifying with a client's story is not necessarily a problem, and it may at times prove helpful. Similar experiences can create some familiarity with the client's territory and provide a foundation for empathetic and caring coaching.

So where might such identification present problems? In general, identification becomes a problem when the focus of the coach's attention moves from client to coach. When we over-identify with a client, we are more likely to assume similarity. Our vision suffers, and we may actually distort reality.

Jose is currently launching his own independent coaching practice. The experience is proving exciting, but also very stressful. As his family's primary breadwinner, he is particularly anxious about money. One of Jose's first coaching clients has recently retired from a successful and lucrative business career and is planning to launch a strategy consulting business.

Jose finds himself unable to stop worrying about the viability of his client's new business, though the client repeatedly assures him that he is at no financial risk. Jose also pushes "solutions" that have worked for him but don't work for the client. His client's real desire, to explore the broader meaning and value of his new career, is not met.

The dangers of identification increase when the "similar" situation or issue is a charged one for the coach. Jose is caught up with launching his own practice. He projects his anxiety, particularly about finances, onto the client situation. As a result, it is hard for him to hear his financially comfortable client's quite different needs and wants.

A coach's work is to help clients resolve patterns of breakdown or reactivity. The client is stuck, and the coach helps the client discover how to get unstuck. To be helpful in this situation, it is critical that the coach is not himself in a state of breakdown or reactivity. A coach's perception of similarity in the client situation or story may cause coaches to assume greater similarity than actually exists. A special challenge is presented when the perception of similarity triggers—or is triggered by—a coach's own active or unresolved issues. When we as coaches are in breakdown ourselves, we may "see" our clients differently.

A number of things can happen when a client's similar situation triggers a coach's active story, as it did in the case of Jose. The coach may

- miss signals;
- become focused on her own story, and lose sight of her client's story;
- buy into the client's story and get stuck with him;
- begin to work "harder" on the problem than the client is;
- push solutions or reject certain solutions;
- be unable to see alternative ways of being or acting; and
- have difficulty challenging the client or discussing a need for change.

All of these possible responses can hamper the coach's ability to help the client.

Coaching leaders in organizations involves additional considerations. We are in effect entering into the organizational "field" with our clients. Leaders function amid a network of complicated relationships and pressures. They must deal with multiple challenges, involving vision and values, competition and conflict, and ultimately success and failure. As a result, there are countless opportunities for us to be drawn into those same pressures and to lose our necessary independence and objectivity. This is especially true when our own issues, reactivity, and blind spots are apparently similar to those of the leader we are coaching, as in the following case.

> Maria made a career switch to coaching after a fairly unpleasant and unfulfilling stint as an organizational leader. She disliked the competition and conflict she experienced in her work, as well as the focus on the bottom line. She became a coach to be able to focus on building positive and supportive relationships with others.
>
> One of Maria's clients is a leader who is struggling to manage a great deal of conflict in his organization. Maria begins to harbor negative feelings about the client organization and is finding it hard to help or support her client. She begins to think that her client would be better off leaving this organization.

In this example, Maria has clear difficulty differentiating her story from her client's situation. Her own unresolved discomfort about the bottom-line focus and conflict in business organizations is aroused by her client's experience of them. As a result, her inability to separate her own reactions from her client's adversely affects her ability to be of help to her client.

Coaches working in organizational contexts need to take particular care to avoid being unduly influenced by their own experiences and stories about leaders, leadership, and organizations. It is interesting to consider that leadership coaches have generally chosen not to take full time jobs as leaders in organizations. What might this suggest about our view of what it is like to be a leader in an organization?

We need to understand these filters through which we see leaders and organizations. These include not only our general values and assumptions, but also the experiences and stories that live deep within us. We might ask ourselves: What do we like most or least about being a leader? What have been our most or least successful and fulfilling experiences? What kind of leader am I? What excites or scares me about it? What does all of this tell me about my own story about leadership and how this might affect how I coach? A similar set of questions could be asked about our experiences in organizations.

Here are just a few of the stories we may hold about leaders and organizations:

- Organizations eat people up.
- Entrepreneurial organizations are better than bureaucratic organizations.
- Organizational leadership is heroic.
- Most leaders are dishonest.
- Successful leaders need sharp elbows.
- The problem with most leaders is: [fill in your own story].

How a coach's own story interacts with a client's particular leadership context can be further complicated when a coach has multiple relations in and with the organization. For example, the coach may

a) have a contract with the organization to coach this client,
b) coach others in the organization,
c) consult in the organization,
d) be on staff in the organization,
e) have a history in the organization,
f) have a relationship with key members, and
g) experience any combination of a) through f).

Besides creating boundary issues, the existence of such relationships can multiply the sources of potential triggers for the coach.

WHAT CAN WE DO TO COACH EFFECTIVELY AND ETHICALLY IN SUCH SITUATIONS?

In one of the vignettes earlier, Judy initially assumes that her client will react as she herself would have and begins probing "for evidence of disappointment and sadness." What Judy eventually learns, however, is that her client is, in fact, relieved. She had been fearful that her boss's assessment would be far worse, and she is also beginning to realize how little she likes or cares about her current job.

By maintaining curiosity and an awareness that the client is different from the coach, good coaches correct for any tendency to assume similarity. Further exploration often reveals client situations and responses to be distinguishable from the coach's experience in important ways. By staying open and curious, Judy learned that her client's reactions were actually quite different from her own.

In another of the vignettes, Jose was launching a new coaching business while coaching a client also in the midst of career change and thinking about next career steps. Here is more of the story, told from Jose's perspective:

> This client's situation triggered me in a number of ways. Along with feeling very immediate financial worries, I was also very committed to the process of self-authoring the next stage of my life. I found myself becoming anxious for and about my client. Since I found structure helpful in my own situation, I advocated structures for him. I also wanted him to pay close attention to generating income quickly. As a coach, I became very result-focused with a client who was much more interested in a philosophical exploration of the possibilities of this next stage of his life. But it was hard for me to see the distinctions between our situations.
>
> A number of steps helped me become more grounded. By spending some time understanding his past, I was able to see how he was different from me. Using the DISC instrument and other "neutral" assessment tools also helped me differentiate my story from his. I consulted with a mentor coach who helped me tune into the problem more clearly. Finally, concerned that my coaching was not proving helpful to the client, I initiated a discussion about my concerns with him. Sorting out what he was and wasn't getting out of the engagement gave us an opportunity to talk through these issues.

Jose got into difficulty because his related story was active and charged. But he also took a number of steps to self-correct and, in doing so, he became much more helpful to his client. The steps Jose undertook included:

1. Staying open to his client's story (as Judy also eventually did)
2. Using neutral assessment tools (examples of such instruments include the MBTI®, DISC®, BarOn EQ-I®, and FIRO-B®)
3. Consulting another coach (conversations with other coaches can help you see what you are not seeing in your coaching)
4. Sharing concerns with the client
    It is often helpful to share with the client what is happening for you as it occurs. The conversation might go something like this: "I am noticing similarities between your situation and one that I

faced recently, and I am concerned that my own reactions might get in my way. I would like to hear more about how you are reacting so that I can understand ways that the situations are similar and distinct." This kind of statement invites a very real communication with the client and helps the coach to keep his or her own experience separate.

Additional steps that are useful are

5. Paying attention to the warning signs (cited earlier, p. 122)
6. Using discretion in sharing stories

Once aware of possible similarities between the client's story and our own, we should take extra care to keep the two experiences distinct. If we decide it will be helpful to share our stories, we should frame this sharing very carefully (i.e., "I am going to share an experience that I had related to this. I am not suggesting that my experience or approach applies to your situation directly. But I offer it in case you find something useful in it"). These kinds of steps help to keep the focus on the client's experience where it belongs.

Effective uses of these action steps depend, first of all, on being aware of the personal issues that may surface in our interactions with leaders. Only through ongoing personal development work are we likely to be able to know which issues belong to us and which belong to our client. In particular, it may be useful to explore our experiences and stories about leadership and organizations. Once we have identified and dealt with those issues, we are less likely to experience the "charge" when one of our issues shows up with a client, and we will be more able to use our own experience without projecting it onto the client. As part of this ongoing inner work, coaches should engage in regular practices of reflection and centering (i.e., journaling, meditation, and bodywork) that support their self-awareness and their presence for coaching.

Self-awareness can also help us know when we are just not the right coach for a client. Most coaches have decided at some point that a particular client is not a good match. This is a hard call, but learning to differentiate a similarity that the coach can manage from one that may interfere is a critical skill to learn.

In the end, our ability to manage identification issues is an ethical concern. The Code of Ethics of the International Coach Federation states:

> I will at all times strive to recognize personal issues that may impair, conflict or interfere with my coaching performance or my professional relationships. Whenever the facts and circumstances

necessitate, I will promptly seek professional assistance and determine the action to be taken, including whether it is appropriate
to suspend or terminate my coaching relationship(s).[3]

CONCLUSION

A final way in which identification operates in leadership coaching
occurs at a deeper, more fundamental level than we have discussed
thus far. Our contemporary understanding of leadership effectiveness
increasingly extends beyond the idea of what leaders do to who they are
as people. "Leadership from within" suggests the notion that leadership has everything to do with the personal attitudes, beliefs, strengths,
and character of the leader. It is these qualities that allow a leader to
navigate the challenges of modern organizations in a rapidly changing
environment. In addition, it is particularly to this dimension of leadership that coaches must ultimately attend. Coaches who are attending
to their own personal attitudes, beliefs, strengths, and character can be
more adept at guiding their clients through that exploration.

Parker J. Palmer writes with particular insight about those fundamental inner qualities that most contribute to a leader's effectiveness.

> We share responsibility for creating the external world by pro-
> jecting either a spirit of light or a spirit of shadow on that which is
> other than us. Either a spirit of hope or a spirit of despair. Either
> an inner confidence in wholeness and integration, or an inner ter-
> ror about life being diseased and ultimately terminal. We have a
> choice about what we are going to project, and in that choice we
> help create the world that is…What does all of this have to do
> with leadership?…I'll give you a quick definition of a leader: a
> leader is a person who has an unusual degree of power to project
> on other people his or her shadow, or his or her light.[4]

In the "shadow side" of leadership, as Palmer describes it, are a
number of common stories that undermine a leader's ability to project
light. Those include deep insecurity about one's own worth, the belief
that the universe is essentially hostile and life a battleground, the belief
that ultimate responsibility for everything rests with oneself, fear of
the natural chaos of life, and the denial of death and the related fear
of failure.

It is ultimately the power of these "shadows" or deep stories that
determines the effectiveness of leaders. For coaches to help clients
identify and work with these core stories and beliefs, coaches must also

understand how these stories are present in their own lives. Work at this fundamental level is most critical when the leader's shadow story is also alive for the coach.

Coach and leader are in a sense on a similar journey. Both are challenged to identify their core stories, to understand how they may affect their work, and, in some cases, to choose new and different stories to live by. For coaches, this ability to recognize and manage these deep stories determines whether we shed light or darkness in our coaching.

NOTES

1. Psychological theorists have explored this terrain in considerable depth. Since Freud, for example, the concept of projection—the psychic mechanism by which one attributes to others one's own unacceptable thoughts and/or emotions—has become central in psychological theorizing. Readers interested in exploring the evolution of this concept should consult Freud, Anna, *The Ego and the Mechanisms of Defense* (London: Hogarth Press and Institute of Psychoanalysis, 1937), as well as a good textbook on psychoanalytic theory, for example, Laplanche, J. and J.B. Pontalis, translated by D.N. Smith, *The Language of Psychoanalysis* (London: Karnac Books, 1966).
2. Adapted from Cashman, *Leadership from the Inside Out: Becoming a Leader for Life*, 39–42.
3. International Coach Federation, *ICF Code of Ethics, Part Three, Number 5* (approved 1/22/2005).
4. Parker J. Palmer, *Leading from Within: Reflections on Spirituality and Leadership* (Washington, DC: Servant Leadership School, 1990), 7.

BIBLIOGRAPHY

Cashman, Kevin. *Leadership from the Inside Out: Becoming a Leader for Life.* Minneapolis, MN: TCLG, 1998.

Coleman, David. "A Coach's Lessons Learned: Principles and Guidelines for Practitioners," in *Executive Coaching: Practices and Perspective,* edited by Catherine Fitzgerald and Jennifer Garvey Burger. Palo Alto, CA: Davies-Black, 2002.

Flaherty, James. *Coaching: Evoking Excellence in Others.* Boston: Butterworth-Heinemann, 1999.

Granberg-Michaelson, Wesley. *Leadership from Inside Out: Spirituality and Organizational Change.* New York: Crossroad, 2004.

O'Neill, Mary Beth. *Executive Coaching with Backbone and Heart.* San Francisco: Jossey-Bass, 2000.

Palmer, Parker J. *Leading from Within: Reflections on Spirituality and Leadership.* Washington, DC: Servant Leadership School, 1990.

CHAPTER 12

CONGRATULATIONS—YOU'RE IN BREAKDOWN!

JENNIFER SINEK

NATALIE[1] LOOKS AT ME HESITANTLY, her normal certainty absent. The strong, confident, self-assured professional seems shaken. As she's talking she looks at the floor, then glances up to see what I think, her shoulders tilted to the side as opposed to her normal strong presence with sustained, direct eye contact and squared-up, face-to-face posture.

Simple and elegant, polished in her appearance but not uptight, she is a white woman in her forties with short, stylish brown hair, wearing a navy pantsuit with a cream-colored blouse. A principal at a large consulting firm, she's accustomed to knowing what to do in any situation and just getting it done. Her current level of doubt is unprecedented in our work together.

Her voice is halting. "I just don't think I can do it."

"I know it doesn't feel like it, but that's really good news." I give her some space so my words can sink in. Her body tightens, and she looks at me with surprise. "It seems as if you've been at the edge of this struggle for a really long time." With that, her back relaxes, her chest and face soften, and she lets out a deep sigh.

"You're right," she responds, "but I don't see how that's good news."

I ask her, if it were good news, how would she be sitting in the chair? Natalie looks at me quizzically, but shifts forward in her chair. She sits taller, her chest and arms more open, and looks up. Her eyes still look doubtful, but there is a hint of a spark in them. If it were good news, what would it open up for her? The spark grows. As we continue, her mood begins to lighten, her energy expands, and we are on our way.

Every effective coaching interaction either has an apparent point of entry, a doorway to spur the client to take action, or one must be created. This is the concept of breakdown—and breakdown is essential to breaking through. Although the word sounds destructive, at its core, breakdown is generative. Breakdown provides the client with both the possibility of a new way of seeing things and a desire for this by "breaking down" the barriers to seeing our lives from a new perspective, making us question our spoken or unspoken assumptions about what's possible or impossible, about what's "true" for us and for others, and about how the world works.

WHAT DO WE MEAN BY BREAKDOWN?

Breakdown is what happens when the outcomes we experience don't match our expectations. We're not talking about a "nervous breakdown" or clinical levels of anxiety or depression—merely what most of us experience to varying degrees at different times as we move through life. Clients may feel as if they're breaking into pieces, and we have a chance to help them see that they are actually breaking through a barrier into greater capacity.

This experience is about seeing things that weren't visible to us before—sometimes an entirely different world. Think of the chick that begins to crack the shell, to break through, and emerge into the world. The shell was protective, but then becomes a barrier—the breakdown is needed for the chick to continue to grow.

However, we don't always notice the breakdown, much less its upside, right away.

For humans, just as in the rest of the universe, inertia is a natural law. We tend to keep doing what we're doing. In addition, if we're not getting or creating what we want, we often do more of what we have been doing, only faster or more intensely. We overlook the adage that the definition of insanity is doing the same thing repeatedly and expecting different results. One must overcome this inertia to effect change.

Consider the "boiled frog syndrome." According to research done in the late 1800s, frogs' nervous systems are unable to distinguish incremental changes in temperature or pressure.[2] Therefore, if you were to put a frog in a pan of water and raise the temperature very gradually, eventually the frog would boil to death without noticing that the water was getting hotter. However, if you put a frog in a pot of water that is already hot or increase the heat quickly, it will jump right out.

We humans tend to behave like the frog in a number of domains. Many of us don't pay close attention to slight changes in our emotional state, health, or performance in our jobs. Raising (or cooling) the water temperature gradually is like the slow version of breakdowns in our lives. It's the job that isn't great, but isn't awful. It's the team that's showing signs of increasing difficulty, but it hasn't really impacted the work— a lot—yet. It's the subtle signs that the organization isn't overjoyed with our work or our management style or our choices. Sometimes it's the coach's job to step in and point out the breakdown, either by naming the story we see being played out or by providing the opportunity for the client to see the "hot water" in a different light.

Often we live with a low level of pain in one or more areas of our lives, to the point that the pain becomes invisible to us. It is so familiar that we no longer see it. On the surface, we may realize that things aren't quite what we want them to be or that we're not as happy as we expected to be, but we tell ourselves that that's just the way life is—our expectations were too high, and we just have to live with it.

Alternatively, we may think we can't change what we perceive to be "wrong." We fear that it will take too much energy or risk, or change who we fundamentally are. And all the while, the pain is sapping our energy, keeping us from the future we desire and deserve.

Natalie shifted from shock at my congratulating her for being in breakdown to joy in just a couple of conversations. She realized that she had to make a major shift; she could no longer just get by, trying to manage the pieces or change them incrementally. Once she achieved this clarity, the energy that was being sapped by her situation (and her angst about it) began to be freed up. She was able to envision a future she truly desired and focus on it, and this continued to fuel her energy and joy.

ENERGY FOR CHANGE

Energy for change comes from what pulls us forward—the vision—and what drives us from behind—the desire to get rid of what we don't want. And when we're creating the future, it is valuable to know what we don't want to include in it as well as to know what we do want.

The push (discomfort, dissonance, and pain) multiplied by the pull (the vision) yields the energy available for change to occur (figure 12.1).

Discomfort × Vision = Energy for Change

Figure 12.1 A formula for change

Our rising awareness of discomfort or dissonance helps us stop and reflect on what we really want. Clear vision of the present allows us then to have a point of comparison for our future vision and shows us where we need to take action to create the situation we desire.

Several years ago, I was involved in a project that turned into a much larger commitment than I had anticipated. It was also different work than I had hoped, much of which I didn't enjoy or experience as bringing my value to the world. The longer-than-expected hours on top of an already busy schedule came out of my nights (sleep), weekends (recreation), and most importantly, my time with my husband and young children. However, I had committed to the project, and my story was that I had to continue, even though it was sapping my energy. I told myself repeatedly that things would change once we had gotten past the start-up phase, an ever-receding milestone. I was so busy trying to get everything done so that I could spend some time with my family, and perhaps get a bit of sleep, that I didn't look at what was happening, how out of line with my values my life was becoming.

Fortunately, something happened to trigger an additional level of pain. I received a call inviting me to be part of a significant project, one that truly spoke to who I am, to my values, and to my continuing development. The pain came from my initial reaction, which was that I had to turn it down—there was no way I could add one more thing, even something I dearly desired, to my already crazily overbooked life.

I experienced even greater pain as a colleague coached me, helping me to explore and paint the picture of this future I desired in even more vivid color. What a fit with my values, my vision! How nourishing being part of this would be, in addition to helping others on their path! As I thought about it more and more, the vividness of that image and the contrasting pain of turning it down brought my life into sharp relief. I started thinking more about the impact on my family, about the percentage of my toddler's life that had already been affected by my being consumed with this earlier project—and I knew I had to make a change. It was no longer a question of finding a way to add this new project to my life—it became a question of how to remove the other project to create open space for what I did want. Once I made that shift in focus, two things began to happen immediately. First, the pain became more real and much less tolerable. How had I been downplaying or ignoring it all this time? Second, my energy became focused both on creating the change—removing myself from this contract—and also beyond that on exploring changes that would help me continue to move closer to living my life according to my values and dreams. This energy was positive—and generative. The process took energy, but like a good workout, it left me stronger, energized, and ready to take action.

Had I not experienced that trigger, the sharp rise in the level of discomfort I was experiencing, who knows how much longer I would have continued on the same, negative path. As it was, the increase in the level of discomfort, combined with the increasingly clear vision and draw of the future I desired, supplied the energy I needed to make the change.

TYPES OF BREAKDOWN

Breakdowns come in all shapes and sizes (table 12.1). Some are externally induced or triggered (i.e., situational or crisis-related breakdowns). This could be the loss of a job, being passed over for a promotion, a team the client just can't get to work together, or a bad performance evaluation. It could be the death or illness of a loved one that causes a client to question how he or she is spending his or her own life. On the positive side, an unexpected promotion or new job opportunity can also trigger breakdowns, raising fears of failure or success.

Some breakdowns are triggered internally. These can fall into a few categories. On the negative side, we might notice the following:

- The client is experiencing pain or dissatisfaction, but doesn't see a clear way out. Sometimes clients just aren't happy—they're tired, frustrated, or something just "isn't right," and they're no longer effective. Sometimes a seemingly positive transition didn't create the change in their life they believed it would.
- The client is feeling numb, empty—not connected to anything they care about.

On the positive side, we might notice the following:

- The client is fairly content with the present, but knows there's more, a next step. In this case the breakdown is about what's next. The itch for growth, for continued transformation, has reached awareness and is calling to be scratched.

Table 12.1 Types of breakdowns

	External catalyst	Internal catalyst
Positive	Unexpected promotion, new job/opportunity → anticipation or fear of failure or success	Looking for the next step in development or transformation
Negative	Crisis-related, for example, job loss, bad performance evaluation, illness, death of someone close	Experiencing pain or dissatisfaction but doesn't see a way out or feeling numb, disconnected

OK, SO NOW WE KNOW THERE'S A BREAKDOWN. WHAT IS THE COACH'S ROLE?

The coach helps clients see or experience more fully the breakdown they're either in or headed for. How? By holding up the mirror that reflects the breakdown as a breakdown. This may temporarily increase the client's perceived level of pain, though the intent is merely to see the situation more accurately and free up energy to create the future the client desires.

With any type of breakdown, it's critical that the internal link is driving the change. If the catalyst is external, then it's important that we help clients translate the breakdown and the subsequent change into something that matters to them, that enlivens them, that has connection to something they truly value and believe in. That's what allows them to move beyond the pain of the breakdown into generating the vision of the future that will focus their energy and pull them forward.

Therefore, as coaches we do the following:

- *Invite our clients to see the breakdown more fully* and experience its impacts on different areas of their life. We might ask them to self-observe for a week or two: "To what extent are you creating the results you want, and what's the story you're telling yourself about that?" Or we may invite more internal reflection: "Where is the friction, where are the nagging, annoying, or empty places?" To go back to the chick analogy, where is their shell becoming too small? We focus on helping them to see their thoughts more clearly as well as the emotions they're experiencing, the physical sensations, and the actions they take. What is the physical "shape" of their breakdown?[3]
- *Help our clients find spots of joy.* Often the comparison or contrast to the rest of the client's life brings the pain in those areas into

sharp relief—and creates both an opening and energy for change. This provides an oasis, a place to rest and recharge during the process of change. When clients think of their joy, how do their emotions shift? What do they notice in their body—sensations, form, aliveness? We help them to own these and build on them.

- *Help them to author an alternative vision*—an external story of a truly compelling future, one that speaks to who they are and what they value. We have them envision this fully—intellectually, and in terms of their mood, emotions, and bearing. How does their body feel as they put themselves in that new future? Shifting attention to their embodied vision helps them to discern where there are opportunities for change and growth and to notice quickly when they get off track.

- *Help our clients generate and live into an alternative story*—an internal vision—one that serves this external vision for the future that they have created. What stories about themselves or the world do they need to write or rewrite to be successful? We help clients ground the new story in skills, but also in mood, presence, and structures of support. This stage of the coaching process can involve developing new moves and physical presence so clients can step into the new vision powerfully and effectively.

- *Help clients keep an eye on the speed limit.* Sometimes when we're working through breakdown, the energy for change increases so rapidly that a client can get carried away. At these times, we offer the suggestion to brake gently, so the clients see the road ahead and manage their speed to navigate the curves safely for themselves and others around them.

- *We must also develop the capacity in ourselves to hold a safe space for clients in breakdown.* If we are tense or get triggered, we make the breakdown experience less safe for the client, and they can end up shaming themselves. Our goal is to normalize what they're experiencing, help them feel it and honor it. Thus, we allow them the space, light, and air for their lives to transform.

WHAT IF WE CAN SEE THE BREAKDOWN, BUT THE CLIENT CAN'T?

We often gather information from our clients' colleagues in addition to what we hear directly from our clients, and this provides the opportunity to use the colleagues' experiences of our clients as a mirror. From here, we can invite clients to consider a different perspective on the situation.

Often, clients have inklings about the issue that become much clearer with additional perspectives and self-observation exercises. We must also realize that clients may not be ready to address the issue at that point in time—or that we may be off-base in our interpretations!

CONCLUSION

Coaches often fall into the trap of helping their clients feel better and decreasing their level of pain. We care about our clients, and we don't like to see people suffer. Although this is a positive long-term goal, sometimes it actually does clients a disservice. Easing discomfort can leave them stuck in their current situation, robbing them of the energy they need to make the move or to take the risk that will help them create the life they truly want.

Sometimes we need to turn up their sensation of the heat by asking questions that focus their attention on the thermometer, providing invitation and support for clients to experience their breakdown in a transformative way. Clients don't want to wake up five, ten, or twenty years from now and say, "What happened? How did I get here?" We help them wake up now, if they're ready, to the gradually changing temperatures in different areas of their lives and see new possibilities for what they want to create.

We point out the breaking down of the coherence in their lives— mind, body, emotions, and spirit—and help them see and take action on new choices to make their lives whole. Therefore, as coaches, we must become adept at both identifying and welcoming breakdown. Our focus must be on how to create the space and the opportunities for our clients to step into their breakdowns, experience them fully, and use them as openings—as invitations to grow into and create the future they desire.

NOTES

1. Name and some details have been changed to protect client confidentiality.
2. Edward Wheeler Scripture, *The New Psychology* (New York: Charles Scribner, 1897), 300.
3. The work of Richard Strozzi-Heckler is seminal in working through the somatic shape of the client to effect and support change. See *The Leadership Dojo* (Frog Books, 2007) and *The Anatomy of Change* (North Atlantic Books, 1997).

CHAPTER 13

THE ROLE OF EMOTIONS IN COACHING

KAREN CURNOW AND RANDY CHITTUM

INTRODUCTION

In ontological coaching, leadership coaches seek to generate long-term transformational learning for their clients by engaging with their clients in the domains of language, body, and emotion. This chapter focuses explicitly on the domain of emotion and the role of emotions in coaching. We propose that without relevant emotional learning, lasting change does not take place for our clients.

Sometimes, leadership coaches bring emotions into their coaching work superficially, using what some call a "cheerleader" approach with emotions. In these situations, the coach seemingly helps the client transform "bad" emotions into "good" ones, supposedly helping to create a happy ending. While clients occasionally need encouragement, the outcomes of cheerleading are short-lived because no habits of mind and heart have been addressed. The real learning for clients almost always lives in the very emotions the cheerleading coach is trying to talk them out of. Deeper learning is possible if the coach and client mine the emotions for what they reveal.

At other times, leadership coaches avoid working with emotions in their coaching altogether because either they don't know what to do with emotions or they mistakenly believe that addressing emotions oversteps the boundaries between coaching and counseling. It's not a surprise that working with emotions is difficult for coaches. The cultures of many organizations do not value expressions of emotion. Emotions can be misunderstood and people labeled negatively for expressing them. Tough-mindedness, which often seems to be preferred as a leadership quality, may be misconstrued as being devoid of or unaffected by emotions.

The fact is emotions are always present. Even when someone is feeling numb, that numbness is an emotion. The beauty is that emotions reveal much about what matters. It is the job of a coach to pay attention to emotions and to invite our clients to acknowledge, listen to, and learn from their emotions. While we aren't in the business of healing deep emotional wounds from the past (this is the work of counseling or therapy), we can open new learning for our clients by listening to and working with emotions. The question for leadership coaches then becomes: what's a coach to do with emotions?

WHAT DO EMOTIONS REVEAL?

Packaged with every emotion are beliefs and behavioral tendencies. Philosophers have suggested that all emotion is propositional, that emotions are connected to a proposition, a belief, an assessment. One way coaches can work with emotions is to invite clients to identify the assessments or beliefs that exist behind their emotions and the actions they are most likely to take in the presence of those emotions.

For example, when someone at work raises his or her voice, some people might feel defensive, because their emotional experience of defensiveness is rooted in the belief or assessment that they deserve to be treated differently and that they can and will protect themselves. Other people may respond to the same situation with overwhelming fear because they believe that they may not be strong enough to handle the situation. Each of these two assessments—the first being a belief about one's worthiness (and the right way to be treated) and the second being a belief about one's weakness—generates a different emotion, which in turn influences what actions one would most likely take in the situation.

These assessments matter because they can predict what people are likely to do and not do. Emotions and the beliefs or assessments connected to them predispose a person to act within a certain range of behaviors. In fact, the word emotion derives from the Latin *ēmovēre*, that which moves a person, that which puts someone in motion, into action. In the previous example, people feeling defensive will likely explain or protect themselves, whereas those in fear will likely want to run away or hide.

Helping our clients see this direct connection between their emotions, beliefs, and behaviors can produce new awareness, helping them see themselves more deeply and clearly. This deepened awareness empowers clients and enables them to make intentional choices about the actions they take.

There are three possible entry points then for the coach working with a client in the domain of emotions: the client's direct emotional experience, the assessments the client holds, and the actions the client wishes to take in the situation.

For clients who are able to articulate what emotions they are experiencing, coaches can help them listen to their emotions by walking them directly through the three portals, asking questions such as:

- What emotion or emotions are you experiencing?
- What beliefs or assessments are linked to that emotion for you?
- What do the emotions and assessments predispose you to want to do?

These simple, direct questions can work very well with clients who can specifically identify their emotions. Clients may not be that emotionally fluent, however, and may need to explore their emotions in a less direct way.

Sometimes, clients cannot pinpoint the emotion or emotions they are experiencing, and coaches can support them by "backing in" to reveal the emotion, starting with the assessments clients have about a situation or by asking them to identify the actions they want to take. Asking clients who are unaware of their emotions a question like "What emotion are you experiencing?" (as suggested above) can leave them stumped, resulting in the probable response, "I don't know" or the common one, "I'm feeling fine." By identifying the assessments a person is holding about a situation, the coach can help the client identify the underlying emotion that is driving the client's reactions and behaviors.

For example, one client was surprised to learn that she had lingering resentment in a work situation—something she discovered only after her coach helped her identify the story she told herself (her assessments) and the actions she wanted to take in response to the situation. Learning that resentment was present allowed the coach and client to look at and test the client's assessments about the situation (as unfair), about her boss (whom she assessed as the "tyrant"), about herself (the "victim"), and about how they both "should" operate.

The client and coach also looked at the actions the client wanted to take (largely about punishing her boss in subtle ways). While she didn't actually *do* these things, admitting what she *wanted* to do was eye-opening for the client and helped her clearly see the resentment and anger that had been brewing for some time.

As a result of this discovery and exploration of resentment (by acknowledging her underlying assessments and predispositions for action), the client was able to identify a way forward that took into account what she cared most about (which included saying what she needed and making requests, among other things). Her new ability to work with her emotions instead of simply reacting without thought freed the client from the grips of the formerly unacknowledged resentment.

Coaching is largely about helping clients see new possibilities. Coaches who are less comfortable including emotions in their coaching may be tempted to focus quickly or exclusively on the actions a client should take. Their coaching sessions may involve having the client articulate a concern and then having the two of them simply brainstorm solutions and action steps.

Working with clients' emotions, as opposed to only behaviors, is more powerful in terms of creating lasting change. For example, a client was given feedback that he needed to be more approachable. Discussing how this client would act if he were more approachable (behaviors such as smiling more and showing interest in others) is likely to leave the client feeling incongruous and to lead to behavioral changes that are not sustainable. However, when we look deeper into the emotions that are present when the client appears unapproachable and uncover the beliefs or thoughts connected to those emotions, we may interrupt the process at a deeper level and generate long-term impact. In this real example, in his moments of appearing unapproachable, this client experienced irritation that was built on a belief that others were not as smart as he. While it took time and practice to challenge that belief and replace it with a more generative and accurate one, when the change came, it was a sea change.

A fundamental question the leadership coach can offer to leader-clients is: Do you have your emotions or do your emotions have you? This question asks leaders to consider to what extent they are aware of their emotional experience. Coaching questions that focus on emotions, beliefs, and behavioral leanings provide a pause in the knee-jerk reaction that emotions often produce. This pause enables our clients to consider their choices and then lead intentionally; in this way, they create a better chance for achieving the outcome they want. Understanding emotions, the beliefs underlying them, and the actions that are likely to result creates leverage for sustainable change.

BEING EMOTIONALLY INTELLIGENT

When our clients get in the habit of looking at the stories behind their emotions and their habitual reactions to events in their lives, they are developing greater capacity for showing their emotional intelligence as leaders. The most powerful leaders understand the power and impact of emotions, including and especially their own. Emotional intelligence experts tell us that decision-making and other key leadership competencies are only possible with the guidance provided by emotions.

You may find yourself working in an organization whose leadership is attempting to practice emotional intelligence. The essence of emotional intelligence is awareness of your own emotions, of the emotions of others, and of the impact of these emotions. Emotionally intelligent leaders know how to put this awareness into action. In an activity we use in teaching leadership workshops, we ask the leaders in the room to identify what makes the most respected leaders in their lives successful. What we consistently find is that based on their own experience, they report that the best leaders are caring, tuned in to the other person and not just the task, able to appreciate and acknowledge others, and inspiring to others to realize their potential. What seems to matter to followers and colleagues is a leader's ability to be emotionally intelligent. While having academic intelligence or technical expertise is also important for leaders, research shows that emotional intelligence is the lever that makes for great leadership.

Many leaders are limited when it comes to accurately sensing and then naming their emotions. They can often get stuck at "good" or "frustrated." Part of our work in helping our clients develop emotional intelligence is to create greater differentiation in our language about emotions. What distinguishes joy from happiness? Anger from rage? Love from admiration? Some leaders claim that they do not have an experience of emotion in normal settings, but being numb to or unaware of emotions is not the same as not having them. There is no emotional neutrality since we are always experiencing some emotion, to a greater or lesser degree.

Asking leaders to keep a log or journal of emotions they notice during the day is one way to build their emotional self-awareness. (You can give them a list of emotions as a starter for building their awareness of emotions.) Regularly asking questions such as, "What emotion were you experiencing when that occurred?" and "How do you think that emotion made possible certain behaviors and limited you regarding others?" can help our client leaders notice patterns that can lead to especially powerful conversations.

Another practice that can help raise our clients' awareness of emotions is to have them tune into their physical experiences at different moments since these body sensations actually reflect emotional states. Most leaders have awareness of when they are hijacked emotionally— and can report their physical reactions in the moment of the hijack (sweating, heart racing, flushed face, etc.). They are often less attuned to their physical responses at other moments. Having them take note of their physical reactions at different moments can support them in developing more fluency in naming their emotions.

Somatic or body-based coaching practices can also support clients in expanding their capacity to be with and to access various emotions. For example, one client with difficulty standing up to an abusive boss developed a daily physical practice in which she shaped herself into the "body of indignation" (which she created during a coaching session, with feet planted solidly, shoulders squared, and an unwavering and serious stare). This regular practice "reminded" her of what that emotion "felt like" physically so that when called for, she could access both the physical posture and the emotion. After doing this practice for some time, this client discovered another emotion that must be in place before indignation can show up: a sense of her own dignity. Using body awareness as a vehicle to understand one's emotions is exceptionally powerful. More on the use of the body in coaching is covered in chapter 14.

Having an awareness of the emotions of others can be daunting for leaders. While coaches might have a natural affinity for attending to emotions, many leaders do not. Without the capacity to notice and identify the emotions of others and to exercise empathy and care, leaders can be blindsided in their efforts to lead. The good news is that leaders who have developed their own emotional self-awareness often become more attuned to the emotions of others as well.

For leaders who are challenged in this area, a helpful coaching practice is to have them simply get in the regular habit of making their best assessment regarding another's emotional state, often by observing the other person's nonverbal messages more carefully. In places and relationships where it feels safe to do so, clients can then also check out their "guess" as a way to calibrate their perception over time.

Finally, leading in an emotionally conscious way is the result of the interplay of emotional awareness of oneself and others. For example, a client got easily flustered and offtrack whenever she had to speak truthfully to people in power. After focusing on her emotions in these moments, she noted that she felt anxious and assessed these conversations as hopeless—that she had "learned" from past experiences that nothing good would come from the risk she was taking. It is not hard to see how an assessment of being hopeless would lead her to feeling flustered. After a coaching conversation, she challenged her "hopeless" story and chose to focus her attention and actions more on the future (hopeful) and less on the past (resigned). While the coach and client could have articulated those useful behaviors, the emotional work of challenging her own assessments and taking actions from the new, more optimistic story created a more sustainable change for her.

THE EMOTIONAL CONTEXT FOR COACHING, LEARNING, AND LEADING

Context is essential in emotional learning. We can be fooled into thinking that coaching is simply something we "do" to our clients, just as the leaders we coach might think that leading is something they "do" to their direct reports. In fact, an essential part of coaching and leading is to cocreate with others the emotional context needed for new direction and learning. Effective leaders are masterful in creating contexts adequate to the tasks they have at hand. Change the emotional context, and you will change the learning and actions that are possible.

In a context of deep trust, for example, people will speak about things they wouldn't otherwise bring up. If the environment is full of anger, there will be limitations on what change is possible for the group. Effective coaches and leaders recognize that much of their work is helping to create an emotional context that will support the future they have declared they want for themselves and others. In a recent interview, Julio Olalla, founder of the Newfield Network, said, "Emotional learning does not happen by command, but rather by immersion. Context is essential in emotional learning. For example, if you coach from a place of tenderness, or logic, or enthusiasm, or resignation, it will show up in your coachee" (from Karen Curnow's interview with Julio Olalla on August 10, 2012.) Wise coaches note their own emotional landscape while they are coaching, since their embodied emotion, whatever it is, is contagious. The art of emotional learning is connected to the art of creating emotional context.

How are these emotional contexts created? Creating a new emotional context will always require stating or recognizing what is not working, understanding the assessments and emotions that are leading to this undesired outcome, and creating a new story that will help generate a different outcome.

SUMMARY

In our experience, the work of emotional intelligence and using emotions in coaching is critical in creating long-term learning that matters for our clients. This learning ultimately affects those who work with and for them. While we recognize the power of working with emotions, we also know that it can feel risky to those who have not engaged in such conversations before. We cannot emphasize enough that coaches must do their own emotional work in order to truly help their clients with understanding the emotions that are keeping them stuck. Using emotion-based approaches can help coaches support their clients in developing a deeper understanding of themselves and others and in creating emotional contexts adequate to the organizational changes they choose to lead. The result is a substantial and sustainable return on investment—for the coach and the leader.

CHAPTER 14

USING SOMATICS TO COACH LEADERS

MARGARET ECHOLS AND SANDY MOBLEY

OUR LEADERSHIP COACHING APPROACH INCLUDES basic distinctions related to language, emotions, and body; we increase our power as observers by obtaining more distinctions in language, deeper and wider access to our range of emotions (and moods), and greater *awareness of our body*. As our own leadership coaching experience has grown, we have developed an increasing recognition and appreciation of the rich possibilities in exploring more deeply the critical role the body plays in the clients' learning and in helping our clients transform. It is routine for coaches to ask their clients, "What are you feeling?" but rarely is the emotion or mood linked to the client's body sensations or body posture.

In working with somatics—that is, the domain of the body—coaches learn to make deep connections between language, body, and emotions, and they learn to become more powerful observers of others and ourselves. We discern what the body can tell us about who we are and how we are living. Before they can assist clients somatically, coaches need to experience for themselves how they are in their own bodies, where they are open and where they are contracted, and where there is possibility and where there is limitation.

To work with leaders *through the body*, coaches learn to observe, in themselves and then in others, when language, emotions, and body are congruent or aligned and when they are not. They learn to observe, in themselves and others, reflexive ways in which people respond to certain triggers or life events. Through awareness and somatic practices, we expand our capacity for action. As coaches practice and cultivate the power of being centered (i.e., connected, present, open, and focused) in more situations, more frequently, they also learn to recover more quickly when off center. They shift from simply being coaches to becoming *embodied* leadership coaches.

UNDERSTANDING THE GAP

An amazingly hard human lesson to grasp is how often we fail at something we've set out to do. Think about the commitments that you've made to keep your desk neat, to return phone calls or respond to e-mails in one day, or to get to meetings on time. Since most of our education had been biased toward cognitive learning (i.e., facts, theory, etc.), we were shocked to learn in an initial Strozzi Institute leadership course how often *knowing* doesn't translate into *doing*.

In a physical (somatic) exercise designed to model making a request, we were told to walk toward the person we were making a request of with our hand out and touch the person just below the throat with an open palm. One coach remembers: "With the best of intentions my hand always ended up on the other person's shoulder. I don't have vision problems, and I could walk up to someone and touch them under the throat, but in the context of making a request, I missed every time. That's when I saw my own gap. My body knew something my mind did not."

For example, many people *know* the importance of making an effective request and can even recite the criteria perfectly. However, under pressure or in certain situations, they often fall into old ineffective patterns. Alternatively, they might say the right words, but their tone of voice or body language conveys an undermining message. Seeing this dilemma made us more aware that, in working with executives, we needed to look for and bridge this gap.

After the somatic exercise, the coach continues, "my awareness was raised further as I listened to how I made requests. To staff I said, 'Please make sure you include me in that client meeting.' But with the boss, the same 'request' sounded like, 'It would be useful to me to attend client meetings.' I clearly *knew* how to make an effective request, yet wasn't able to *do* so in some situations. This made me curious about what happens in that knowing-doing gap."

Human beings are conditioned through upbringing and culture to behave in ways that might have served at one time, but are no longer effective. These behaviors are so ingrained that we don't realize we have a choice. For example, a leader we know was taught as a child to *not* make direct requests of others. This behavior became so automatic that it occurred whenever she wanted something; she had buried the ability to make direct requests. "I can remember being at my aunt's house when I was eight years old, desperately wanting an Eskimo Pie ice cream from her freezer and knowing that I dared not ask for it. I could only make a series of hints. 'My throat is burning up,' I said, prompting my aunt to offer water. 'No,' I responded, water won't do it; it needs to be *colder* than water. Perhaps some milk, she suggested. 'No, milk won't work; I don't like the taste of it, but that is closer to what I'm looking for.' Finally, my aunt asked if I'd like an ice cream." Imagine the inefficiency and waste of time if someone used that process at work!

Instead, the leader in our story above learned to make powerful requests of the staff that left no room for interpretation. By bringing this skill into her conversations with her superiors, she realized she would save herself a lot of aggravation and disappointment when they couldn't decode her veiled requests. "Until I became aware of this conditioned response, I could only hint and hope that others would know what I desired and respond positively," she says. To undo the conditioning, awareness of the behavior had to come first. To be effective, coaches must help leaders recognize the ingrained, habituated responses that they can't see and assist them in adopting more productive behaviors.

Clients aren't disembodied heads, required only to *think* leadership. Without the ability to *act*, leaders can't motivate others, align behavior, or influence change. Action occurs through the body. Action follows awareness, so it is important to notice what we are paying attention to. For example, if a leader is focusing on keeping others happy, he may not make requests that he feels are unpopular. On the flip side, if the leader is only concerned with getting the work done and not how others feel about doing the work, he runs the risk of alienating the workforce.

A key factor for effective leadership is authenticity—alignment between saying and doing. People evaluate their leaders more by what they *do* than what they *say*. Albert Mehrabian from UCLA studied this behavioral difference. He found that when people communicated feelings if there was dissonance between what was said and how that person behaved, the audience judged the person's actual words to have only a 7 percent impact, while the person's voice and body language had much higher impact, at 38 percent and 55 percent respectively.[1]

Clearly a person's actions and voice, with a 93 percent impact, carry far more weight than the words a person uses.

In his book *The Anatomy of Change*, Richard Strozzi-Heckler writes, "Somatics . . . defines the body as a functional, living whole rather than as a mechanical structure. Somatics does not see a split between the mind and body but views the soma as a unified expression of all that we think, feel, perceive, and express."[2] Somatic coaches show clients how their body language correlates with often hidden and limiting inner feelings, narratives, and mindsets. Specifically designed, somatically based practices allow these internal states to shift, enabling clients to take new actions to achieve their goals. For example, if a man grew up being told that "nice boys" don't brag, he may drop his voice and look away from his peers when asked to talk about his projects in a team meeting. He may have no awareness that hiding his talent is limiting his career progression. Once these behaviors are brought to his attention, he will still need time and somatic practices to keep his voice strong and maintain eye contact when talking about his work.

GETTING CENTERED AND USING SOMATICS FOR COACHING

To understand somatics and apply it to coaching, you must be attuned to your own body and your feeling. Many people have become anesthetized to feelings and tell themselves—that is, tell their bodies—what they can and can't feel. A person may feel sad at the death of a relative or the loss of a meaningful job, but feels compelled to put on a happy face and dismiss the feelings. Another person whose boss yells at her several times a week may say, "Oh, he is under pressure and doesn't really mean it." For both people, their bodies ache nonetheless. Denying feelings doesn't ease pain. In addition, numbing painful feelings decreases the capacity to experience other feelings—joy, fear, surprise, and so on.

On the other hand, some people can be overloaded by the intensity of their feelings to the point that it becomes intolerable and they boil over in rage or panic. Daniel Goleman refers to this in his book *Working with Emotional Intelligence* as an amygdala hijack.[3] In these situations, the primal part of the brain senses an old and uncomfortable emotion, and the person is thrown into one of three basic responses—fight, flight, or freeze. The higher-functioning part of the brain is cut off, and the behavior that results is seldom pretty.

To avoid having to swallow feelings or to be ruled by them, it helps to have a place of safety inside oneself that allows time for choice and greater ranges of possibilities. The first step to finding that internal oasis in the body is to learn what it feels like to be centered. Being centered in your body is like shifting to neutral in a car with a manual transmission. It is the place of flexibility that allows for easy movement in any direction. It is a place where you can access your power, focus on what you care about, and tap into the inner wisdom of your body, feelings, and emotions.

There are times when being centered can mean the difference between life and death. Consider the police officer who has a split second to decide whether the person in the heavy overcoat coming his way is carrying a bomb, a weapon, or something harmless such as a cell phone. Being centered can affect whether you win a negotiation, get a job, or hear what is really bothering your teenager.

Somatics begins with you as a coach. It is important to be centered before beginning a coaching session. This allows you to be open and connected to your client. You become a more powerful observer because your focus is on your client and his needs, not your worries about what to say next or whether you sound intelligent. Centering keeps your internal chatter at bay and opens you to hear what the client has to say. Your ability to center helps your client center as well. Think about how one scared horse spooks the others in a corral, or the impact on others of a hysterical person at the scene of an accident. Being open, centered, and confident helps the client become open and calm, too.

To center, pay attention to your breath. Is it low in your belly and moving fully through your body? Bringing your attention to your breath helps you center. Notice your posture. Are you slouched or rigid? If so, sit or stand tall with your weight evenly distributed on each side and from front to back. What about your forehead—is it wrinkled or relaxed? Notice your eyes. Are they staring fixedly or wide open like a deer in the headlights? Relax your eyes—let them soften and increase your peripheral vision. How about your jaw? Is it held tightly? Are you grinding your teeth? Open your mouth as wide as you can and then relax your jaw. How about your shoulders? Are they pulled up tightly near your ears as you carry the weight of the world? Tighten them more and then relax them, feeling the tension slide away. These are some of the key areas where we hold tension. Tension dilutes center. If we are feeling tightness or pain, our attention goes to these areas and away from feeling centered.

It may be useful to do a centering practice with your client at the start of your session. Coaching sessions often take place in the middle of a busy day. Helping your client get centered allows her to let go of other concerns and be fully present for the session. The more you can bring your client's awareness to her stance and sensations, the better. Pay attention to your client's body. Are her shoulders high? It could mean she is taking on too much responsibility. Notice tightness in the jaw area. This may indicate the need to control things or that she is *chewing* on a difficult problem. How is her eye contact? Do you see a "deer in the headlights" look, an intense stare, a sleepy gaze? What do these things mean to you? You are helping your client see what has been invisible to her. For example, you may point out that she smiles broadly when she is saying no. Then she wonders why people don't accept it when she turns down a request.

Rather than keep a checklist that says if you see this, it means that, it is more useful to be curious. You might sometimes mirror what you see to the client and ask what that posture or look provokes in her. That tends to give you more insight about what the client is experiencing, and she in turn sees herself from new perspectives.

HOW IT WORKS: SOMATICS IN ACTION

To illustrate how you, as a leadership coach, can incorporate an understanding of somatics into how you would coach a leader, here's how one coach we know recounts her own experience:

Carol is a senior government official in an important position with the Department of Defense. I assumed she'd be somewhat rigid in her posture, buttoned down and stern. When a slight woman dressed in a flowered blouse and light blue skirt, with wispy blonde hair and a shy demeanor, met me on our first appointment, I presumed she was Carol's administrative assistant coming to escort me through security. Imagine my surprise when she introduced herself as Carol.

Carol possesses a brilliant mind and is one of only three women to rise above the director level. I learned that she is an excellent project leader, able to see the big picture while still keeping track of all the details needed to make a project succeed. Possessing strong influencing skills, she would thrive in a more collaborative work environment, but her difficulty making direct requests allows others to take advantage of her in this competitive workplace. Carol was referred to me because to meet her goals, it is essential that she get other parts of the organization to work together. To do this she must learn to make requests effectively.

When I asked Carol to show me how she makes requests, her body and words betrayed her intent. She blinked her eyes nervously, her mouth twitched, and her posture became slumped. She appeared to be begging. Her language became indirect, prefacing her requests with words like, "I would like it *if...*" or "We need..." or even "I wish..." She told me people would respond to her with nods, but rarely would anyone take action. She was burning out from lack of support.

I asked her to give me examples of assertive people in her organization. She described only men. I asked her to tell me about some assertive females. She said there were two, both of whom she described as aggressive, attacking terrors who frequently raised their voices, barked out orders, and never listened. She could not identify a single woman who was assertive in a positive way. In her world, women were either vicious sharks or meek little mice. She felt revulsion at the thought of being a shark.

I began by demonstrating a continuum of behaviors between Mouse and Shark. First I made a request at the Mouse end. I rounded my shoulders, crouched down, looked up through my eyelashes, avoided eye contact, and said in a soft voice, "It would be nice, uh, uh, do you think maybe we could finish the project today?" Carol observed that the Mouse-me was so hesitant that she was unclear what my request actually was and felt no urgency to comply. I asked her to match my Mouse posture. She did it easily and said that this stance felt all too familiar.

I then demonstrated the Shark-me. I puffed up my chest and demanded, "I want the completed project on my desk by the end of the day, or you can look for work elsewhere." She took a step back, her face froze into a mask, and the light went out in her eyes. I asked her what she experienced and she said she felt afraid. "But," she added in a feisty voice, "if you didn't have the authority, you could hold your breath before I'd respond to a demand phrased like that." I noted that she sounded angry. She agreed and said, "People who abuse their power really infuriate me." I asked her to notice her posture. She was standing tall and making direct eye contact. "This is you stepping into your power," I said. "Notice how it feels." I suggested there might be some benefit to harnessing her inner Shark. "For example, you notice this feeling when someone has stepped over a boundary. Instead of shrinking, you can use the feeling to get in touch with your power and prevent someone from pushing you where you don't want to go."

I then demonstrated a centered, confident, and direct request for her. I stood with my feet shoulder-width apart, my back straight and aligned with head over shoulders over hips over feet, all in one continuous line. I made direct eye contact. Breathing in a relaxed manner, I spoke in a strong, even voice, "Please have the project on my desk by the end of the day." As I made the request, I noticed that Carol also seemed relaxed. She met my eye contact and her posture shifted from slouched to more erect. She was surprised that I could be so strong without being offensive, and she said she felt "invited" to hear my request.

For the rest of the session, I modeled and she practiced moving in small increments along the Mouse-Shark continuum. Sometimes when people make a change, they go too far in the opposite direction. My goal was for Carol to know what degree of directness was appropriate for her. Awareness is the first step toward making a change. At the end of the session, Carol was aware not only of her inability to lead her organization from the Mouse end of the spectrum but also of a range of responses and their impact on her. As we walked toward the elevator, a colleague walked by and called her Cheryl. I asked if her name was Carol or Cheryl. She admitted it was Cheryl. She had let me call her Carol throughout the entire first session because she was embarrassed to correct me.

Cheryl's homework for the next week was to practice making requests in a direct, not indirect, way—such as asking her change-resistant secretary to redo the filing system or asking her coach to call her by her correct name. When we met again, Cheryl had made requests, and for her, that was a positive step forward. I began by calling her Carol. She quickly asked me to call her Cheryl. As she described successes, it became clear that she had made most requests of people she thought would be amenable. For the following week, I challenged her to make more difficult requests and to notice her body language and what she was feeling and make notes for us to discuss at our next session. My goal was to help Cheryl *feel* how to make requests from a centered place and to notice her own and others' responses when she did so. I wanted her to embody making strong requests and not lapse into her Mouse body, which made requests that were easy to ignore.

At our next meeting, she reported that she had been able to make more challenging requests of her staff, such as asking them to take on more project responsibilities. Most of her difficulty had occurred when asking peers in other departments for help. She recounted many instances when she had helped others with resources, provided support for their proposals, and even times when she shared money from her budget to help fund others' projects. However, when she needed assistance, her peers consistently failed to reciprocate. Two things became evident: (1) she never let others know that helping them was a cost to her, so they thought she had excess budget and resources, and (2) she never stated her expectation that they reciprocate. She had set up an expectation of a one-way relationship (she gave, they didn't) and they were happy to keep it that way.

Underlying Cheryl's difficulty was her quaint notion that if she did nice things, people would naturally reciprocate. She wouldn't *have to* make requests. I asked her how she would feel making a request of her peers. She said she actually had several requests in mind. Her posture was strong and I could see that she was harnessing her Sharkness. She said that she was tired of their ignoring her and never offering help with her projects. I asked her to remember the sensation in her body when someone called her by the wrong name and instead of ignoring the feeling, to use it to get in touch with how irritating it feels to be dismissed and ignored.

Her homework for the next session was to continue making challenging requests and to pay attention to her feelings when she made them.

When we met again we discussed requests she made to her peers. She reported several successes and one devastating failure. She had asked Tom, notoriously rude and the most alpha dog on the team, to loan two people from his department to assist with a project that had a tight deadline. He ignored her and simply walked away. She felt angry and hurt, but rather than bury the feeling, she followed him to his office and made the request again. He didn't look away from his computer as he said, "Look, my people are overworked. I can't help you." She didn't know what to say then. She felt so low she could have slipped under the door.

I suggested we practice. I role-played Tom and asked her to make a request of me. As direct as Cheryl had been in a previous session when she asked me to call her by her correct name, her posture reverted to Mouse with resigned body, slumped shoulders, and downcast eyes. I asked her what she noticed. She said that as much as she wanted to be strong, she felt all her emotions pulling her to be indirect. "What feelings?" I asked. "Be specific." "I think…just the pain of being rejected," she said. As a peer, she had no power to reverse his rejection. Tom's "no" represented disrespect and powerlessness and she feared that when he rejected her request she looked even weaker for asking. This was another layer that kept Cheryl from making direct requests. It brought back all the shame she felt as a teen asking her father for money when he said no, most painfully when she asked him for money to go on a class trip and he said no. Moreover, it brought back as well the sadness of having to tell her friends that she couldn't go with them and her loneliness the week they were gone.

I wondered if Cheryl realized that making a request means the other person has the power to say no as well as yes. I asked her if she was making a request or if she were *demanding* that he do something. "I hoped he would agree, but realized he could say no." She took a deep breath and sighed. I asked what the sigh was about. "Maybe I never feel that *I* can say no," Cheryl admitted, "so I resent it from others." Now, another layer had surfaced. Cheryl didn't allow herself to say no, so she didn't think others had the right to do so. Furthermore, she felt someone saying no to her request was a sign of disrespect. Working through the body is interesting because at each step, the body reveals more of what is being held back.

The next step for Cheryl was to learn to accept a "no" without relapsing into her internal story of disrespect and powerless. As in learning to make direct requests, gaining the ability to accept a rejected request took three sessions before Cheryl could maintain her poise without crumbling into Mouse. One key to change for Cheryl was to recognize that when her shoulders curled and her chest tightened, she could practice dropping her breath into her belly and get centered. From here, she recognized that she felt less afraid. It brought back the memory of how she anchored before a track meet in college—the crouch in the blocks before the starting gun. Accessing her center deactivated her Mouse-body, where her breath was high and her chest felt tight. As in making requests, Cheryl found being centered made all the difference in calibrating how forceful to be. Later that day, she asked her boss for an additional person. Although he said no, she said the rejection wasn't hard to take at all. Moreover, she felt proud of herself for having the courage to make the request.

A few weeks later, I got a surprise telephone call from Cheryl. "This amazing thing happened," she said. "Tom said no to me again." "Then why do you sound so happy?" I asked.

She related that while making the request she had been able to drop her breath, stand tall, and stay centered the whole time. She felt the strength of her stance made him pay attention to her. And even though he said no, he looked up at her and said courteously, "Sorry, I can't help you this week."

"He was so polite I thought maybe an alien had invaded his body," Cheryl joked.

I asked how she felt. She said she felt courageous and inspired to ask for what she wanted and to say no when she needed to. "What does that feel like in your body?" I asked. "I feel tall and powerful like when I crossed the finish line in a race," she said, "like I can take care of myself."

CONCLUSION

To achieve our goals or be who we long to be, we must be able to take new actions. New ways of engaging can feel uncomfortable, sometimes even unsafe. Being centered allows us to try new moves and to make the moves in ways that work. Having a coach as an ally to weather the discomfort of learning new actions and calibrating how far to go makes it easier to take risks. Consider the pain Cheryl, in the story earlier, felt at being taken advantage of and feeling unsupported by her peers. To learn that she could get support by behaving differently was a life-changing experience for her. Imagine how many possibilities opened when she became able to make direct requests and decline others' requests.

When we consider that we all have behaviors that limit our effectiveness, we gain an even greater appreciation of the power of somatics to increase our awareness and capacity to change—both in our clients and in ourselves. Thinking about a change is a necessity, not an end. Change must be embodied. Over time new behavior becomes deeply rooted and can be relied on to produce the results we want.

NOTES

1. Albert Mehrabian, *Silent Messages* (Belmont, CA: Wadsworth, 1971), 77.
2. Richard Strozzi-Heckler, *The Anatomy of Change: A Way to Move through Life's Transitions* (Berkeley, CA: North Atlantic Books, 1984, 1993), 9.
3. Daniel Goleman, *Working with Emotional Intelligence* (New York: Bantam Books, 1998), 74–76.

CHAPTER 15

DISTINCTIONS FOR COACHING LEADERS

BETH BLOOMFIELD

COACHING LEADERS IS, IN MANY WAYS, different from coaching everyone else; and yet, in many ways, it is much the same. Leaders are, after all, human beings first and foremost. What's different is the special pressure of being "in charge," ultimately responsible for people and results, which means they are "on" all the time, under constant scrutiny, subject to endless second-guessing and their own impossibly high standards. In my work with leaders in a variety of organizations, I find that most of them struggle with the same issues of managing themselves, characterized by the set of distinctions examined here. Readers beware: There are no easy answers, only thoughts and ideas, and of course, more questions.

MANAGEMENT VERSUS LEADERSHIP

Why do executives all want to be known as great "leaders" but worry that the words "good manager" in their performance review are the kiss of death to higher aspirations? The notion that management is bad and leadership is somehow good has grown out of a decades-old idea that there is a dichotomy between the two.[1]

Management skills are denigrated or completely overlooked in the popular literature of business these days, while books on leadership are perennial bestsellers. Management is frequently characterized as old school and fear-driven, while leadership is seen as enlightened and trust-based. Management is seen as the province of number-crunching mid-level drones, while leadership is the creative work of extraordinary or even heroic figures.

My own premise is that although there is a distinction, the dichotomy here is a false one. Management skills and leadership "jazz"[2] are both essential elements in building and sustaining a healthy and productive organization in today's world, and good management is complementary to, rather than opposed to, strong leadership. It's curious that American businesses spend vast sums annually on leadership development without any real evidence to show that it actually works, while training in the fundamentals of management is neglected in many organizations.

Management practices are what bring order and focus to an otherwise chaotic environment, and good management is a distinct professional set of knowledge and activities that is necessary to achieving consistent and reproducible results. Successful leaders must be adept at strategy and execution, vision and organization, creativity and structure, motivation and measurement.

Leaders can better align the organization by including a set of core management practices along with core business processes and core values. They should focus on developing a common set of management practices that can be explained and taught to managers at all levels. Here are a few questions to ask the leader you are coaching:

- What are the current management practices in your organization? Where are the areas of commonality? Where are there differences, and why?
- Is there a good understanding of management fundamentals by all levels of managers? Are the fundamentals being practiced? If not, why not?
- Are your management practices tied to your organization's strategy, goals, and expectations for its managers?
- What management practices need to be developed to address key gaps in your organization's performance and business results?
- Is there a system in your organization for mentoring and coaching managers in the fundamentals of good management, and how to apply them to your particular organizational context?

Looking at management as a part of the whole system of the organization will help the leader develop a more appreciative understanding of its value to the bottom line. Good management should fit hand-in-glove with a leader's approach to leadership. Without one, the other isn't very likely to succeed.

POWER VERSUS INFLUENCE

One of the hardest lessons of leadership for those new to the role is that practically everything they have to get done must be done by others. For those accustomed to excelling as individual contributors, the transition to leadership can be a bumpy ride, especially in today's workplace. They can no longer rely solely on the power of their position in the hierarchy to command and control their employees because today's leaner organizations depend on more fluid structures and collaborative processes. Effective leadership requires the ability to influence people in a variety of ways, across a range of organizational structures.

We all influence others in some way, it's just that we seldom realize that we do or how we do it. By becoming more intentional in the use of influence, and by practicing it more consciously, it's possible for a leader to build some extra "muscle" and get noticeably better results. The foundation of influencing skill is "personal power," as distinct from the power of the leader's position. Leaders are the ones in control of their personal power. It's up to them to build the necessary trust, respect, and commitment of others.

To influence others to do something we want them to do, the first place most of us go is logic. We marshal the most logical and rational arguments in favor of our proposal, in an effort to appeal to the intellectual and analytical capacities of the stakeholders. To sweeten the pot, we cite lots and lots of good data in our appeal to their minds. If we're especially shrewd, we make sure we make the pitch in terms of the best choice for their interests or the most benefit to them. Most of us are good at making rational arguments.

That would be fine if people decided what to do only on the basis of logic. But of course, people are more complicated—they have emotions, and they are frequently not aware of how much they rely on emotion to make decisions. Therefore, if a leader wants to be a more powerful influencer, she'll also appeal to a person's values, his or her self-image and sense of belonging. She'll couch her request in terms of a larger purpose or vision and express confidence in the person's ability to accomplish the job. To be most effective, she'll need to listen well for clues about what really motivates them. Finally, she'd be wise to appeal to the need for connection and relationship that we all share. By building connection, she invites a more solid and continuing commitment by others to his proposal and his broader goals.

Begin coaching on influencing skills by asking the leader you are coaching to notice the many ways in which he seeks to influence others and to note which avenue he typically uses—logic, emotion, or relationship. If he relies too heavily on one, he's missing opportunities to bring people along. Ask him to practice extending his range in different situations, and notice how people respond. The objective is to develop his own style of influence, and build his own personal power to get things done.

INTELLIGENCE VERSUS CURIOSITY

What distinguishes the truly strategic thinkers from the larger group of general managers in most organizations? Certainly well-honed analytic skills and intellectual sophistication are the price of admission. We can also point to a recognized set of carefully cultivated habits of thought and action and maybe to some innate qualities of being as well. One thing I've noticed in my work, though, is that the biggest thinkers are the habitually curious people.

In this day and age of specialization, niche marketing, and technical expertise, it can be tough to make the leap from "go-to" person in one particular area to "big picture" player on a larger stage. It's hard to let go of the very thing that has made you so successful—up until now. But strategic leadership lives in the very broad context of history, culture, politics, economics, demographics, science—the rich broth in which we all swim. To get strategy right, you have to be conversant in all these domains.

Given the perpetual busyness of life today, that might seem impossible, not to mention downright unappealing. That's where curiosity comes in. If a leader can reframe the question of how to manage the torrent of information coming at him, to one of how to manage himself in the midst of the flow, the entire picture changes. If he can remember what it was like, at other times in his life, to have what some Eastern cultures call "beginner's mind," he's well-positioned to think big. Stay curious about the world and all things in it, and the world will open itself to you.

Here are six practices you can use in coaching a leader to build healthy strategic thinking "muscle" by getting curious and getting smart about her particular strategic context:

1. Become a "first-class noticer," as novelist Saul Bellow put it. Survey the people and places in which you find yourself during the course of your day. What's different, unusual, or interesting about them?

2. Develop your peripheral vision. Broaden your focus beyond what's in front of you. Cast your glance from side to side. What do you notice that's out there on the fringes?

3. Acquire a voracious appetite for knowledge and understanding. There's nothing too small or too subtle for you to notice and learn from. What would it be like to see the world from these various vantage points?

4. Cultivate a discerning eye, ear, and mind. Learn to tell the difference between quality and quantity in news, information, and opinion. Which sources are trustworthy, which providers are reliable? Be mindful of what your purpose is, and where you want to go. What criteria will you use to sort out the meaningful from the merely interesting along the way?

5. Learn how to speed-read, both figuratively and literally. Build your skills for scanning both the information environment as a whole, and the mountain of reading material that's available to you. What's the "take-away," the one priceless nugget you want to remember from any given book, article, program, speaker, Web site?

6. Exercise ruthless editing. Cast your net widely, but be prepared to cast off most of what you catch. Once you've read, seen, or heard enough to form a strong impression, you can pare away the nonessentials. What's the simplest and most direct way to describe something you have observed or learned?

BALANCE VERSUS INTEGRATION

I often hear requests for help in achieving better "work-life balance" from senior executives who are stressed out by incredibly busy lives and impossibly competing commitments. That sense of being constantly out of balance between the demands of the job and the requirements of the home and family seems to afflict women executives more than men, but it certainly isn't exclusive to them. Sometimes it seems as though equality of the sexes in the workplace has just spread the pain of being torn in different directions.

Usually, these busy leaders are looking for the magic bullet, for some powerful methodology or practice that will neatly resolve the dilemma for them. "I need a better time management system" is one I hear a lot. Alternatively, "I need to figure out how to do more of my work at home." I usually point out that none of us can "manage" time, time happens with or without us at the same rate of speed. It's what we choose to do with it that creates the problem, so what we have to manage is ourselves.

There is another way to appreciate the balance question, found in the distinction between living a "balanced" life and living an "integrated" life. Webster's defines the verb *integrate* as "to form, coordinate, or blend into a functioning or unified whole."

Applied to how we live our lives, that's a powerful paradigm for change. For leaders who can't realistically set rigid boundaries in time and space between work and home life, integration offers a model that intuitively feels right.

Here are seven strategies you can introduce to the leaders you coach—choices they can make for an integrated life:

1. Give up the idea that there's "work" and there's "life." Isn't it *all* life?
2. Design your work to fit the life you want, and your life to complement your work (versus to support it). Think about when, where, and how you want to work so that it blends more seamlessly into when, where, and how you do your life.
3. Be "out there," in both work and life. Live as though you are your work, versus your work defines who you are. Get curious about your world and everything in it, and get comfortable with not knowing all the answers all the time.
4. Decide what your life is about, and live *all* of it that way. What is your purpose? Seek authenticity in all domains of life, be who you really are, all the time.
5. Work with people you want to be with. Why not be friends with your clients, colleagues, and customers? It's less about setting boundaries than it is about being respectful and compassionate towards others, and being "clean" (honest and appropriate) in your relationships.
6. Give up the idea that you can "achieve" balance (or integration!). You will always be a work in progress, and you will never get there. So? Forgive yourself for not being perfect.
7. Not everything in work and in life is that serious. It's not *all* about life and death. And, it's not all about you, either. Try thinking about "my life as a comedy" once in a while to bring yourself back to earth.

STAMINA VERSUS RESILIENCE

Leaders at all levels these days are expected to have the stamina of an Energizer Bunny, to "go the distance" and "stay the course" no matter what. The physical and psychological demands of "extreme jobs" are unquestioned in many organizations today, with little heed to what that really means for the individual or the people he must lead. However, as an older and much wiser colleague always used to say, "Nobody goes through life unscathed." If you live long enough, sooner or later "stuff happens." Why do some people snap back, while others snap under the stress of unanticipated occurrences? The quality of resilience is very often the determinant of success in work, as well as in life. Studies show that resilience matters more to sustained high performance than do education, experience, or training. Resilience, more than stamina, is crucial to effective leadership.

Here's the dictionary definition of "resilience": (1) The ability to recover quickly from illness, change, or misfortune; buoyancy. (2) The property of a material that enables it to resume its original shape or position after being bent, stretched, or compressed; elasticity.

The important thing to note here is that we are *not* talking about being unaffected by events and forces in our world but rather about the capacity to move with them and then reestablish a working balance.

According to experts, the main building blocks of resilience are the capacity to accept reality and stand up to it; the ability to find meaning in life; and the ability to improvise. Other important factors are a strong sense of self; the belief that you are the author of your own life; and the ability to be flexible. It's an interesting mix of mental, emotional, physical, and spiritual qualities, all of which can be cultivated. My own experience in coaching leaders in a variety of organizational settings confirms the observation.

Authors Jim Loehr and Tony Schwartz have researched how winning athletes train for high performance, and they translate their findings into practical strategies for corporate leaders in their book, *The Power of Full Engagement: Managing Energy, Not Time, Is the Key to High Performance and Personal Renewal*.[3] Fundamental to their approach is the idea that you can't manage time—you only have a fixed quantity—but you can manage the energy available to you, and the quantity and quality of that is not fixed.

We build mental, emotional, and spiritual capacity in the same way we build physical capacity—by expending energy beyond our usual limits and then recovering. So, effective energy management in all domains requires cycles of expenditure (stress) and renewal (recovery) of energy. Building resilience means mastering the practice of these rhythmic cycles. Resilient leaders have developed rituals that help promote cycling—going to the gym at the same time every day, for example, or sitting down to dinner with the family every night.

Loehr and Schwartz note that the demands on today's executives dwarf the challenges faced by professional athletes.[4] Executives must sustain peak performance while athletes play in relatively short bursts of energy. Athletes spend most of their time training and very little performing—executives just the opposite. Athletes have off-seasons, while most executives are lucky to get three or four weeks of vacation. An athlete's career averages five to seven years, while most executives will work for 40–50 years. As a coach of leaders and those aspiring to leadership, it's very important that you work with your clients to help them develop lifelong habits that will support resilience in the face of the inevitable personal and professional setbacks they will experience in the course of that long career.

FOCUS VERSUS REFLECTION

Survey after survey, bolstered by anecdotal evidence from virtually all my executive clients, indicates that work is expanding almost exponentially. There's no end to this trend in sight, and the stakes are increasingly high for executives who must deliver solid business results from whatever project or assignment they have taken on. Leaders need an edge to keep up, and it had better be a sharp one if they want to sustain peak performance.

The top three challenges faced by executives today are time pressure, financial pressure, and the imbalance they feel between work and life. They often feel out of control, as though they are perpetually reacting to events. To help my leader/clients regain a sense of control, of "authorship" of their own lives, I frequently begin with the development of a critical skill: focus. The ability to focus on what's important, when it's important, is one of the things that distinguish successful from unsuccessful leaders.

Focus is a learned skill, and it also can be practiced until it becomes habit. In addition, as with any other habit, it lives in the body, our biological being. That's important, because most people tend to think that focus is strictly a mental process and a matter of emotional self-discipline. When we talk about someone being "unfocused," we often conjure an image of dishevelment and incompetence, almost a morally deficiency.

Focus, when practiced well, is not about homing in on one thing to the exclusion of all others. It is an essential element in what is often called "flow," and it involves agility and grace, the ability to move almost seamlessly from one thing to the next with a minimum of settle time. The key to developing this kind of focus is what I call "attention training"—the physical practice of mastering a mental shift. Here's a set of practices you can adapt for the leader you are coaching to help him achieve better focus:

- To focus, you have to set aside all the things you are *not* going to focus on—you have to define the universe of what's important by eliminating the unimportant. Begin by tracking all the things you do in a day, a week, a month, and choosing *not* to pay attention to the distractions.
- Choose one important matter to attend to for an hour or more each day, working with a clearly articulated goal in mind, one that includes both a time element and a quantitative measurable outcome. While you are working, if something else comes up, turn it away until your focused work session is complete.
- As you increase your ability to concentrate on this one matter for a prescribed period, add another important matter, treating it in the same way. Use physical actions—turning off your phone or computer, closing your door, asking your assistant to screen calls and visitors—to reinforce your focused attention.
- Limit the number of important matters you will attend to to three, and as you reach your goal for one, move another new matter to your set of three. As other matters come to your attention, pass them on to others, or turn them away.

At the beginning, it may seem impossible to control this much of the time in a day. If the leader treats this practice as a conscious choice, though, and puts physical structures of support in place, she'll begin to build the muscle for focus. After a while, this way of attending to what matters will become habitual, and the habit will be reinforced when she enjoys the fruits of success. By training her attention, she'll develop a felt sense of greater autonomy and control in work and life, and discover the secret to sustained peak performance.

The requisite partner to focus is reflection, the complement to the reactive or "process" thinking that tends to govern our waking hours. Reflection is necessary to cement the things you are continually learning in your memory, because it enables you to assign meaning to the myriad of experiences you have every day. Reflection is the "time out" your brain needs to process the mix of sensory perceptions, emotions, and communications you are being bombarded with all the time. Reflection is how you figure out what you think, and therefore who you really are.

Frequently my leadership coaching clients tell me they can't find the time for reflection, or they don't think they know how to do it. Very often, when we probe what's behind those assessments, we discover that there's another really huge or "master" assessment, namely that if you're not constantly in action you aren't really accomplishing anything. This is such a powerful assumption in these times that it is often literally impossible for people to see how driven by it they are. It's as though we were all afflicted with some profound variety of attention deficit disorder.

Why are we so reluctant to sit quietly with our own thoughts? Is it because of our modern existential phobia of inactivity as akin to death? Alternatively, perhaps our physical addiction to the adrenalin rush of constant busyness? Suffice it to say that if you aren't reflecting in a conscious way, your brain is doing it for you automatically, running the program in the background—and you might not like the logic it is using while unsupervised by you. Dedicated reflection practice will raise the whole thought process to the conscious level, and it is a necessary precursor to planful action. If you skip this step, you're far less likely to get to where you really want to go in business and in life.

The good news is that the leader you coach doesn't have to retreat to a mountaintop to bring more reflective thought into his life. Ask him to start wherever he is and build some reflection time into his daily routine. If he already exercises most days, suggest that he turn off the iPod for five or ten minutes and turn his thoughts inward as he walks or jogs on the treadmill. If he already keeps a journal or a "learning log," throw in a good question for deep reflection once a week or so. If he does the dishes every evening, ask him to turn off the TV and enjoy his time at the sink by spending it with his own thoughts.

Your coachee will soon see that reflection happens regardless of the surroundings or the length of time he may devote to it. She may find it adds to the experience to set up a regular reflection ritual, perhaps settling into a favorite armchair with some soft music and a cup of hot tea. However, the brain doesn't require any of that. A good "quieting" practice, such as taking a few deep breaths or centering himself, will quickly put her into the posture for good reflective thought. Anywhere, anytime.

NOTES

1. An influential thinker on this point was Abraham Zaleznik, a professor at the Harvard Business School, who published an oft-cited article on the social psychology of managers, "Managers and Leaders: Are They Different?," *Harvard Business Review*, May–June 1977, 67.
2. Max Depree, *Leadership Jazz* (New York: Currency Doubleday, 1992).
3. Jim Loehr, and Tony Schwartz, *The Power of Full Engagement: Managing Energy, Not Time, Is the Key to High Performance and Personal Renewal* (New York: Free Press, 2003).
4. Ibid., 8–9.

PART III

USING

CHAPTER 16

ALIFE™: A LISTENING MODEL FOR COACHING

CHRISTINE WAHL AND NEIL STROUL

A GROUP OF COACHES, SITTING AROUND a conference table, sharing their best practices. Batting ideas around. Getting juice from the life in the discussion. One of them, Neil Stroul, offered up a framework that he had developed to organize the stories he was hearing from leaders, and he said that this framework helped him calibrate how he listened. We talked about what a leader has to do, what and how a leader thinks, and how a leader ought to learn. One of the other coaches, Karen Gravenstine, mused aloud that these organizing principles could be reordered to create an acronym "ALIFE." We've used it that way ever since.

ALIFE™ stands for Authenticity, Leadership, Intentionality, Fear/Courage, and Execution. Each of these concepts has distinctions that coaches can use to work with leaders. We have found that just by listening through the lens of ALIFE™ when we listen to leaders' "stories," we can zero in on areas that the leader may be blind to.

Over time we have refined our thinking about these concepts and offer it to our students as a grounding model for beginning coaching. We have also presented it to a number of audiences—coaches, leaders, HR managers, and OD consultants—that have given consistent feedback on its usefulness. This chapter outlines key attributes of the ALIFE™ model.

AUTHENTICITY—WHAT DOES IT MEAN TO BE AN AUTHENTIC LEADER?

Authenticity is one of those terms that people hear and understand on some level—but don't really "get." Many people think of it as just being yourself—but we don't see it that way. It's deeper and bigger than that.

As coaches, we are supremely interested in helping our clients bring their authentic selves forward; at the deeper levels our clients need to learn who they are when they are showing up as their "best self," and our task as coaches is to help them identify what that authentic, best self is capable of, and how to assist them in summoning forth that best version of themselves. In our view, it is essential to being a great leader. For most of us—coaches and leaders alike—it is a lifelong process.

How can you tell an authentic leader? Most of us can *feel* it when someone is authentic, and so we can say that it has something to do with one's *presence*. Moreover, we feel connected to them in some way. An authentic leader creates trust. An authentic leader is generative. An authentic leader draws from deep internal source material, understands that people aren't perfect, and works with them anyway.

An authentic leader tells his/her "truth" in such a way as to invite dialogue that embraces the "truths" of others.

At a deeper level, being authentic means that we express our fundamental sense of purpose and that we are working, with awareness, to be the person we aspire to be, the person we *must be* if we are truly to feel that our deeper sense of purpose is being fulfilled.

Most people in organizations learn to "play the game" at some level, and they may push their own deeper needs to the background. However, this is a story that does not serve the leader and inevitably generates an inauthentic way of being. The human operating system can support a certain amount of this, but over time, too much of it leads to being out of synch with ourselves, and our authentic self becomes buried. Another version of "playing the game" looks like this: completely ignoring your own quiet voice in favor of those louder ones, inside of you and outside of you, that encourage you to do what everyone else does to get ahead—multitask, be accessible nearly 24/7, work longer, harder, faster, get more done, stay later, and come in earlier. You get the picture. These belief systems that keep you in the more-harder-faster-better loop are debilitating over time, and they override your authentic voice. When we hit a crisis of burnout, illness, or some other sort of suffering, it may be our authentic self demanding our attention. The coach's job is to help clients notice their flagging energy and see opportunities to more fully express themselves, so their authenticity begins to come forward.

A leader striving to be more authentic has the pull to stay in touch with the vision of the person s/he aspires to be, and to challenge him/herself more and more to *be that person* by noticing daily exactly what life is calling for. The coach's job is to encourage and support the leader to live in the question, "am I bringing my best self forward?"

Our belief is that every day, each of us has the chance to greet life from a more authentic stance. That's the beauty of it—we get opportunity after opportunity to show up as the person we aspire to be.

As coaches, we listen to our leader clients tell us about the obstacles they face at work, what they want to get done, and what makes it so hard. In many cases, what they are describing is their desire to bring their fuller self forward. We listen for those places where their authenticity is thwarted, where their presence diminishes, and where they feel no power. This is always an opening for coaching.

The poet David Whyte[1] offered the concept that the soul would rather fail doing what it must do, than succeed doing what someone else thinks it ought to do. This is the mission deep within our operating system, the one that helps us bring our authentic voice forward. Awareness is the first step on this path.

LEADERSHIP

In listening to stories that leaders tell us, we are discerning how this person sees him/herself as a leader. We are wondering what distinctions related to leadership exist in the client's mind. Is he a leader in title? Is he a leader in spirit? Does he embody leadership? Does he walk his talk? Does he communicate his leadership, both in speech and action? Do others perceive him as a leader? What does he know about the demands of being a leader? To what extent, does he operate with a "leader's mindset?"

Let's look at leadership as a series of public acts. In our minds, being able to *be* a leader is based on reflection and self-knowledge, and executives "show up" as leaders when they move into action. It does no good to just think grand leadership thoughts. Every leader has chances, both big and small, to embody leadership through their daily actions. Another distinction important to consider is that leadership moves more toward the future than management, which stays more in the present. Leading often requires a strategic focus, while managing requires an operational focus. The question we are wondering as we listen is how is this client showing up daily? Is this client "out there" acting as a leader? Is this client focusing on the future, on what is possible? Is this client thinking strategically?

Now, let's view leadership as a mindset. Actions that a leader takes will be fueled by the context she is in and the story she tells herself about that context. If a leader lives in a story of possibility, her actions will reflect that. If a leader lives in a story of resignation, her actions will reflect that. In each case, the possible outcomes can have a dramatic impact on the leader's organization. A leader's actions are informed and supported by the amount and quality of self-reflection she engages in, how well she knows her "self," and how well she takes lessons from feedback.

Powerful leaders today are those who can read a situation and know how to act within it. They do not assume that their "style" is applicable to every challenging situation. There are times to be autocratic, authoritarian, supportive, inspirational, and logical. Coaches need to listen to the leader's distinctions about being a leader and help the leader shore them up wherever necessary.

INTENTIONALITY

Leadership without intentionality will lead you to move in a direction that may well be contrary to where you actually want to go. Notwithstanding the occasional magic of serendipity, we believe intentionality is key to great leadership and is based on integrity and authenticity. Intentionality is also integral to achieving a vision. Intentional means purposeful, focused clearly on an outcome. Most of us have worked for leaders who lacked intentionality—and the result was chaos. It reflects the classic metaphor of a ship adrift, with no one at the helm.

One client we worked with needed to discover the power of intention. He did not have a big goal; instead, he blew with the wind. Whatever the organization needed, he would try to mold himself into that. In the process, he lost a sense of energy and gained a sense of resignation. His authentic self was buried somewhere under the external expectations he was trying to meet. He clearly needed a sense of intention. When his team was faltering, he tried something new. He *declared the intention* of pulling them together and inspiring them to do better. He became willing to step up to the plate and envision a new kind of success: intention in action.

We have frequently encountered executives who have inherited an agenda from a predecessor or senior executive and have not worked out a way to integrate the previous mission with their own aspirations. As a result, their intentions become vague and lack potency. The coach's task is to help leaders attain the requisite clarity so that they can then become intentional.

Think of intention as the point around which a leader can rally energy and ignite the energy of followers. A leader can have intentions around just about anything, such as:

- personal development as a leader
- commitment to develop others
- commitment to wholeness, for yourself, and others
- commitment to clear communication
- commitment to partner with colleagues
- commitment to increase market share
- desire to bring the organization to a new way of thinking
- desire to create an image of your organization that is admired and valued by others
- desire to create an organization that is respectful, innovative, and welcoming for everyone who works there

The list can be endless. Coaches listen for a leader's intention or lack of it and help the leader choose those areas to focus on that will create energy and leverage for self and for the organization. Coaches help leaders create a crystal-clear intention, make a commitment to it, and live it! As a result, the leader will be quicker to make decisions (intention is a compass pointing north), will generate creativity, and will stretch beyond what was thought possible.

FEAR/COURAGE

Fear—it is often difficult to admit that we feel afraid. We try to suppress its insidious hijack of our purpose, and regardless, fear will hold us in its thrall. Humans (even leaders) are hardwired to be fearful. It rightfully protects us from threats that we feel. Yet, sometimes the threats are not real. The famous quote, "there is nothing to fear but fear itself" may ring truer than most of us imagine, partly because when we imagine the worst, it's easy for us to see how possible "the worst" could be, and we begin to believe the imagined scenario.

Fear keeps us small. Courage helps us live larger. Courage is not the opposite of fear, but it helps us past our fears. Imagine a great leader acting out of fear. What if, for example, Churchill had acted out of fear? Or Roosevelt? Acting courageously is something every leader must do. Powerful people are able to *transform their fear into courage*. Leaders must find courage to lead, make the hard decisions, and move past their fears, all in service of preserving an organization's integrity and supporting its future.

Coaches who listen for the leader's fear, however hidden or nuanced it may be, can help the leader step to the other side of the fear to lead more courageously. In many instances, leaders are simply unable to recognize that they are fearful. It is the coach's task not only to help the leader "put her hand in the flame," but also to give the fear a name. Naming a fear allows a leader to *claim* (own) the fear that is the first step in regaining their personal power and moving into courage.

Personal courage is necessary for leaders. There are times when the demands of work life unabashedly trounce on boundaries of balance—little or no time for personal pursuits outside of work, for family, for reflection. In many systems, it takes courage to model balance and effectively nourish an ability to be present. "Systems" will take as much as a leader is willing to give them. Who sets the limits?

From a coaching perspective, fear takes many forms. Fear shows up when a person has to speak publicly, have a difficult conversation, defend an argument, stand up to authority, or go against the norm. Leaders can have a fearful response to e-mail! It matters not if it's a big thing or a little thing that causes fear; the point is to recognize ways past it whenever possible. Getting to the other side of fear is empowering and energizing.

We had a client who needed to hire a second-in-command. The client procrastinated, made excuses, laid blame for not hiring at the feet of the HR recruiters she was working with. Months went by, and the position was still vacant. Although she lamented her workload and verbally wished for a strong leader under her, the truth was that she was afraid that if she hired someone strong, they would take over her position and she would be out of a job. Once this fear was identified, and the client could come to terms with the dragons that were managing her mind around this issue, she was able to comfortably hire someone remarkable and reap the benefits of strong leadership supporting her vision and mission.

EXECUTION

Execution is key to the cycle of action and key to leading others. Anyone who is a leader undoubtedly has a mandate to create a future and make things happen. Leaders who are unable themselves to move into action and get others to move into action fail to deliver on their mandates. Recognizing *what is* and *what needs to be* is the first step. Filling the gap to get to what needs to be is where execution or action is necessary.

Execution, therefore, is necessary to leadership.

Leaders do not have the luxury to just sit and think big thoughts. Though thinking big thoughts is necessary (we encourage every leader to find time—and hold it sacred—to kick back and think big), thoughts and ideas need to be translated into action. Declaring a big thought—a new future, for instance, is not enough. Though the declaration is the first step, it is not the only step. Leaders need to execute on their ideas and engage others in moving forward. The job of a coach is to listen for the ways that the leader moves into action, such as balanced versus rushed, thoughtful versus spontaneous, in partnership versus lone-ranger-like, and networked or system-oriented versus tunnel-visioned. Then, a coach helps the leader notice the timing of the action and its effects on the leader's organization.

We have found over time that this model offers a very deep and rich way to listen to a leader's story. We share ALIFE™ with the leaders that we coach. As the coaching progresses, our coachees often start our conversations by saying, "today, we will talk about fear" or "today, I need help refocusing on intention." And off we go. The richness that comes from listening through this lens never fails to show an opening where the leader can respond to a development opportunity.

Below are some questions for reflection in each area of the ALIFE™ model. They can be used for conversation, journaling, or daily reflection, and we encourage our readers to share them with leaders to deepen their understanding and commitment to leading authentically, courageously, intentionally, and producing amazing results.

PERSONAL REFLECTIONS

AUTHENTICITY

- When I'm experiencing "life is at its best," what am I able to notice about how I'm feeling, what I'm doing, what's happening around me?
- If I could hear others eulogize me at my funeral, for what would I want to be remembered and how would I want to be described?
- What talents or abilities do I possess, that, when I'm applying them, I feel a sense of rightness or wholeness?

LEADERSHIP

- Who lives in my memory or imagination as examples of great leadership? What qualities do those leaders embody?
- What am I able to notice about my own experiences as a follower? Are there universal principles of leading that inspire others to follow?
- What do I stand for? Do I hold key values that could form the basis for a leadership agenda?

INTENTIONALITY

- When I reflect on possibilities, is there a particular future that I could be committed to creating?
- What do I know about my key stakeholders? What do they want/need from me?
- If I'm feeling thwarted or bogged down, what do I know about the obstacles to success?
- What would it take for me to declare an intention, find support for fulfilling it, and stay committed to it?

FEAR/COURAGE

- Am I able to recognize where fear lives in my body? Am I able to recognize when I'm afraid?
- What do I know about my own defensive habits? Are there patterns I follow when I'm afraid?
- Am I able to recollect episodes from my own history when I successfully converted fear into courage? What allowed me to shift?

EXECUTION

- Is it possible that I am my own source of interference? In what way? Are there actions in which I need to stop engaging in order to be more effective?
- What do I know about my own sources of resistance and avoidance? Might there be actions that I need to initiate that I have been procrastinating?
- Are there actions I have not taken because I am insufficiently competent? What might I need to learn?

NOTE

1. David Whyte, "The Three Marriages: Work, Self and Other" (presentation, Georgetown University Coaching Reunion, Sterling, VA, 2005).

CHAPTER 17

BEHAVIORAL PRACTICES MADE SIMPLE

SCOTT EBLIN

IN ESSENCE, OUR PRIMARY FUNCTION as leadership coaches is to help our clients make behavioral changes to achieve new or different results. Of course, we can't do this for our clients; we can only help them identify and stay on the path to get there. Like coaches in other fields of life, we can increase the likelihood of success for our clients by structuring and making the most of practice. In our case, the practice focuses on behavior.

The idea of getting better through behavioral practice goes back to at least the ancient Greeks. They had a word *"praxis,"* which, roughly translated, means the act of becoming a certain way by doing the specific things that someone who is known for that characteristic regularly does. For instance, if your goal was to be more loving, you would come up with a list of loving behaviors and do a few of those things every day. Eventually, you would actually be more loving.

Aristotle captured this idea in a nutshell when he said, "We are what we repeatedly do. Excellence, then, is not an act, but a habit" (http://www.quotationsbook.com). Breaking a goal down into discrete, tangible behavioral practices is not a practice that is exclusive to Western thought, however. The Japanese manufacturing process of *kaizen* relies on the same idea. It's based on the principle of continuous improvement through small steps.

One of the greatest coaches of all time, the late UCLA basketball coach John Wooden, applied the same principle in leading his teams to ten NCAA championships. In explaining how he consistently turned green freshmen into national champions, Wooden said, "When you improve a little each day, eventually big things occur. Seek the small improvement one day at a time. That's the only way it happens, and when it happens, it lasts" (http://www.hoopsu.com/99-wisdoms-from-wooden).[1]

So, there's a lot of heavy-duty philosophical and experiential grounding in behavioral practices. Interestingly, all of that insight can be found on the back of a shampoo bottle on the part of the label that says, "Lather, rinse, and repeat." In its simplest form, that's all a behavioral practice is—doing something like lathering up, rinsing it out to observe and learn from the effect, and then repeating the process until you own it. If a leader does that often enough, ideally with some helpful guidance from a coach, then, voilà, she's the proud owner of a new habit that helps her achieve a different result.

THE SCHOOL OF REAL LIFE

It can be that simple and, these days, most likely needs to be. One of my primary observations in over a decade of executive coaching is that leaders have more and more on their plate every year. The economic and technological realities of the marketplace require them to do more with less and do it faster. More often than not, their calendars are racked and stacked with very little white space between commitments. As much as we would like for that not to be the case, that's the reality for most of our clients. To help them at all, we have to meet them where they are and make it as easy as possible for them to get started with the behavioral practices that will have the biggest impact on the results they're trying to achieve.

A solid behavioral practice, therefore, will rely on what's going on in our client's calendar. Indeed, most likely they have to do all of the stuff on their calendar (at least that's the assumption they start from). You may therefore want to ask your client, "If you're going to do all of the stuff on your calendar anyway, why don't we look for one or two habits you can practice in your daily life that will help make you an even more effective leader in achieving the results you're trying to get?"

There are a couple of points I want to make about the way I framed that question. The first is that you probably noticed I used the word "habits" rather than the term "behavioral practice." That's because I think we have to do everything we can as coaches to avoid using "coach speak" with our clients. Busy people with a lot on their plates are turned off by jargon. As coaches, we have to make our language accessible and easy to understand. The second point regarding the question is embedded in the way it ends—"achieving the results you're trying to get." Busy people usually need to understand the payoff immediately before they agree to take on additional work. A behavioral practice cannot be an end in itself. To matter to our client, it has to be a means to an end. That's why it's so important to tie the practice to the results the client wants to achieve.

I'll be the first to acknowledge that all of the above can sound really tactical and small ball. On first blush, it doesn't seem to address the more transformative outcomes we'd love to see for our clients. That might be true, but remember the words of Coach Wooden, "When you improve a little each day, eventually big things occur." We have to meet our clients where they are, and that usually means addressing their most immediate and obvious pain points. We can do this by guiding them into practices forming the habits that will help them with their biggest challenges. This is what I call coaching in the school of real life. If we help our clients master the little things that will help them right away, there's a good chance they'll form the habits that will eventually lead to bigger, transformative results. We all have to start somewhere, so let's start with helping our clients use their calendars as an opportunity to try some new things that will make a difference and help them learn in the school of real life.

FIVE CHARACTERISTICS OF
AN EFFECTIVE BEHAVIORAL PRACTICE

If there were an overarching principle of helping a client to identify an effective behavioral practice, it would have to be to keep it simple. If clients can't remember the practice, they won't do it. Simplicity, therefore, rules. To break this down a little further, here are five characteristics of effective behavioral practices:

1. They involve doing something on a regular basis. There's a reason that the first word in the term is "behavioral." An effective practice requires the client to actually do something different. The strong assumption is they'll have to do it on a regular basis over a period of time. That's how habits are formed. If they don't follow through, nothing will change. One of our primary functions as coaches is to encourage clients to follow through and learn something in the process.
2. Other people can see them. Since behavioral practices involve doing something different over time in the school of real life, the

client's colleagues should be able to see what the client is doing differently. This takes practices such as journaling off the list. That practice might have great reflective value for the client, but no one else is going to see that.

3. They are simple, practical, and immediately applicable. One way to determine if a behavioral practice meets the principle of simplicity is to check whether the client considers it practical and immediately applicable to the work that must be done every day. If the practice doesn't seem practical and applicable, a busy leader is unlikely to follow through on practicing it long enough to build a new habit.

4. They are easy to do and likely to make a difference. It's actually possible to graph whether or not a behavioral practice meets the criteria of simplicity, practicality, and applicability. Here's how to do it.
   a. Label the vertical axis "Easy to Do."
   b. Label the horizontal axis "Likely to Make a Difference."
   c. The scale for both axes is low to high.

   We want to help our clients come up with practices that they consider to be in the upper right hand corner of the graph—highly easy to do and highly likely to make a difference. Experience shows that those are the practices on which busy people are going to follow through.

5. Less is more. One of the benefits of using the approach of easy to do and likely to make a difference is that it helps clients build some "quick win" momentum that gives them the confidence and foundation to take on more challenging practices later. Reinforce that momentum by insisting that your clients limit themselves to one or two new practices at a time. Less is more. They'll make a lot more progress by going deep on one or two new behaviors than by trying to spread their time and attention across five or six practices. If you want, keep a list of things to get to later, but sequence the work. Busy leaders will likely need your help with that.

REAL LIFE EXAMPLES THAT SHOW HOW IT WORKS

By now you may be thinking, "OK, principles and characteristics are all well and good, but how does the simple approach to behavioral practices work in real life?" I'll share a couple of real-world examples (with names changed to protect client confidentiality) to illustrate the points I've made so far.

SUE'S STORY

The first story is about a project manager named Sue. When I coached her, she was leading a team working on a $20 million project that was deep red on a green, yellow, red status reporting system. When I conducted a 360-degree assessment for Sue, one of her lowest rated behaviors from her direct reports was "Demonstrates an understanding of the effect of his/her comments and actions on the morale of the organization and makes appropriate choices." In the open-ended comments part of the report, a few direct reports mentioned that Sue was basically "Debbie Downer" in the weekly project status meetings. It didn't matter if there were some things that were going right; Sue focused primarily on the things that were going wrong. As a result, the morale of the project team was in the basement.

To her credit, Sue owned the feedback. With my encouragement, she shared the results of her 360-degree assessment with her team and asked: "What could anyone who was working on doing a better job of managing the impact of their comments on group morale do to be better?" The team had a lot of ideas, but the one that really stuck and that Sue agreed to follow through on got her team involved in the process.

Sue and her team agreed that if she started to become totally negative in a project meeting, the team members were allowed to hold up three fingers as a sign that she was doing it again. (We all agreed that three fingers were better than one particular finger!) In the first couple of weeks of this practice, Sue was surprised by how often she saw the three-fingered salute. In the next couple of weeks, Sue noticed that she wasn't getting the sign as often. She also noticed that the meetings were improving. Encouraged by that, she started thinking before the meetings about positive points she wanted to emphasize in addition to calling out the problems that needed to be solved. The team started participating more. Ideas flowed. After a few months, there was no need for the signal from the team. Was the practice easy to do? Yes, definitely. Did it make a difference? Apparently so. By the end of Sue's six-month coaching engagement, the project status was green, and her team gave her much higher scores on her overall and behavioral effectiveness in a follow-up survey.

BOB'S STORY

Another story comes from a senior manager named Bob. Trained as an engineer, Bob was the kind of manager who really wanted to get into the details. In his 360-degree assessment, he scored low on most of the behaviors that a micromanager would score low on.

As I did with Sue, I asked Bob to follow up with his team to learn more about what was going on. He reported back to me that one of the things that came up more than once was the frequency of what his team had come to call V-Bobs. It turned out that a V-Bob was the name for the version of a PowerPoint deck or a memo that Bob would send back to his team after he had reviewed it and made comments. It was not uncommon for a revised deck or memo to get up to V-Bob.5 on the way to a final product. He was driving his team crazy.

Fortunately, Bob realized that there were many downsides to this and was willing to work on changing his ways. In a follow-up coaching conversation, I asked him how many V-Bobs he thought he sent out in an average week. His guess was five or six. I asked him what he thought a reasonable weekly limit would be. His answer was two. I then said, "So, how about we get your team in on this. What if you told them that for every V-Bob over two a week that you'll put twenty-five dollars in a team party pot that will pay out three months from now? You could still have multiple V-Bobs a week, it would just cost you twenty-five bucks for every V-Bob over two." I could hear Bob gulping over the phone as he said, "How about five bucks?" With a chuckle, I told him five bucks wasn't enough; it had to be a big enough number to make him ask: "Is this worth it?" He said he'd have to run it by his wife. She gave her OK, and Bob let his team in on the deal.

Every week for the next three months, his team was waiting for the third V-Bob of the week and jokingly goading him to send one. He never did. The practice of asking himself, "Is this worth twenty-five bucks?" changed his behavior. In the process, Bob learned that his team actually operated pretty well without so much of his input. With the time he freed up by not writing V-Bobs, he got involved in some cross-functional initiatives that made a difference for the company and strengthened his profile as an organizational leader. And, by the way, he threw a party for his team a few months later even though he never had to put twenty-five bucks in the pot.

SOME BEHAVIORAL PRACTICE BEST PRACTICES

There are some best practices embedded in the Sue and Bob stories that can help make just about any behavioral practice more effective:

CALL IT OUT

Leaders don't work in a vacuum; they work in a system including other people. For behavioral practices to make the biggest possible difference they have to be noticed by the other people in the system. Whenever I have clients who don't agree with the conclusions of a 360-degree feedback report or who start justifying why they do what they do, I'll usually let them vent for a while and then say, "Everything you're saying may be right, but the fact is their perception is your reality. For you to be fully effective, you're going to have to change their perception." One of the most effective ways for leaders to do that is to tell people what they're working on and then ask for their help. Perception change almost always lags behind actual behavior change. We can help our clients accelerate the rate of change on both fronts by encouraging them to name the behavior they want to change (often based on 360-degree feedback from colleagues) and then asking colleagues to watch for (or observe) the behavior change.

GET COLLEAGUES INVOLVED

As coaches, we have a limited perspective on how our clients actually show up day in and day out on the job. That's why it's so important that clients get their colleagues involved in helping them follow through on their behavioral intentions. With a little guidance from us professional coaches, clients can develop a cadre of peer coaches at work who can provide ideas on the behavioral practices that would make a difference and keep our clients honest in following through on their intentions.

MAKE IT FUN

Life is too short to not have a little fun. A behavioral practice does not have to be a superserious slog in order to be effective. In fact, it's probably not going to be effective if it is a slog. One of the real gifts we as coaches can bring to the process of changing behavior is to help make it fun. Adults of a certain age likely remember reading *Highlights* magazine in the waiting room of the doctor's office when they were a kid. The slogan of *Highlights* was "Fun with a purpose." Those are good watchwords for us as we help our clients identify and follow through on behavioral practices.

SUMMARY

I've been using the simple approach to behavioral practices for over six years as I write this and have the metrics to prove that it works. In follow-up 360-degree surveys for over 500 clients that are coming to the end of a six- to seven-month coaching engagement, over

85 percent of their colleagues agree that the leader was significantly more effective in the behaviors worked on. The average assessed change in behavioral effectiveness is 53 percent of the maximum on the assessment scale.

As Coach Wooden might say, if we support our clients in accomplishing little things each day, eventually big things occur.

NOTE

1. John Wooden was basketball coach at UCLA for 27 years, from 1948 to 1975.

CHAPTER 18

COACHING IN ORGANIZATIONS

RANDY CHITTUM

IN THE SAME WAYS THAT COACHES and clients come in all shapes and sizes, the environments in which coaching occurs are all different. For the sake of discussion, there is a distinction that needs to be drawn. The first type of coaching is "life" coaching. This type of coaching is more likely to focus on the client's life ambitions, which may or may not be related to work, career, and leadership success. The second type of coaching is "organizational," or "leadership" coaching, and it is the focus of this chapter.

It is a misnomer to suggest that life coaches and their clients do not deal with living and working in systems and organizations. It is similarly misleading to suggest that leadership coaches do not deal with "life" and issues greater than the role of leadership. That said, for the coach whose expressed interest is in coaching in organizations, there are implications beyond mastering the art and skill of coaching. This coach must also give due diligence to understanding organizational systems in general, and the client's system in particular.

This chapter attempts first to outline and discuss some of the considerations of coaching leaders in organizations, and second to address some of the issues related to entry or contracting.

ISSUES RELATED TO WORKING IN ORGANIZATIONS

ORGANIZATIONS AS SYSTEMS

Coaches, like the leaders being coached, are subject to the powerful influences of organizational systems. By their nature, systems are complex and nuanced and often serve primarily the continued survival of the system. Social psychologists led by Lewin, argue that we consistently and significantly underestimate the impact of the environment on our behavior. This is called fundamental attribution error. I would suggest that coaches, with our focus and even fascination with the person, could be especially ignorant of our tendency to err in this way. In organizational development parlance, there is the notion of being "co-opted" by the system. When someone becomes co-opted, she begins to unknowingly act in ways that are consistent with system influences and expectations. She is likely unaware of this co-opting process because of its very power. It speaks to our desire to fit in and to be accepted, among other things. Coaches who work in organizations can be co-opted and may be likely to underestimate the power of the system and environment on their clients.

ORGANIZATIONAL DYNAMICS

Bolman and Deal (1984) suggest that to understand an organization, four perspectives must be considered. The first is structural. Most organizations have an organizational structure that details reporting relationships, roles and responsibilities, authority and so forth. For the novice, there can be a temptation to stop at the structural understanding. It all seems so clear and easy to understand when you print the strategic plan, business plan, and organization chart! The coach with deeper distinctions about organizations will understand that this lens, although useful, is far from a complete picture.

The second perspective is the political. Simply defined as competition for scarce resources, politics are an important part of how organizations work. Who has budget authority? Who makes decisions about resource allocation? How are alliances formed and utilized? Where is there missing transparency in the organization and who benefits and who is harmed? What topics are off limits, and with whom? These types of questions will help you understand the political landscape of an organization.

The third perspective is human resources. This perspective addresses how people are tended to. How are employees recruited and hired? How are they oriented and trained? Evaluated? Rewarded? What is the philosophy of succession and development? What is the stated goal related to diversity and what is the reality? How are employees treated formally (benefits, policies, and procedures)? How are employees treated by managers?

Finally, understanding an organization requires attention to the culture or spirit of the organization. What stories are told that create a sense of organizational identity? What rituals and celebrations exist and what do they teach us about what the organization truly values? For example, what would it tell you if a "performance-based" culture celebrated only longevity? Reading organizational culture takes a great deal of mindfulness and time in the organization.

The leadership coach in an organization may not have to fully diagnose the organization in the ways described earlier. However, the basic distinctions are important because this is the world in which you work. Given our tendency for fundamental attribution error, it seems even more important that we acknowledge the sway of the systems in which our clients work.

TEAMS

Teams are ubiquitous in today's organizations. You can almost certainly expect that any leader you coach will both be a part of a team, and probably lead a team, if not more than one. The extensive use of teams has aided organizations to be more effective through better use of human capital and more clear opportunities to strategically align efforts. However, being a leader or member of a team increases the level of complexity. There are several important distinctions to notice when working with leaders in the context of a team-based environment.

The first issue is that leading a team is different than leading a group of individuals, more commonly thought of as a functional department, or perhaps a working group. A team implies shared purpose and interdependence. The strength of teamwork is found when synergy is created, thereby making the team greater than the sum of its parts. Therefore, leading a team is dramatically different from leading a collection of people. The team leader has to have the capability to balance declarations with consensus, manage relationships among others, enroll others in a shared vision, and manage planning processes. Also, since the work of teams happens through meetings, the leader of teams should be a skilled facilitator, with a strong understanding of group dynamics and processes.

The second issue to consider is that teams are sometimes compensated differently. Team members may be rewarded for individual performance and for team performance and success. Managing compensation and rewards is a unique and perhaps necessary skill for the leader of teams.

ORGANIZATION INITIATIVES

When you enter an organization, you may find yourself in the middle of any number of organizational initiatives. In fact, you may be there to help a leader engage in one or more of those initiatives. Some of the more common possibilities are listed here.

Strategic planning is a common organizational effort that consumes much energy from leaders. You may encounter leaders who are immersed in that process. Having broader strategic vision is one of the most cited developmental needs for leaders, particularly those who are being developed for more senior leadership positions. Strategic planning processes are often a wonderful time to be coaching because it is all about creating a new future, which coincides nicely with most coaching philosophies. It is also an interesting time to be coaching because it is often stressful for the leader, giving you a glimpse into how the leader handles stress.

Succession planning is becoming ever more popular as organizations realize that the demographics of retiring leaders do not support the need for long-term leadership at the very top levels of the organization. Many organizations are preparing for the expected competition for leaders as current leaders retire. The most likely intersection for the coach is that you may be coaching a leader who is in a succession management program. This coaching may not vary significantly from coaching a leader who is not in a succession management program. The possible sources of interference include the awareness of greater evaluation by senior leaders, the potential feeling of competition between leaders, and the desire to impress decision makers.

It seems that organizations are in constant change, some planned and some not. Leaders today must excel at leading change efforts. It is likely that the leader you are coaching is either responsible for, or influenced by, or both, a significant change effort. The midst of this uncertainty presents great opportunities for coaching. Some would argue that leading in change is the best test of leadership. As the coach, you get to see the client in all sorts of challenging situations. It will be in your best interests to have some distinctions about managing organizational change.

ASSESSMENTS

One of the great benefits of coaching in organizations is that you have ready access to feedback about the client. It may take the form of past performance reviews, or leadership assessments that you might do or others might have already done. It is increasingly popular to do a verbal 360 review in which the coach interviews direct reports and other people in key relationships with the client. All this data is available to the coach and client. There is a danger in thinking that what you hear from a client while sitting in his/her office is the whole picture. The leadership coach often needs additional information to be effective. For example, I have had many clients who had stories or mental models that limited what they could notice. What clients notice is often significantly impacted by his/her beliefs. In one case a client was completely convinced that he listened well and made others feel included. As he described his view, I found it very compelling, in part because of the conviction of his beliefs. Had I not looked other places for contrary data I might have headed down a less fruitful path. This client was shocked to hear that others did not share his view of his listening skill and quickly became committed to improving.

Many organizations have leadership competency models that have been developed to paint a picture of the effective leader in that organization. Competency models are often the framework used for promotion and hiring, performance reviews, and compensation. Competency models are behavior-based, researched models that typically explain the difference between very high performers and average performers. The behavioral evaluation is often multirater, or 360 in nature. It is an excellent opportunity for leaders to learn how others perceive their leadership on a variety of dimensions. The organizational implication is to get more people to behave more like the high performers. For those reasons, they can be of great importance to the person being coached.

Although the idea of such a model has an appeal, there is a potential downside. To the extent that the model becomes that which the client must become, possibilities are limited. There is much evidence that truly effective leadership is an "inside-out" process. Coaching or teaching to the model is the opposite, an "outside-in" process. Each coach must find for him/herself the balance between using organizational tools such as competency models and a more generative approach.

An organization may request that a leadership assessment be performed using a standardized assessment tool. The advantage to this method is that these assessments often provide a benchmark against other leaders. Leaders often like to know how they "measure up." It is important when using a tool such as this that the client know exactly what questions will be asked and of whom. It is beyond the scope of this chapter to recommend specific assessment tools. Reliability and validity studies should be readily available for the more reputable tools. Perhaps most important, be sure to choose an instrument that will be consistent with the organizational culture and will speak to the client.

The reports are usually very formal, with lots of graphs and data to be absorbed. It may take both coach and client some time to ascertain the implications of such a report. There is one word of caution when using these tools. Clients can sometime assign great importance to these reports, in part because they look so official. Be mindful that they are one view into one aspect of a very complex person!

There is ample, and growing, evidence to suggest that there is greater leverage in focusing on developing a few clear strengths as opposed to trying to develop every possible dimension of leadership. For example, Zenger and Folkman (2002) in *The Extraordinary Leader* write, "Our research has led us to conclude that great leaders are not defined by the absence of weakness, but rather by the presence of clear strengths."[1] They go on to say that 84 percent of the leaders they studied have no clear weaknesses but are not perceived to be strong leaders. This is a very important concept to discuss when debriefing a leadership feedback report. I find that leaders are generally first interested in improving in areas of weakness and find the "strengths" movement counter-intuitive.

ISSUES RELATED TO ENTRY AND CONTRACTING

ACCOUNTABILITY

The coach in an organization quickly learns the importance of transparency around accountability. Consider the possible complexity of a coach hired by the human resources officer, to work with the leader of a division, who reports to a vice president. For whom do you work? Who is your real client? It is naïve to assume that you work only for the person you are coaching. Organizations invest in coaching with the expectation of seeing a positive result. You and your client are bound by those expectations.

I have recently heard organizations defined as "collections of agreements." This is one place where the coach can be a good role model for establishing clear agreements. What constitutes that agreement will differ for each of us, based on our need for certainty and our coaching offer.

One school of thought is total transparency. Meet with everyone at once and clarify the relationships and expectations. Clarify your role with each person so that all are clear. Be especially careful to reach an agreement about confidentiality. You can make any agreement you want, but make sure it is clear, transparent, and that you honor it. I generally try to make the agreement that the only way I will discuss the coaching is if the person being coached is in the room at the time. This provides some assurance to the person being coached that he/she will always be aware of any discussions of his/her performance.

Finally, here are two specific words of caution. First, be very careful of being used by the boss to deliver news that he/she was unwilling to deliver. In addition to leaving the person being coached more effective, I would like to leave the relationship with her boss more effective. That is best accomplished by helping the client and supervisor learn how to have a meaningful and truthful dialogue. Second, beware of being asked to fix "broken" clients. My experience, and that of most coaches I know, is that this is a risky proposition. The temptation to help is strong. The danger is rooted in the possibility that this person has essentially already failed and you are the last effort to prove that the person cannot be "fixed." The timelines for change may be unreasonable. The possibilities are severely limited. The emotions are often so overwhelming that purposeful, future-based coaching can hardly occur at all.

The story of one of my very first coaching clients comes to mind. I was hired by the board to coach the executive director of a nonprofit organization. Her performance had suffered for years and a frustrated board had reached the point of bringing in outside help. Convinced I could help, I agreed to the six-month window for her to show "significant improvement." Unclear as to what that meant, she and I moved heroically down the path of self-discovery. Six months later the board deemed her cured and all was well. Three months after the coaching engagement ended she was fired. What I failed to understand was the extent to which the "coaching" had deteriorated into "managing perceptions." Although this felt and looked good at the time, six months was not long enough for her to recover emotionally and make significant transformative change.

OUTCOMES

Today's organizations want to measure everything. The mantra seems to be, "that which is measured, gets done." This organizational edict may wend its way to your coaching relationships. You may be asked to demonstrate ROI, or speak to how the organization will benefit from your coaching presence. In fairness, remember that the organization does not exist to provide you with opportunities to coach! They are rightly interested in how you can help them to achieve their organizational mission, through enhanced leadership capacity. This is another area in which there is no right answer. You will have to determine what your coaching offer means in light of expressed goals on the part of the organization.

Here are a few things to consider. How will you respond if the desired goals do not match up with the client's interests? What if the client is seriously considering leaving the organization? Knowing that transformative work involves the client exploring new possibilities and reaching his/her own conclusions, how will you proceed if those possibilities will take the client further from the organization's stated objectives? How will you respond to the internal pull to "teach to the test?" Your responses to these, and other questions like these, should be part of your offer and discussed up front. The ultimate question at stake here is, "Who is my client?" If my client is the person I am coaching, I will likely respond one way. If my client is the organization, I may respond differently. The most harmful wrong answer is to not have an answer in advance.

The organization into which you enter will have an assessment of the value of coaching long before you arrive. That assessment might include how open one should be about having a coach; in other words, whether it is a bad thing to have a coach or a good thing to have a coach. Either assessment will open certain possibilities for the coaching and close down others. I have found it useful to explore this issue early in the relationship, often in contracting. Some of that exploration is factual—how many leaders in this organization have coaches? For what reasons are coaches typically hired? What have been the outcomes of the last three or four coaching engagements? Some of that exploration is emotional—how does it feel to have a coach? How do you imagine feeling if others know you have a coach?

CONCLUSION

This chapter has likely raised more questions than it has answered. One key issue is being clear about who you are as a coach and about your coaching offer. Another is to stay mindful of the organization and its influence on you and your client. Chris Argyris is noted for, among other things, his writings about "espoused theory" and "theory in action." He suggests that we have two theories, the one we state to the public and likely believe, and the one that actually guides our actions. I believe that these differences are explained in large part by the power of the environment. Beyond your own mindfulness, I find it useful to have coaching partners with whom I confidentially share coaching experiences. Sometimes the brilliant insight to which I seem blind is right there in front of me.

Coaching leaders in organizations is a rich and rewarding experience. This coaching allows for the opportunity to use context and backdrop to enhance the coaching relationship. The opportunities for significant learning are endless.

NOTE

1. Zenger and Folkman, *The Extraordinary Leader: Turning Good Managers into Great Leaders*, 20.

BIBLIOGRAPHY

Argyris, Chris and Donald A. Schon. *Theory in Practice*. San Francisco, CA: Jossey-Bass, 1974.

Bolman, Lee and Terrence Deal. *Modern Approaches to Understanding and Managing Organizations*. San Francisco, CA: Jossey-Bass, 1984.

Lewin, Kurt. *A Dynamic Theory of Personality*. New York: McGraw-Hill, 1935.

Zenger, John and Joseph Folkman. *The Extraordinary Leader: Turning Good Managers into Great Leaders*. New York: McGraw-Hill, 2002, 20.

CHAPTER 19

MOVING THE CLIENT FORWARD: DESIGNING EFFECTIVE ACTIONS

FRANK BALL AND BETH BLOOMFIELD

AS COACHES OF LEADERS, we are quite skilled and practiced in building rapport with our leader/clients, asking penetrating questions, listening deeply, and understanding our clients and the worlds in which they live. When we're with them, great things often happen. A new distinction is seen, a helpful insight is grasped, and the leader can often begin to write a new story for himself during the meeting. Powerful though those interactions may be, the question remains, "how do we keep the momentum moving forward between sessions?"

One of the most critical skills of a coach is the ability to design effective, purposeful activities for clients to engage in between coaching sessions. This is how the coach helps the client continue to move the action forward when the coach isn't there. If our work with our leader/clients is to be more than the sum of the individual meetings, we need to think beyond those conversations.

In this chapter we introduce a process to link the coach's assessment of the client's current state and coaching goals to specific activities to help close the gap between them. We also explore five specific types of activities coaches can ask their clients to engage in between coaching sessions, during the middle part of the coaching "Life Cycle." We define and describe each activity in turn, provide examples, and show how they produce the desired results. These activities are unique

Beginning		Middle	End
Up-front work	Program design	The coaching itself	Closing
Contracting • Duration • Frequency • Payment • Agreements • Other terms *Rapport & Trust Building* • "Intake" • The Story *Investigating* • Presenting issues • Assessment instruments • Interviews • Workplace observations	• Current state • Goals/Objectives • Grounded assessments • Format • Timeline • Conditioning • Methodologies	*During the Session:* • Purposeful conversations • Immediate concerns • Exploring the story • Staying in the question • Models, tools, role-plays, etc. • Congruence of mind, body, emotions • Reviewing commitments • Results of insights; learnings • Feedback for coach and client • Recontracting/new agreements • Noticing & offering distinctions *Between Sessions:* • Inquiry • Self-observations • Practices • Exercises • Resources (books, poems, videos, etc.) • Structures of support (day planners, exercise buddies, etc.)	• Pre/Postcoaching comparisons • Action plan • Next steps • Evaluation of program • Feedback for coach • Ritual/gifts

Figure 19.1 The flow of coaching
Source: ©Frank Ball & Beth Bloomfield

to coaching and distinguish the skillful coach from those whose impact is more limited.

In the "Life Cycle" of coaching every coaching engagement has a beginning, a middle, and an end (figure 19.1). If you think of the beginning only as contracting, intake, investigating, and rapport building, you'll miss an important opportunity to be purposeful and intentional in your coaching through design of an individual coaching program using coaching-specific activities. Why should you as a leadership coach be thinking in terms of a "program" for your leader/client? Working programmatically provides structure to the engagement, ties the coaching to measurable outcomes, and places coaching in a systems context—all important aspects of coaching leaders in organizations.

THE ELEMENTS OF PROGRAM DESIGN

We can identify five key characteristics of a well-designed coaching program for a leader/client:

- *Purposefulness*: "Begin with the end in mind."
- *Rigor*: This makes possible purposeful conversations (versus merely interesting).
- *Impact*: Purposeful conversations are what give coaching its impact and distinguish it from other approaches to personal and professional development for leaders.
- *Consistency*: Through the rigor of good design, you achieve consistent results for the leader.
- *Breakthrough results*: Good design is the only way you can be sure of getting *breakthrough* out of "breakdown."

Program design is done together by coach and leader/client, in a process of "co-creation." Both work together to describe the leader's current state, using the information and insight derived from the up-front work of investigation and assessment (whether through means of formal assessment instruments or a more organic process of inquiry). As a coach, you help the leader see "the way things are," focusing especially on what's missing and what's getting in the way of the leader reaching his goals. The leader has the prerogative of describing his own desired end state, although the coach can help ensure that the goals are realistic and attainable, while at the same time big enough to stretch the leader and build his capacity for continuing growth and development.

Out of this work, the coach must formulate theories or working hypotheses for why the leader is who he is, why he behaves as he does, and how change might happen for him. These are actually "grounded assessments" of where the gaps are between current state and desired outcome. As the coach, you may choose to make these assessments together with the leader or keep them to yourself until later on in the coaching process, if you assess that the leader's tolerance for hearing potentially unwelcome news is low. In that case, part of your work will be to increase his capacity for receiving feedback, however unflattering to his ego. We should add that our preference is for direct communication with the leader/client from the beginning of the engagement; a key coaching competency is delivering feedback and well-grounded assessments in a way that is respectful, useful, and kind.

Up until this point, we have been working with the "what" of the individual coaching program design. Now we will move to the "how"—how are you, the coach, going to help the leader/client bridge the gaps? This is where the design of effective actions is integrated into the structure of the overall coaching program. Key elements of this part of the design include those that mainly involve your effort as the coach and those that mainly involve the leader's effort. The coach is responsible for determining the sequencing of coaching-specific activities—what's the order, what are the milestones—and for conditioning the client—is he "in shape" for coaching? If not, what actions will you request he take to get himself ready for the hard work ahead?

The leader, on the other hand, is in charge of his own learning style—what does he know about what works best for him, and how does he communicate that to the coach? He is in the best position to assess his own learning gradient—how quickly can he integrate change? How steep is the slope? In addition, both coach and leader/client should seek some early wins, to give them both a strong foundation to build on as the coaching progresses.

With all these elements in mind, it's up to the coach to plot a pathway, using coach-specific methodologies, including learning activities specific to coaching. It's good practice to share the roadmap with your client, and to invite his comment and reactions to it. That way, the coaching process becomes more transparent and the coaching program you have designed together becomes a touchstone that you can both return to periodically to gauge your progress along the path, and if necessary, to change your route. Remember the ultimate purpose of coaching is to build capacity for learning and self-generation in the client.

DESIGNING ACTIONS

At last! You're coaching! You have entered the middle phase of the coaching engagement, and it's time to put your program design to the test. And now, also, you are called upon to supplement your powerful coaching conversations with some powerful activities for the leader to use to continue and perhaps to accelerate her learning between sessions. During the program design process, you should have thought through the types of activities that you want to use, but the commitments you ask the leader to make—whether you call them "homework" or "fieldwork"—should be specific to the issues and concerns raised in the coaching itself, and so may be difficult to anticipate ahead of time.

For that reason, most leadership coaches maintain a "toolkit" of activities they can turn to and adapt to the particular needs of the individual leader/client at that point in her coaching. We categorize these activities, specific to the middle of coaching programs, into five basic types:

- Self-observations
- Practices

- Inquiries
- Exercises
- Structures of support

SELF-OBSERVATIONS

To the extent that leadership coaching is about helping the leader see differently so that he can then act differently, becoming able to observe oneself more skillfully is the first step leading to change (table 19.1). This enhanced ability to observe oneself is also the source of the leader's ability to self-correct and is the ultimate source of sustained excellent performance. Well-designed self-observations are a key tool coaches use to take the first step of creating insights. We define them as:

> A precisely defined set of observations that a client performs over a period of time, whose purpose is to create self-awareness, provide grounded assessments for decision making, and build capacity for self-correction.

Self-observations can be focused on either the leader's interior landscape of thoughts and emotions or his exterior landscape of actions and results. For example, the leader might be asked to notice his thoughts and feelings when in certain situations. On the other hand, the leader could be asked to notice the volume of his voice, his rate of speech, posture, and gestures in certain situations. The intention is to focus the leader's attention on a place where he is not now focusing to bring new things into his awareness.

Shifting and increasing awareness is the first step leading to change. For example, if a client declares that he intends to lose weight this year and doesn't start to pay attention to what and how much he puts into his mouth differently than before, it's unlikely that he will lose weight. The new practice of dieting is reinforced through observation of himself in action (what and how much he eats). Through observing himself in action he develops the means to self-correct and self-manage in a

Table 19.1 Steps to create self-observations

---

1. Identify an opening or situation you want to know more about.
2. List questions on how you think, show up, and act in that situation.
3. Split yourself in halves: an observer and an actor.
4. In real life, have the observer watch the actor using one or more of the questions in step 2.
5. Record what you observe and learn. Look for patterns and trends.

---

way that supports the change he has declared he wants to call into being.

Details that contribute to the effectiveness of self-observations include specifying times or occasions when the observations are to be made. The leader/client will be asked to collect data over time. This is where the practice of journaling comes in; the two support each other. By keeping a record of his observations, the leader will be able to discern patterns and trends in his own behavior and what prompts it. Over time the leader will be able to notice what works and what doesn't, and when he is effective and when he is not. Many of our leader/clients may have difficulty slowing down enough to self-observe.

Often the coach will ask the leader to engage in a practice of "not doing," such as meditation, to slow the leader down and support the self-observation.

PRACTICES

To the extent that self-observation leads to insight and new understanding, the next coaching-specific activities that build on this learning are practices (table 19.2). They are focused on building the leader's ability to take effective actions through embodying the learning self-observations and other activities described in this chapter. A practice is:

> a behavior that is performed iteratively with the intention of improving a quality or competence, and building automaticity and transparency in the client.

Practice doesn't make perfect. Practice makes permanent that which is practiced.

In addition to building new capacities for effective actions within our leader/clients, practice can also be used to interrupt the action or cause a break in the leader's automaticity. For example, a leader who is working to include others more into her decision making may adopt a

Table 19.2 Steps to create practices

---

1. Gather data (observe).
2. Set a goal: What do you want to change, learn about, or deepen?
3. Create a practice to do often (at least daily).
4. Reflect periodically on what you're learning.
5. Self-correct—fine-tune the practice or create a new one.

---

practice of asking "what do *you* think?" whenever a colleague presents a problem needing resolution. By stopping her automatic response to answer the question right away, the leader creates the possibility of a different outcome. When accompanied with a self-observation to notice when it is easy or difficult to engage in the practice, the leader can learn more about those factors that affect her ability to act with purposefulness and skillfulness. Practices and self-observations, then, support each other.

Often in the beginning of the coaching relationship the coach may ask the leader to begin one or more practices of self-care regardless of any other practices agreed upon. These contribute to the process of getting the leader into condition to be coached.

In contrast to self-observations that can focus on thoughts and emotions as well as actions and results, practices usually involve the domain of the body and have the leader doing something in the physical world. In a sense they can be thought of as the means through which learning is made permanent through embodiment of the learning. This is what happens when you learn any new skill—playing the piano, or tennis, or riding a bike—you can read or hear about it, you can watch it being done, but not until you practice it repeatedly do you build the muscle for it.

INQUIRIES

The capacity for reflective thought is a hallmark of an effective leader, yet in today's blur of events and activity, few of us have the opportunity to engage in it. We hear repeatedly from our executive clients that allowing themselves to pause for reflection is one of the great benefits of coaching. Part of our role as coaches is to help them make the space for reflection in their lives well past the conclusion of the coaching engagement.

Inquiries are the tools we use to open up the leader for reflective thought (table 19.3). We define an inquiry as:

> an investigation of values and beliefs; moods and emotions; behaviors and actions; connections and relationships; and social, cultural, and historical contexts, in order to build awareness and understanding of a client's situation and ultimately to build the client's capacity for self-correction and self-generation.

Inquiries are questions coaches ask leaders to "sit with" between coaching sessions and often over an extended period. One of the key

Table 19.3 Steps to create an inquiry

---

1. Identify an opening or situation you want to know more about.
2. List questions on how you and others show up, behave, and interact in that situation.
3. Observe and ask, "What's behind that?" (at least 3 times).
4. Record what you observe and learn. Look for patterns and trends.
5. Ask new questions.

---

elements of an inquiry is that its purpose is not so much for the leader to find an answer to the question asked as it is to inhabit the question in a way that heightens understanding. In some ways, asking a leader to "sit with the question" is like a coach using silence during a coaching session rather than speaking or asking. Much richness can arise when the space is afforded for that possibility.

It has been our experience that people lose all their curiosity about a thing (i.e., stop learning) when they think they have the answer. One key, we've found, to the effectiveness and impact of an inquiry is to ask the leader to avoid answering the question to permit new thoughts and alternative explanations to surface.

EXERCISES

We have noticed a fair amount of confusion among both our leadership coaching students and sometimes our executive clients about the use of the term "exercise" as distinct from self-observation or practice. To be clear, in the coaching context we view an exercise as having a specific meaning stemming from its function; an exercise is:

> a focused activity, finite in scope, that a client performs with the purpose of gaining clarity or understanding, in preparation for (or in support of) a shift in the client's consciousness or behavior.

As distinct from practices, which are repeated over time, exercises generally tend to be one-off activities used to provide the client with new information or new understanding—clarity. Examples include written exercises such as the "Future Self" exercise described in *Co-Active Coaching: New Skills for Coaching People toward Success in Work and Life*[1] or a "Day in the Life" written exercise.

STRUCTURES OF SUPPORT

Finally, we recognize one other category of activity, the creation or adoption of what we call a structure of support (table 19.4), defined as:

Table 19.4   Creating a structure of support

- Who
- What
- When/how often
- Where
- How

A mechanism, object, social construct, or person(s) that supports a client in putting new practices or behaviors in place.

Frequently, a structure of support builds in accountability for the leader in staying with new practices and behaviors. Examples might include calendars and planners, an exercise buddy or trainer, an assistant, or a traditional support group. Some would say that hiring a coach is a structure of support in itself!

Structures of support can be as simple as a post-it note on the computer screen to remind the leader to self-observe or a sign on the desk with "WAIT" written on it to remind him to ask "*Why Am I Talking?*" In our dieting example earlier in this chapter, attending weight watchers meetings could be a structure of support for the client.

A FEW OTHER CONSIDERATIONS

It's always best when the leadership coach and client can cocreate the various activities the leader will commit to engage in between sessions. There will be occasions, though, when the leader will be so stuck in his story that he will not be able to imagine an exercise that will yield a new insight or build the capacity to act in new, more effective ways. The coach must be prepared to step in and design an activity, using one of the five methods presented here, to get the leader unstuck and moving forward with new eyes and new actions. Moreover, even if you aren't feeling particularly brilliant in the moment, you can always promise to research and send one along soon after the coaching session.

It's important to be clear here that we are not advocating the use of "tips and tools" in some sort of cookbook recipe for good and effective coaching for leaders. Absent a fundamental grasp of the distinctions of leadership coaching and some meaningful experience in their application to real leaders with real coachable issues, the kinds of coaching activities we describe here are little better than interesting diversions. Coaching is both science and art, and the skillful practitioner brings both to the design of coaching programs and actions that are unique for each individual being coached.

What's required is a thorough understanding of the mechanisms at work in each type of coaching activity, and a dash of inspiration that can come from virtually anywhere. Some of our favorite sources of inspiration, beyond the ubiquitous self-help and business books, include interview questions asked by thoughtful journalists, stories told in novels or films, metaphors suggested by poetry, and even games played by children. Lightness and wonder help set the stage for learning, and both should inform your design of coaching activities for your executive clients.

The five coaching-specific activities described earlier are often combined to great effect. For example, a new leader/client might be asked to complete the "Future Self" exercise described in *Co-Active Coaching: New Skills for Coaching People Toward Success in Work and Life*.[2] Based on the results of that exercise, the coach might assign a specific inquiry for the leader to sit with over time, collecting thoughts and insights using a journal (a structure of support.) Based on the insights gained through inquiry and journaling, the leader and coach might codesign a series of practices and self-observations through which the leader can build the capacity to take new, more effective actions and observe himself in action in a way that permits self-correction and thereby sustained excellent performance. Finally, structures of support can assist the leader in the journey from where and who they are now to where and who they aspire to become.

Something to consider is the gradient of the learning curve you are asking your client to climb. Your leader/client is already living a life full of other commitments, and anything you request he take on in support of his learning and growth will be competing for space in an already very full schedule. So one aspect of gradient is the quantity of the additional work we ask our executive clients to do between coaching sessions.

The second aspect of gradient is the degree of difficulty of the activities we're asking them to complete. For example, journaling or starting a practice of seated meditation may be very easy for some clients and very difficult for others. We must gauge our clients' receptivity and readiness to take on and be successful at those activities we assign them.

Likewise, it's important to pause periodically, perhaps at mutually agreed milestones in the coaching engagement, to recalibrate the program with the leader, to check your assessments about him, and if necessary, to revise your design or change your planned activities and methodologies.

Another consideration for the coach is to make sure that the activities you ask the leader to engage in address all domains of learning—the cognitive, the emotional, and the body. This is especially important if the client is dramatically underdeveloped in one or more of the domains. Big breakthroughs are possible if the coach has the courage to take the leader where he hasn't spent much time before. Sometimes it's also easier to work in the less familiar domains because the person is less well-defended there—his story that is keeping him stuck isn't as strongly entrenched there.

When asking leaders to engage in specified activities between coaching conversations, the coach is wise to have them complete the activities over an extended period before either adding more practices or changing them. In the case of self-observations, for example, their impact is much greater if the leader self-observes over an extended period to allow for trends and inconsistencies to emerge. Using a journal to capture those observations as they occur then provides a sound basis for insight, learning, and growth. Although insight can occur in a flash in "coaching time," deep change of the sort coaching seeks to bring about takes a long time and a lot of hard work to become permanent.

In a coaching relationship, growth and learning occur over time in a way that is cumulative. One of the roles of the leadership coach, in addition to designing and assigning great activities for the leader/client to engage in between sessions, is to insure progress and accountability.

Coaches often dedicate a specific portion of their coaching sessions to a check-in around the assignments since the last time they met with their client. Key aspects of the discussion include whether the assignment was done, what difficulty (ease) the leader experienced in completing the assignment, what outcomes the leader achieved, and what he learned about the topic, himself, or coaching. This conversation is where key learnings are identified, where the efficacy of assignments can be measured, where course corrections can be made, and where progress can be noticed and celebrated.

The coach and leader then have a sound basis to either drop, modify, or continue the assigned between-session work to continue the learning and growth experienced in the direction of the coaching goals agreed upon at the beginning of the relationship. This process is yet another way in which rigor is insured, and the leadership coaching relationship is purposeful and not merely interesting.

NOTES

1. Laura Whitworth, Henry Kimsey-House, and Phil Sandahl, *Co-Active Coaching: New Skills for Coaching People toward Success in Work and Life.* (Palo Alto, CA: Davies-Black, 1998), 216–221.
2. Ibid.

CHAPTER 20

ASSESSMENTS FOR INSIGHT, LEARNING, AND CHOICE IN COACHING

SUE E. McLEOD

YOU'VE PROBABLY HAD THE EXPERIENCE of coaching a leader when you were sure that how they saw themselves wasn't consistent with their behavior or what you believed was authentic for them. These people seem to be playing a role, or focus on their intentions—what they meant to do, what they were thinking at the time, or the story that they tell about themselves—rather than what actually happened. Assessments can play an important role in generating self-awareness in the leaders we coach, and provide information, beyond the leader's self-perceptions, that can be directly applied to their most challenging situations.

As coaches, we create opportunities for new insights that open the doors for improved performance and authentic leadership. Assessment data can open new ways of thinking or behaving, by bringing to light new information that the leader couldn't see before. It can also affirm what the leader already knows, but thought was hidden or invisible to others. It often provides a powerful mirror to allow the leader to say, "Yes, that's me" and to take more responsibility for his or her own behavior and how it impacts the people and results of their organizations.

We seem to expect that leaders will be unaware of their weaknesses and the negative impacts they have on others. I have seen this quite a bit in my experience. However, I'm always struck by the leaders who do not fully know their strengths and their natural gifts, or appreciate how their gifts help to make them successful. By giving an objective and neutral perspective, assessments can be powerful tools for "accentuating the positive" as well as "eliminating the negative."

WHAT ARE ASSESSMENTS?

Assessments are, in general, information that assesses selected aspects of the leader's behavior, skills, performance, styles, or preferences. In this chapter, I'll refer to using the following types of assessments in coaching[1]:

- Self-assessments of personality and style assessments that indicate preferences for behaviors, thought patterns, attitudes, or approaches under normal or stress situations. I'll refer to the results of these assessments as preferences. I like that language because it implies choice and flexibility, which is what we're trying to engender in the leaders we coach.
- External assessments of behavior or results that use data from sources other than the leader, such as 360-degree assessments with data.

It's important to note that these assessments are just that—assessments. They are one view of the leader, from the leader's own eyes or from the eyes of selected others, created at a particular point in time using a particular frame of reference. They are not "the truth," they are not the definition of the whole person, nor do they completely describe the past or predict the future. Given that perspective, I take the results seriously—they have meaning and are valuable—and hold them lightly, especially when using them to create new actions in the future.

FROM "AUTOMATIC" TO CHOICE

In my coaching, I first want to understand the leader's "automatic" approach. "Automatic" is the way the leader reacts without advance planning or thinking. For example, as an intuitive type, my automatic response to new information is to ask, "Why is this important? What's new and different about this approach?" Someone with an automatic approach that is more analytical might ask, "Where's the proof that this will work? What's missing?" These are two very different responses to hearing new information.

Once we understand the "automatic," we start noticing whether it works or not, or, more specifically, *when* it works and *when* it doesn't. For example, my automatic response doesn't work well when the situation requires a critical eye for the details. The analytical approach may not work well when it's time to brainstorm creative, new approaches.

In situations where the automatic isn't working, the leader and I can turn our attention to new choices that might change the results.

Assessments are tools that can be used for each step of this process. They tell us about the leader's past and current behavior. They provide data about what the leader is doing well—what's working—and where the leader may have difficulties or challenges. They present this information in an objective and neutral way, taking out the judgments and negative (or positive) connotations that we associate with certain traits. Assessments also give leaders new insights into how they are seen by others. This can uncover the gap between their intentions and the impact they are really having. Finally, many assessments provide a well-researched conceptual model of human behavior that can be used to generate new options for action.

SELF-ASSESSMENT

There is a wide variety of self-assessments on the market today, many with strong research behind them. They measure many things—personality types, thinking style preference, values, leadership traits, critical thinking skills, emotional intelligence, body and energy patterns, behavior patterns, and so on. The most effective assessments will be the ones that you, as coach, can use effectively. This means you should be trained or well studied in the conceptual model, have practice interpreting the results and applying it in the coaching context of creating new awareness and new future behaviors.

The training and study in the assessments you use should prepare you to introduce the assessment and interpret the results with the leader. Here we focus on the coaching aspects—creating distinctions and insights and finding openings for new actions.

INSIGHTS FOR THE LEADERS

What insights can you create for your leaders with these self-assessments? First you can develop an understanding of their "automatic" responses or behaviors. Some assessments even include measures of responses to stress. In your coaching, explore the stories of how they see their preferences day to day. Can they distinguish their preferences from the set of possible preferences in the assessment? Can they describe and recognize the preferences of others? With your guidance, they can understand the distinctions of styles, types, or preferences in the conceptual model behind the assessment.

Another insight to create for leaders is how their automatic preferences translate to behavior. You want them to "see" their preferences in action, so they can recognize their behavior when it happens. For example, understanding how I process information gave me more insight into how I conducted meetings. My agenda follows my preference for information to be presented in a particular order. When others present information to me using their own preferences, different from mine, I find myself bored, disengaged, or frustrated because they didn't give me the "foundation" information that I wanted.

Finally, the ability to step out of their "automatic" to choose another response requires your leaders to be able to think about a situation objectively before behaving. Use the assessment model to discuss some of the challenging situations they find themselves in. Ask what style is *appropriate* that might be very different from what they *want to* do. I have one leader who has a strong preference for creating new ideas, seeing the big picture, and being innovative. This doesn't work in some of the things he needs to do well to be successful, such as managing budgets or executing a structured decision-making process that is working well. Make the connection between his preference and the less-than-stellar results, and you have an opening for new action. By having your leaders think about what's needed is a situation, then mapping their own preferences and behaviors against what's needed, you can help them see how their preferences impact their success.

PATH TO UNDERSTANDING OTHERS

The assessment that you use for the leader to understand herself can also help her understand others. Sometimes just the awareness that other styles exist and that people think and behave differently is an important thing for leaders to understand. Without that understanding, they can carry unstated expectations that others think, feel, and behave the same as the leader, with the resulting frustration when those expectations are not met.

I hear so many complaints about people who "should have" done something or used a different approach. I've found this reflects the leader's assumption that others would approach the situation the same way he or she would. Yet, most of us use our most comfortable styles when we approach our work. Our intention is to do our best, not to frustrate others by doing it a different way. For example, the person who seems to be sabotaging the new policy by repeatedly bringing up how people who are affected might feel during the change may just be asking that his preference for considering people and feelings be included in the decision making.

The assessment puts a neutral and objective picture of humanness on the table. Once you can see that someone is operating out of a preference for a different approach, the emotion can subside. Then it's easier to consider the other point of view, ask what the situation needs, and make a choice. In the earlier example, considering how people will feel is an important component of developing and communicating a policy change. Changing the perception of "sabotage" to "adding a valuable perspective" can make a tremendous difference in the success of the policy change, as well as smooth the relationship between the "saboteur" and the leader.

Here are the basic questions to ask your leader when coaching using a self-assessment:

1. How do you *want* to act, given your preferences?
2. What can you *expect* from others, given their preferences?
3. What's *needed* in this situation for the project, initiative, or task to be successful?
4. How *will* you act and what will you ask of others, to be successful?

EXTERNAL ASSESSMENTS

External assessments provide a different view of the leader's behavior, impact, and results within the organization. This view is a valuable addition to the leader's self-perception. The external view gives both leader and coach more information about the impact of the leader's behavior on the people with whom she works most closely. These assessments can also give an organizational or leadership context for the coaching.

Three-hundred-sixty-degree assessments collect information from all sides of the leader—self, supervisor, direct reports, and peers. Some are even designed to get the perspectives of other key people with experience and insight into the leader, including friends, family members, customers, and suppliers.

THE VALUE OF AN OUTSIDE PERSPECTIVE

It's important to remember that the inside perspective (from inside the leader) is just one perspective and is often clouded by the leader's knowledge of his or her intentions and internal standards of behavior or performance. Ability to gauge impact on others depends on the level of awareness and the amount of time spent reflecting on how others reacted. By gathering information from other people in the organization, the coach and leader discover how other people see the leader, what expectations they have, and how the leader is measuring up to those expectations. Hearing about performance and impact from outside also makes it more difficult for the leader to "hide" from the impact and implications. We all have the illusion that our mistakes and faults are overlooked—it's often an awakening for the leader to realize that everyone sees his weak points, in action! Alternatively, some leaders' performance doesn't measure up to their own incredibly high standards. It can be a relief to find that others are satisfied with their performance.

Getting multiple perspectives is also valuable. Each person's view of the leader is colored by his or her own filters and experiences of the world. By gathering data from multiple sources, the coach and leader will begin to see patterns in the feedback—what's consistent, what's different among the people asked. The areas where there are consistent messages are more difficult to ignore. As one of my leaders used to say—if one person calls you a horse, you can think about it; if three people call you a horse, you might consider buying a saddle.

Another advantage to multiple perspectives is insight into how the leader is perceived in different layers in the organization. Is this someone who "manages up," spending time and energy impressing the boss while ignoring direct reports? Or is the leader protective of direct reports to the detriment of building relationships with key peer organizations?

TYPES OF ASSESSMENTS

Three-hundred-sixty-degree assessments can be formal instruments developed and scored by companies who specialize in studying and assessing leadership behavior. These can be "off-the-shelf," that is, commercially available for use in any organization, or they can be custom designed for an organization, often based on a model of competencies that the organization deems are necessary for success. Like the self-assessments, I recommend that you be well-versed in these formal assessments before using them in your coaching.

If a formal assessment isn't available, or doesn't seem appropriate with the leader you are coaching, you can offer to collect 360-degree feedback using a set of structured interviews. This method allows you to tailor the information you collect to the specifics of the leader's situation.

You're also likely to get some interesting insights through these conversations that don't usually come out of the more formal instruments. For example, in one set of interviews, I heard about the leader's behavior that was causing difficulties for her staff, but they also talked about their perceptions of her attitude toward them. This made for a much richer conversation, and more impactful coaching, because these attitudes were affecting her ability to lead, much more than the actual behaviors.

Interviewing the people who work with your leader has some additional benefits. First, it lets these people know that your leader is working with a coach and working to improve performance and results. A leader who models self-development and introspection can create an environment in which others will do the same. Second, it lets people know what areas your leader is focused on and gives them the opportunity to suggest additional areas for improvement. This can generate a feeling of respect and empowerment among these people, as they are being asked to provide valuable information that may impact the leader and the organization. Third, it may cause them to reflect on their own performance. Just by interviewing people about the organization's performance, there is an opening created for others to take action because they see that the leader is supportive of changed behavior.

Work with your leader to prepare for the interview or the survey. Discuss the areas to focus on and what information would be helpful. Work together to generate open-ended questions that explore how the leader is perceived, what actual behaviors are noticed, and the impact the leader is having—positive and negative.

Some basic questions you can ask are:

- What does this leader need to do well to be successful in this position and to get to the next level?
- What strengths does this leader demonstrate that helps her to be successful?
- What would you like to see this leader do differently? Do more of? Do less of?

After the prepared interview questions, I ask "What haven't I asked that is important for this leader to know?" I've often seen leaders get the most value from these "free-form" comments (these are often included in the formal 360-degree survey instruments, too). For example, one leader knew that she was working too hard and not taking care of her physical health, and, she thought those sacrifices were important to help her team succeed. It was only when she read one of these comments that she realized how concerned her employees were about her health. They liked working for her and were worried that she would leave because of burnout or some other effect of being overworked. Once she saw the negative impact of her "sacrifices" on her employees, she was willing to take some time off of work for self-care.

When the interviews are complete, you will need to generate a report of findings that conveys the feedback in a neutral and objective way and preserves the confidentiality of the people who were interviewed. Look for themes and patterns, and specific examples to ground the feedback (especially if you think it will be difficult to hear). Some categories I've used include:

- People describe you as...followed by a list of adjectives that I heard in the interview.
- What's expected of you in this position and how to get to the next level?
- Strengths people see.
- What people would like to see more of in the future?

By keeping it simple and focused on what's needed for them to achieve their development goals, it makes the messages more meaningful and useful for the coaching to come.

REVIEWING THE DATA

Once the data has been collected, the coach and leader should each have the opportunity to review the information before discussing it. There are some good questions to pose to the leader for them to consider while they review the data, such as:

- What surprises you about this data?
- What patterns do you see?
- Where are your strengths?
- What's most important to address now?

The coach, too, needs to approach the data with some specific questions—and be open to discovering new insights that the data may show. Here are some areas that I look for:

- Consistent messages—from within groups or across groups of people who completed the assessment.
- Conflicting message—do different groups see the leader differently?

- Outliers—if data about individual responses are available, look for the "spread" of responses. Some very high and some very low scores within groups could indicate "in group/out group" distinctions held by the leader.
- Leader's self-perceptions relative to others' perceptions—does the leader consistently over or under rate himself?
- Clear strengths—what are the areas where everyone (even the leader) sees they have strengths? These are areas that you may want the leader to take full advantage of and "claim" as their own.
- Clear blind spots—similarly, areas that everyone (including the leader) sees as a weakness can point to something the leader may want to address, with the caveat that he should understand the impact of that weakness and consider options for filling that gap in his leadership.

The coach's role is not to draw any conclusions, but to look for new questions to pose to the leader, new avenues to explore, and new insights into the working relationships and environment that can help to focus the leader on how to be more successful.

Most important, however, is to note the areas where you are curious about something or where your intuition tells you there is something interesting to explore with the leader. One leader I worked with had very strong results overall and just a few of his direct reports who said that he didn't listen to them. My intuition told me this was a place to explore, although I had no idea why. When I brought it up, the leader denied that he exhibited this behavior. He always listened to everyone. As he went on protesting, I pointed out that he wasn't listening to me or to what the data (his direct reports) were telling him. He protested some more, and we dropped the subject. In our next session, he told me that I had really hit on something. He didn't *really* listen, and he did keep people at a distance and, from there, we began the exploration of why and what were the impacts on his staff and his leadership and how he might want to change in the future.

In your conversations with the leader about the feedback, it's important to remember your job as coach. You are not expected to have answers, but to create opportunities for self-exploration, learning, and action in the areas that are the most relevant for the leader.

Let the leader know that you've looked at and thought about the data. Give her an overview of what you saw. Since most of my leaders focus on the negatives, I start with the positives, telling them where I see their strengths, affirming where others see them as performing well. I give them my overall sense of their leadership. "You are a leader who sets clear direction and holds people to high standards. You're tough, and your boss is satisfied with your business results."

Then I ask them for their perceptions and for what they've learned by looking at the data. I ask questions about where I'm curious. "You have two bosses who rate you very differently. What's going on?" Leaders have much more insight into the working environment than I do, so I avoid drawing any conclusions before I hear their story about the data.

Then I ask, "What's most important to focus on here?" Moreover, we follow that path. Connecting the feedback to what's most important to the leader at this time—maybe a particularly challenging project or relationship—will give the feedback life beyond the feedback session. I give myself permission to come back to items that I think are being avoided and that I believe are important. One leader, for example, again had strong scores and one peer score that was consistently lower than the others. When I first pointed this out and asked about it, he admitted that there was one peer with whom he had a very strained relationship. He wasn't willing to look at changing it; he was OK with the way it was. When that relationship came up again in another coaching session, I came back to the feedback and asked about the impact of this strained relationship on his direct reports. How did it affect their ability to do their jobs? What kind of example was he setting about collaboration within the company? After looking at these impacts, he saw the importance of improving this relationship and added that to his action plan.

GOAL SETTING AND ACTION PLANNING

In leadership coaching, we want our leaders to be moving toward specific results. The 360-degree data can give very specific areas for goal setting. By analyzing the feedback and connecting it to real situations the leader is facing, you can create specific goals for changing behavior and perceptions. The assessment itself can become a mechanism for evaluating results if the assessment can be repeated in six to twelve months.

None of us can change too many things at one time. I ask leaders to choose no more than three areas of focus for their action plan based on the feedback. I ask that they be relevant to their main responsibilities, the organization's goals, or the leader's personal goals. We don't just focus on improving areas where they are weak. I also ask them to look at areas where they can use their strengths more prominently.

The action steps can be "doing" focused, for example "hold meetings with your staff more regularly, particularly the ones who are feeling out of the loop." They can be "being" focused, for example "be present when your direct reports come to your office to talk with you. Give them your full attention so they feel heard and appreciated." They can focus on the leader's inner thoughts and attitudes, for example "turn off the inner critic for a week, and watch the impact you are really having on your people. Learn to appreciate the 'good enough' rather than constantly striving for perfection."

Give your leaders every opportunity to embrace what the assessment data says and be successful at making the shifts and changes that will help them be successful. Understand that receiving feedback is often difficult and our natural tendency is to explain it away, defend ourselves, and look for reasons to maintain the status quo. Be gentle and understanding as you work with this feedback. Moreover, be challenging and hold firm to the belief that you are this leader's coach because he or she wants to change.

NOTE

1. There are other types of assessments—including tests of skills and abilities, external assessments from just direct reports, and others. The approach to using all of these tools is similar. I focus on these types here to stay focused on the coaching, rather than the assessments themselves.

CHAPTER 21

THE ART AND PRACTICE OF GROUNDED ASSESSMENTS

LEE ANN WURSTER-NAEFE AND JULIE SHOWS

I can't believe I have this meeting with my boss's boss about something that is so critical to me and this organization, yet I can't seem to get the time of day with him. He comes into this organization like a know-it-all, and he is just trying to make his way to the top skimming over the really important stuff. Everybody knows that if you aren't connected to someone who matters to him, you don't get his ear. I am so frustrated and angry.

Now my boss has gotten this meeting with him, and she is all excited and wants me to be the one to pitch our proposal. I keep thinking it is a waste of time because this dude isn't paying attention to me and what I do. He barely acknowledges me in meetings and walks right past me in the hallway without saying a word. But I don't want to let my boss down. I really do want this proposal to fly, but I feel like it is a waste of time. It doesn't really matter how I feel, though, because the meeting is Friday, and I need to buck up and get it done. I can't put my best foot forward when all of this is going on. No one understands the importance of this project, especially him.

I'd like to get my act together. I'd like to organize my thoughts so I can be articulate and influential in this meeting. This is, after all, one of my major goal areas for coaching—to communicate better with senior-level leaders.

THIS WAS THE BEGINNING OF THE coaching session with Sue. After this painful monologue from her, as the coach, I had to gather my thoughts about what I had just heard and observed and reflect on what is appropriate to share with her. I noticed whenever she talked about the upcoming meeting, her shoulders rounded, she slumped down several inches in her chair, and her voice grew soft and monotonous. When she let out several deep sighs and threw her hands up in the air, I felt her exasperation. I understood her sense of hopelessness and resignation: that she had given up before she had even started the conversation with the boss's boss.

I thought sharing this impression with Sue might add to her frustration, yet I knew this was a safe space for us to pull things apart so she could gain greater awareness and check to ensure alignment with her intentions. I decided to tell Sue what I noticed about her slumping posture, gestures, and monotonous voice. I also played back phrases she used a few times: "waste of time"; "it doesn't matter"; "I'm angry and frustrated." I told her what she evoked in me was a feeling of resignation. I then asked how she felt and if this aligned with her intention for how she wants to show up as a leader in this upcoming meeting.

Does this situation sound familiar? Have you found yourself experiencing or observing something significant about your clients in real time while they discuss one of their focus areas for coaching? As coaches, we have a wide variety of "moves" to make during the conversation, such as mirroring back what we just heard, serving as a brainstorming partner, making a request, suggesting a resource/tool, and making grounded assessments, to name a few. In this chapter, we will focus on the art and craft of making grounded assessments.

We have found making grounded assessments to be one of the most powerful and least understood and utilized moves by new and practicing coaches. When we proactively name what *we* see, hear, observe, or sense in the moment with our client, we can help the client see something she was unable to see before. Helping our clients to ground their assessments and sharing *our* grounded assessments as coaches widens the lens, and this facilitates new possibilities for understanding and new action. This is often a gift to our clients, for they may not have another person or venue for obtaining this level of candor and feedback.

So let's cover a few basic definitions and see how we might use grounded assessments more skillfully and confidently as coaches.

WHAT ARE GROUNDED ASSESSMENTS AND WHY DO THEY MATTER?

Assessments are our own personal interpretations, opinions, and judgments. We as humans live in assessments. They are an important part of how we make meaning of the world and how we relate to it. This is true for the coach as well as the client. A *grounded* assessment provides the evidence, data, and facts upon which the assessment is based. What did I see or hear that led me to this conclusion? We make these assessments externally by what we say and how we hold our bodies, our presence. We make these assessments internally by what the voice in our head says to us and how we feel.

Assessments are often confused with feedback. We hear beginning coaches ask permission to share an assessment with the client. Yet, what they are actually providing is feedback, a suggestion on what the client can do better or differently the next time. Feedback is an effective coaching move and core coaching competency. However, it's important to be clear with yourself and your client when you are giving feedback and when you are giving an assessment.

As we listen to our clients, we are observing the internal and external landscapes and looking for alignment (or lack of it) between body, language, and emotions. This produces assessments in you as coach/observer. (This is what happens in the workplace and in life with your leader client, too.) The job of the coach is to sift through the incoming data and the myriad of assessments she is making and select one that syncs up and supports the client's ultimate intention/focus area for change.

This is important. The assessment is not about calling out everything the coach sees or experiences. This can be confusing and/or irrelevant to clients in the context of their coaching goal(s). Coaches must first consider why they are offering the assessment. What's the value to clients in the context of what they are trying to bring about in their life? For the sake of what purpose does the coach offer this insight, feedback, or intuitive reaction? Is it to create awareness? Is it to disrupt or break the coherence of the client's story? Or is it because the coach wants to look smart, competent, or in control of the session? Answer this question honestly, and you will stay in service to your client. When intention equals impact, there is success. When intention and impact are incongruent, there is interference, and the coach can now work with the client to explore and eliminate this gap.

GROUNDING ASSESSMENTS IN THE DOMAIN OF LANGUAGE

Assessments live in our language, emotions, and body, and they are observed in all these domains. In accordance with the work of Fernando Flores and the foundation of ontological coaching, we base ourselves on the belief that language is pivotal in helping humans create their reality. In this understanding of language, how we speak to each other and how we speak to ourselves in our heads determines what is possible in our world. Along with this view that language generates possibilities comes the responsibility of coaches to develop their listening as well. Speaking and listening are inseparable. Learning to listen at a deep level to the language clients use and the meaning they are making allows coaches to ground the assessment they hear the client making with the client.

Grounding assessments gives our clients the opportunity to observe for themselves whether the language they are listening to inside their heads is: creating the outcome they want in the world. They can then decide whether their actions support or limit their ability to create what they want. When they can see the incoherence or coherence, they can make a choice to act differently to open up different possibilities.

As a coach, you should be aware of two perspectives when grounding assessments. First, what assessments are you noticing in the client, and second, what assessments are you noticing about yourself?

Let's look first at the assessments by Sue in the example above. What assessments are you hearing in the language that Sue is using? What are the descriptive words that you hear in her story? What are the generalizations that you hear Sue making? What in her language might give you a hint about the story she is telling herself internally? How is she making meaning of this situation? What are you noticing about Sue's underlying story? What assessments might be driving her behavior? What are the standards that Sue is holding herself to? What is it that Sue wants to accomplish? Do you sense coherence or incoherence?

Your answers to these questions will determine how you would ground the assessments with Sue.

Another internal story is about the assessment that Sue has about her boss's boss. Asking the same questions might allow Sue to become aware of whether or not the assessment that she is living in about her boss is supporting her or limiting her options.

In the domain of language, let's start to ground Sue's assessments. Once Sue gives her permission, you might say, "As I listen to you, I am noticing an underlying message that you might be telling yourself. It sounds like: 'I am going to be ignored' or 'I don't matter.' What might that mean to you?"

Another example you might point out to her is her statement that "no one understands this project." Does she mean no one? What is true about the situation? Sometimes when we can get our clients to realize that the story they are telling themselves is not the truth, new possibilities open up. When you hear generalizations, for example, "Everybody knows" and "No one understands," there is an opportunity to inquire into what is true. You might also inquire into the story you are hearing about her boss: "I hear that your boss is a know-it-all. What has he done that makes you say that? Or you say that you can't get the time of day from him, what have you tried?"

At the same time, you have to be aware of the language you are listening to in your own head. As you read the story about Sue, what were you telling yourself? What's going on with you? What are you listening to? Where are you listening from? How might your assessments be interfering with your listening? Were you thinking that Sue was a victim, a capable woman, or a whiner? Or were you thinking that Sue was a very successful leader who would be able to meet her goal of having this proposal accepted? What about this story is similar to a story in your life? Notice how your questions might come from very different places depending on what assessment you are in and what you are listening to internally.

There are limits to dealing with assessments only in language. Lasting change requires a shift in your way of being. This also involves a change in the domains of emotion and body.

GROUNDING ASSESSMENTS IN THE DOMAIN OF EMOTIONS

People are always in a mood or emotion. We are listening for the emotion in our clients' stories, and we must also be aware of the emotion that we are listening from. The power of emotions and moods is that they influence action. They play into the opinions and judgments that form our assessments and these, in turn, affect the results that are possible for us to create. Our assessments, especially our core assessments, have a strong emotional grip. To be able to change our way of being, we have to be able to change our moods and emotions. That process starts with awareness.

Sue told us she felt as though what she was doing was a waste of time. She was angry and frustrated. How is anger and frustration supporting Sue in this situation? How might these emotions interfere? How does the emotion of anger appear in her communications and overall leadership presence? What other emotions do you sense?

As coach, you might ask, "What is the emotion you are experiencing right now? From that emotion, what is possible for you in this situation? What emotion would allow you to be at your best in this situation? How might you move into that emotion and embody it?"

It's important to remember that as coaches we must be aware of the emotions and moods we are in as well. The emotion we are in will predispose us to listen in a certain way. What emotion are you in right now? What was your mood as you read the story of Sue? How did that influence the assessment you made about Sue? Being able to be an observer of your own emotions in the moment will allow you to shift your way of being so that you are in service to your client.

Taking the art of grounding assessments further, we often find emotions show up in our client's energy, presence, and the somatic domain.

GROUNDING ASSESSMENTS IN THE DOMAIN OF SOMATICS

What is a somatic assessment? "Soma" (from Greek origins) means "the living body in its wholeness." The somatic domain includes all of who we are—the mind, our mood and emotions, the physical aspects of the body, such as posture, gestures, facial expressions, breath, energy, actions, how we move in the world, as well as the quality of our being-ness or presence. For you as a coach, it is critical to hone your awareness and distinctions in the somatic domain for yourself and with your clients. It's another piece of data coming through your senses to inform you and your client of roadblocks and possibilities. When your thinking and speaking can no longer propel a shift in action, it's the body—where action resides—that can be a useful and exhilarating means for self-awareness and transformation.

As you sit with your client face-to-face or listen to his or her voice over the phone, there are two places to notice: your body and the client's. There are also two dimensions to observe: the interior and the exterior. (Note: If you are phone coaching, you will need to listen deeply *and* invite your client to self-report.) Questions to assess the internal dimension include:

- What's the quality of your client's presence? Is it open or closed? Is there an inward or outward focus? Is she centered and connected? Or is she off-center and disconnected? How would you answer these questions for yourself?
- Where is the breath located in your client's body? Is it high up in the throat or upper chest? Is it lower in the heart center or coming up from the belly? What is the pace of the breath? Overall, what does this state of breathing produce in the client? What do you notice about your own breath? What about your breath's location and pacing? What state does that evoke in you?

- What sensations does your client experience, e.g. tightness/constriction or openness/flow; numbness or pain; hot or cold; pulsations; others? What sensations do you experience?
- What is your client's self-talk? What is your self-talk?
- What emotion(s) is your client experiencing? What emotion(s) are you experiencing?

Often, we move from one conversation or meeting or task to another without checking in with our whole self in this way. As coaches, we believe an ongoing cycle of self-checks or self-scans is necessary throughout a coaching conversation because the body is always present and receiving and responding to external stimuli. However, our mind may be so focused on spoken words that we miss, override, or discount cues and information coming to us from the neck down. The same holds true for our clients.

Questions to assess the exterior dimension include:

- Overall shape—how would you describe your client's physical presence? How would you describe your own?
- What's the volume, pace, and pitch of the voice?
- As your client stands or sits, is he or she extending to full height or collapsed? How about you?
- Is your client leaning forward, backward, or to the side? How about you?
- How much space does your client take up from side to side? How much space are you taking up from side to side?
- What do you notice about the eyes, forehead, and jaw? Are they relaxed or constricted?
- Are the arms and hands open, closed, or clenched?
- What do you notice about your client's gestures and movements? How do they sync with and support what she or he is saying? Or is there a disconnect or incongruence? How about you?
- What's the quality of your client's overall energy? What words come to mind? What's the quality of your overall energy?

Let's go back to Sue. I offered a grounded assessment that included the emotion and somatic domains. We now have two places to intervene—the story or assessment Sue is holding for herself in this situation ("I am going to be ignored" and "I don't matter") and the body, which is holding and revealing the resignation and hopelessness. Could I be successful and effective in working with Sue solely in the language domain? Possibly. But what if Sue's intention is to communicate in this meeting and project with confidence and passion? Then she will need to build the body to support these thoughts and emotions. What does the body of confidence and passion look like for her? How will she move and speak with confidence and passion? And what practices can she develop to anchor and embody these qualities so that they are available to her not only for this immediate conversation and project, but also for future leadership opportunities?

CONCLUSION

Returning to the conversation with Sue, by grounding the assessments, Sue was able to step back and see where her actions were not in alignment with what she wanted to accomplish. Sue realized that the story she was telling herself was limiting her possibilities, and she was then able to make a more empowering choice. She could observe that she had been hijacked by her anger and frustration but was less tuned into her overall mood of resignation. From this new awareness, Sue was able to facilitate the meeting and achieve her goal of being articulate and influential with senior-level leaders. This was an example of a coach being courageous and delivering a grounded assessment involving all three domains: language, body, and emotion.

The following is a three-step framework to help you ground assessments with your clients in the same way I did with Sue:

1. **I notice** _____.
   Name what you hear, see, or experience in the client.

2. **I want to share this because** _____.
   State the purpose of your observation. How does it relate to the bigger picture for the client and what the client is trying to bring about?

3. **I notice for me** _____.
   Name what you notice about your self-talk, emotions or body – posture, energy, presence.

Remember, as you practice making grounded assessments:

- As humans, we do not live in one domain alone. Develop your ability to become aware of assessments in all domains.
- Your assessment is your truth—your interpretation—your viewpoint. So hold it as one possibility for your client and let go of the need for perfection! We make assessments all the time.

If you offer a grounded assessment, and it does not resonate with the client, let it go. You will have other opportunities. And remember that it may take the client time to process what you are offering. Days or weeks later, the client may advise that your assessment provoked awareness and movement in a new direction.

- Assessments are most powerful when they are short, simple, and direct; our clients can only absorb so much information.
- Name specifically and clearly the evidence for your assessment.
- Share your observations with your client. Help your client to recognize their own assessments, so that they will be able to make choices that help them create the reality that supports their goals in life, in business, and in leadership.

We hope that you will discover there is real magic in the art and practice of grounded assessments.

BIBLIOGRAPHY

Brothers, Chalmers. *Language and the Pursuit of Happiness*. Naples, FL: New Possibilities Press, 2005.

Flaherty, James. *Coaching: Evoking Excellence in Others*. 3rd ed. Burlington, MA: Elsevier, 2010.

Kimsey-House, Henry, Karen Kimsey-House, Phil Sanford, and Laura Whitworth. *Co-Active Coaching*. Boston, MA: Nicholas Brealey, 2011.

Sieler, Alan. *Coaching to the Human Soul*. Blackburn, Victoria: Newfield Australia, 2003.

Strozzi-Heckler, Richard. *The Leadership Dojo*. Berkeley, CA: Frog, 2007.

CHAPTER 22

COACHING AND LEADING AS STEWARDS FOR SUSTAINABILITY

LLOYD RAINES

COACHING, LIKE LEADING, lends itself to endless innovations and evolution. The evolution of leadership has covered a lot of territory—Theory X, Theory Y, situational, values-driven, emotionally intelligent, and Level 5 leadership, among others. Likewise, coaching has evolved over time, including performance-based, behavioral, cognitive, systems thinking, neurolinguistics, emotional intelligence, somatic, and holistic coaching, to name a few prominent ones. One of the beauties of evolutionary biology is that in any of its forms it builds on what is, innovates, experiments, and evolves. It's nature's gift to life—continual awareness, feedback, learning, and experimentation.

I see in the progression of coaching and leadership a parallel theme. Each in its own way is about stewardship and sustainability. What coaches and leaders do is steward vital resources. To be a steward is to care for and cultivate the things that matter in life and work. What we are here to do with our lives is to be stewards of that which we are given—whether it be as responsible stewards of our bodies, emotions, minds, spirits, families, communities, nations, global human community, wildlife, domesticated critters, or natural resources. When we steward these domains well, we act not only from a sense of self-interest, but from an *enlightened self-interest*—holding the long view—for individual sustainability as we live nested within, and inseparable from, the health and well-being of larger life-supporting systems.

Stewardship is a *mental model*: an orientation held toward work and life. It assumes care for the integrity of social life that includes working to ensure dignity, health, mutual accountability, and fair opportunities (including access, development, and rewards). In doing so, lives are nourished in ways that support our resilience and sustainability within the broader world. *Stewardship* is a basic life orientation, and *sustainability* is its goal. In adopting this mental model in my coaching, I've noticed shifts in the ways I observe, listen, and engage in inquiry with leaders. I now see any aspect of coaching as an element or factor in the leader's overall sustainability—as a person, leader, and organizational contributor.

Common sense and self-interest call us to care for what matters and is meaningful in life, and more and more we're seeing how global factors affect local conditions (the human and financial costs of war, terrorism, energy prices, pollution, global warming, etc.). When we, as coaches and leaders, connect the local and global, the part and the whole, then our self-interest matures into an enlightened self-interest, bringing us into conversations that are bigger than the personal and organizational. Grasping the interconnectedness of humans worldwide and the open-loop systems of nations and nature, we can engage in the conversations and challenges of our time.

Since the late 1990s, books such as *A Roadmap for Natural Capitalism* (Hawkins, Lovins, and Lovins), *The Natural Step for Business* (Nattrass and Altomare), *Biomimicry: Innovation Inspired by Nature* (Benyus), *Green to Gold: How Smart Companies Use Environmental Strategy to Innovate, Create Value, and Build Competitive Advantage* (Esty and Winston), and the annual editions of *State of the World* (Worldwatch Institute) have provided business and government leaders with the trends, statistics, guiding principles, and new conceptual maps needed to address the collision path between our economies and the sustainability of the natural world. These principles and maps are familiar to coaches who have studied Meg Wheatley, Peter Senge, Joe Jaworski, Fritjof Capra, E. O. Wilson, and Elisabet Sahtouris. Holistic systems thinkers address the broader context of organizational life and leadership, drawing from insights embedded in nature and articulated through chaos and complexity theories.[1]

Just as coaches are evolving toward a more holistic approach, leaders too have moved beyond bottom-line considerations and command and control leadership. Many well-known corporate leaders are stepping forward in the absence of political leadership and assuming stewardship responsibilities that go well beyond compliance with regulations and environmental law. Scores of major companies, including Nike, 3M, GE, Starbucks, and DuPont have moved to double or triple bottom-line (financial, social, and environmental) integrated strategies. They see their enlightened self-interest in care that goes beyond maximizing quarterly shareholder returns.[2] Today, given what we've been seeing in terms of global warming and environmental tipping points, it seems essential that we add another integral element—the environment—that is the context within which life, work, and culture take place. In coaching and leading, stewardship is an active holistic application of care and love for the value of our inheritance and continued contributions as we pass it along to future generations through the ways we choose to work and live in nature.

In coaching, the following four interdependent dimensions of stewardship can be explored with leaders:

- Care for one's self
- Care for others
- Care for work
- Care for nature

Taken together, these four stewardship relationships (figure 22.1) comprise a basic infrastructure of life, offering a simple yet robust lens for holistic coaching.

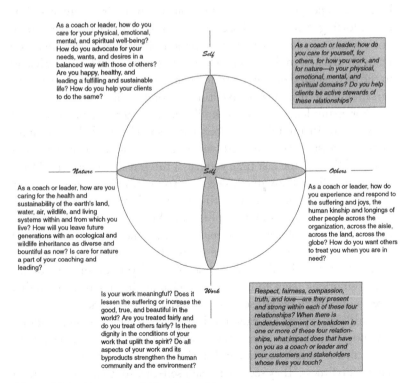

As a coach or leader, how do you care for your physical, emotional, mental, and spiritual well-being? How do you advocate for your needs, wants, and desires in a balanced way with those of others? Are you happy, healthy, and leading a fulfilling and sustainable life? How do you help your clients to do the same?

As a coach or leader, how do you care for yourself, for others, for how you work, and for nature—in your physical, emotional, mental, and spiritual domains? Do you help clients be active stewards of these relationships?

As a coach or leader, how are you caring for the health and sustainability of the earth's land, water, air, wildlife, and living systems within and from which you live? How will you leave future generations with an ecological and wildlife inheritance as diverse and bountiful as now? Is care for nature a part of your coaching and leading?

As a coach or leader, how do you experience and respond to the suffering and joys, the human kinship and longings of other people across the organization, across the aisle, across the land, across the globe? How do you want others to treat you when you are in need?

Is your work meaningful? Does it lessen the suffering or increase the good, true, and beautiful in the world? Are you treated fairly and do you treat others fairly? Is there dignity in the conditions of your work that uplift the spirit? Do all aspects of your work and its byproducts strengthen the human community and the environment?

Respect, fairness, compassion, truth, and love—are they present and strong within each of these four relationships? When there is underdevelopment or breakdown in one or more of these four relationships, what impact does that have on you as a coach or leader and your customers and stakeholders whose lives you touch?

Figure 22.1 Four stewardship relationships
Source: © Lloyd Raines, 2004+

CARE FOR THE SELF

In the first few sessions of coaching a new leader, I'm eager to learn about her relationship with herself. Leaders, by and large, are hard drivers—of themselves and others. They tend to work long hours, put the organization first, and overlook some basic awareness regarding self-care. For me, coaching from a holistic perspective begins with addressing the presenting issues while listening and observing in other dimensions to discern connections (and disconnections) in the leader's self-awareness and self-care. This is a process of raising the leader's awareness about what matters—from the inside out, around the individual's personal and professional effectiveness, health, and well-being. And, in turn, I'm probing how this person's behaviors impact the effectiveness, health, and well-being of others.

Whatever is being expressed through a leader's language, body, emotions, and spirit is a window through which I begin to learn about his or her world. Being in the interior of many leaders' worlds is a chance to notice similarities. After a while, I've come to notice a kind of universality, that leaders have roughly similar needs, wants, desires, and challenges in common, as well as with their stakeholders. What leaders (and people) have in common outweighs their differences. This is comforting. Sometimes I see this commonality when leaders are in crisis mode or when they are in a period of relative stasis. There are many similarities in the look and feel of angst and calm from one leader to the next. A kind of simplicity and complexity is present in each conversation with fresh puzzles awaiting exploration and discovery.

For many leaders, their overall health is not a concern until it becomes so. In my initial sessions with new clients, I do a comprehensive assessment of their self-care and ask questions such as the following: When is the last time you had a full physical check-up? What is your diet like? How much sleep are you getting? On average, how many hours a week are you putting in at work or on work? How are your caffeine, sugar, and alcohol intake? What is your exercise regimen? What time of the day are you most alert and, do you do your best work? How is your general state of mind? How would you describe your mental health? What mood do you find you are in most often? What emotions seem to be the most challenging for you to handle? Are you finding a deeper sense of meaning in your work?

Initially, leaders are caught off-guard by some of these questions, yet soon they begin to see the obvious connections between their physical, emotional, mental, and spiritual well-being and their overall leadership fitness. They see where their self-care (or lack thereof) either adds or drains energy from their *being*, affecting in turn their capacity for *doing* the work of leadership. Each question draws their awareness and focus to the *ecology* of their energy—where and when their energy is high and low, stable and frazzled. By paying attention to what affects their energy, leaders are able to be more intentional in building their overall resilience and sustainability.

Asking questions that evoke reflection on the connections between body, emotions, mind, spirit, and social relationships, leaders can experiment with self-observations or behavioral practices that bring about slight or significant shifts in their awareness and self-care. Those shifts can have immediate benefits for their health and well-being, including enhanced emotional resilience for difficult, tense situations at work and at home. If exploring connections and disconnections stopped at the personal level, however, it would be an inadequate picture of the leader's reality.

A leader's self-care also includes the well being of her or his important relationships—the ones that nurture her health and stability in her private and professional spheres. Care for oneself shares a permeable boundary with care for others. Reciprocity and mutuality in our relationships help balance and make life meaningful, cultivate empathy and compassion, and transform transactional life into intimate life. This sense of mutual accountability is positive and generative and not a burden.

Our personal integration and development as human beings does not occur in social isolation. Self-realization without social realization warps the ego, making it difficult to manage and self-correct one's weaknesses and personality shadows. The brilliant contributor who lacks empathy or is unable to listen to or collaborate with others is not likely to remain sustainable over time in an organization, or if he or she does, others will be forced to leave in his or her wake.

CARE FOR OTHERS

Beyond the leader's care for family and friends are the relationships with her or his organization's employees and stakeholders—those internally and externally affected by the leader's and organization's behaviors (including actions and inactions).

To gain insights into leaders' thinking regarding *care for others*, I might ask them questions like these: How are you regularly inviting the ideas and feedback of people throughout the organization? How are you making decisions that respect the dignity, health, well-being, desire for inclusion, and capacity for contributions from not just those with influence but also the less visible, less powerful stakeholders? What are the ways you reach out and strategically build trust and confidence with internal and external stakeholders? How does your organization reflect the broader demographics of the population and how does it benefit (or not) from diverse representation in the leadership ranks and throughout the organization? What recruitment, development, and reward policies reinforce a diverse workforce? How does your organization help develop and give voice to leaders at all levels? What do you do to regularly, informally solicit feedback from a wide range of stakeholders to learn how to improve as a leader? How do you make it safe for employees to speak truthfully and easily to those in positions of power?

To assess the effectiveness of a leader's social relationships, I conduct half-hour interviews with five to ten key stakeholders to gather anecdotes and data to help me understand current perceptions about the leader's strengths, midrange abilities, and areas in need of development. In addition to any questions the leader may want me to ask, I pose two other questions: What is Laura currently doing well as a leader that you would like to acknowledge and reinforce? And what could Laura be doing more of, less of, or differently to be even more effective as a leader? These questions have a positive, safe, and generative tone and mindset. It is easier for a stakeholder to suggest a few things Laura could do more of or less of than it is to say what Laura is doing wrong.

To explore a leader's mindset around care for others, I ask: What differences, if any, are there in the ways you approach conversations with each stakeholder group? What assumptions do you make about your power and authority and how you think about and interact with external customers, supervisors, peers, direct reports, and other support personnel? How do you express care for others interpersonally, in team meetings, in larger organizational settings, in decision-making practices, and in other areas of organizational life?

When leaders are good stewards of their *internal* ecologies (mind, body, emotions, and spirit) and their social relationships, they are more likely to be experienced as centered, trustworthy, humble, curious, confident, and nonjudgmental. These simple elements of congruence and social connection express a kind of leadership *presence* that attracts the confidence, commitment, and loyalty of others.

When leaders are good stewards of their *external* ecologies, they model leadership presence on a larger stage with broader impact. There are many conscientious, socially attuned leaders we can look to as models. Industry leaders at Patagonia, The Body Shop, and UPS have strategically integrated sustainability and social well-being into their core principles, values, and goals. They conduct their businesses with care for the quality of human life (locally and globally), for the environment, and for profits. Their employees know their daily work contributes to a better world, and it inspires them. These are high performance organizations with high morale, low turnover, and superior customer service.[3] Moving from being a steward for healthy profits alone to a steward for people, planet, and profits is complex for leaders and their organizations and requires a redesign of a company's vision, identity, systems, knowledge integration, practices, relationships, and culture.

We affect each other; our actions and inactions are contagious. Permeable boundaries absorb *from* and emit influences *into* our shared domains of life. The flux and flow of life, leadership, and coaching are alive in a jitterbug of polarities between creation and destruction, emergence and dissipation, stability and change, certainty and ambiguity, abundance and scarcity, courage and timidity, love and fear. That dynamism is also reflected in the evolution of the stories we live—how we react to life and fashion the story of who we are as individuals (as nations and as a world community), how we relate to and work with others, the substance of our contributions in our communities, the mood we absorb and feed into our subcultures and into the broader mainstream culture.

CARE FOR NATURE

Individual leadership behaviors are nested in and influenced by many other factors. Every dimension of a leader's world is informed by many systems and ecologies: culture, politics, economics, geography, location, contemporary mindset, family, health, emotions, spirit, set of social relationships, generation, gender, nationality, and so on. As obvious as it seems, all of these ecologies are ultimately dependent on the health and well-being of nature's ecological systems (air, water, land, resources, critters large and small, and biosphere) and the stabilities or instabilities of weather and climate. Like our health, nature's primacy is invisible until some basic condition that had previously been taken for granted is no longer stable. Consider the impact and social and financial costs associated with increasing rates and severity of violent storms, droughts, floods, and heat waves. Our survival and well-being are directly, inextricably tied to nature and our care or abuse of nature and the biosphere. To the degree that we act with an impoverished sense of stewardship, instabilities in climate will in turn wipe out homes and infrastructure and impoverish us in real terms. Our health and nature's health are bound up with each other. Humans are sustainable only if nature is healthy, stable, and sustainable.

Since the early 1970s and the advent of the environmental movement, early adopter companies like those mentioned earlier have been designing green (environmentally sustainable) organizations. The coaching profession is gradually expanding beyond its holistic focus on the individual to include a broader whole systems view, seeing care for nature as naturally integrated into leadership coaching—and with good reason. We have never been so aware of the intimate connection between the state of our environment and our individual and social well-being.

As coaches and citizens we have long been aware of trends regarding global warming, the deterioration of the environment, and pollution as well as the gap between the rich and poor and the persistence of poverty and homelessness. Yet, for the most part, we have seemed not to know what to do with that information or how to incorporate it into our work. These pressing moral and professional challenges are often alien to our job descriptions, workplace concerns, and our coaching conversations. Our world is fragmented to the point that we see these problems as externalities to our daily work and as the responsibilities of others: government agencies, social services, nonprofits, and volunteer organizations.

At the same time, there are growing numbers of leaders in the private and public sectors developing a comprehensive green approach in their organizations. They have found ways to tap into the natural symbiosis of financial, social, and environmental drivers and have seen that it is in their long-term self-interest to go beyond the single bottom line to a triple bottom line commitment. Well-known companies such as 3M, Unilever, Shell, Proctor & Gamble, and a growing number of others have designed for synergy and discovered ways to combine the best for people, prosperity, and the planet.[4] As one example, the US Environmental Protection Agency created the "3P" focus—people, prosperity, and planet—to spur an integrated strategic approach to conversations in government agencies.[5]

As leadership coaches, we also have a choice to stretch our professional awareness to what is going on around us and actively partnering with that evolving story. This is the great challenge of our era: the alignment of human activities to be in harmony with the natural world and social care for those who are vulnerable, dispossessed, and unable to enjoy the blessings of democratic life.

Leadership coaches and leaders are able to stretch and even transform their mindset and worldviews, and the range of expressions and connections they look and listen for. It is one of the primary reasons we as coaches engage in learning and developmental activities. We attend conferences, take additional coursework, write articles, engage in learning communities or communities of practice, and other methods of continuous learning. Our awareness and action can tend toward being relatively small and self-interested or large and in service to the global well-being. Where once coaching was primarily focused on linguistics, psychology, and performance behaviors, it now has an expanded perspective that includes domains such as the emotions, somatics, care for the environment, and care for stakeholders near and far. And, of course, coaching and leadership are continuing to evolve. Just as the shift to a green perspective in the business world continues, bringing sustainability conversations into the business mainstream, something similar may happen with leadership coaching. And with that progression, a worldview that was broken into fragments by the scientific and industrial revolutions may regain its wholeness in an integrated, socially focused cosmology.

CARE FOR WORK

We live and work in global interdependence—dressing in clothes made in China, Pakistan, the Philippines; eating fruits and drinking coffee imported from South America; driving to work in our internationally made cars with foreign oil and gas. Once there, we power up our computers made with parts produced worldwide, and "google" into the global brain for information in an instant. Since we anchor ourselves in the social world through work and the sharing of products and services produced worldwide, we are in a global network of relationships. To the degree we choose to be conscious of those relationships and interdependencies, we awaken to a fundamental dimension of stewardship. We engage in commerce and civil relations with others as partners for mutual benefit instead of some exploiting others for gain.

When coaches and leaders are attentive stewards at work, we reinforce values of dignity, meaning, and community while also benefiting prosperity and the planet. Stewardship values inform and guide leaders throughout an organization in strategically using and deploying the organization's resources. A holistic approach to coaching leaders is curious about leaders' sense of fulfillment, dignity, health, and well-being in relation to the work they do as well as the effect of their decisions and organizational policies on others and the planet as a whole.

For leaders, coaches can press them with direct questions such as these that go to core values: In the face of the challenges of the day, how does your work and your organization's vision and stance in the world bring meaning and honor to your contributions? In what ways does your work inspire you? How do you feel that your work is making a difference in the quality of life for other people in the world?

Leaders can be attuned with themselves, with others, and with nature—yet, if they are not also attuned with the work they are doing, they will not likely be living to their full potential. Because leaders (like people anywhere) are designed for continual growth, work that once was engaging and fully satisfying may be less so after three or four years. Old questions need new answers as leaders continue to scan the horizon of their own lives and of the larger world around them for motivation, meaning, and creativity. It is common for leaders reaching their professional high-water marks to look for opportunities in which they really believe. Holistic coaching probes a leader's opportunities for introducing into his or her current leadership work and into his or her organization new ideas, principles, and values that could make a difference in the meaningfulness of the work *right now.*

Here's an example of how holistic leadership transformation can happen. At Interface, a billion-dollar global company, CEO Ray Anderson read Paul Hawken's book, *The Ecology of Commerce: A Declaration of Sustainability*, and had an epiphany. Virtually overnight, he became convinced that his company's way of working and producing carpet and office supplies had to change. He committed to transforming Interface from oil-based carpet production into completely natural, recyclable carpets. Further, he engaged his entire company of employees in an education around sustainability that was far beyond what was currently going on in almost any other company.[6] When Anderson and his employees committed to sustainability goals together, they captured a kind of "lightning in a bottle." Employees are excited about what they do because they know they're working for a better world every day, and this inspires them. Leaders who capture a vision that inspires the dedication of their workforce garner the advantage of intrinsic employee motivation along with tapping their collective intelligence. The concepts of stewardship and sustainability have the potential to engage deeper levels of commitment, innovation, meaning, and productivity at all levels of organizational life.

When coaches are aware of these innovative movements in marketplace and leadership development, coaching conversations can explore more expansive possibilities. By probing, inquiring, and provoking new ways of observing what's possible or by introducing an article or book at the right moment, coaches can help fundamentally shift a leader's core mental model.

HOLISTIC COACHING AND MORAL DEVELOPMENT

For leaders, leadership coaching is an invitation for *growth by design*. In the ways we as coaches hold nonjudgmental safe space, listen, inquire, challenge, and trust, we enable leaders to coax from themselves their human potential, wisdom, and courage, and in turn help them understand how to cultivate that in others.

Like any profession, coaching is constantly evolving and growing in ways to awaken more breadth and depth in us and in leaders to act responsibly through our actions with a growing moral sensibility. This process moves developmentally toward greater integration, in moral and spiritual terms through stages. In my coaching conversations with leaders, I initially use a three-stage model developed by Carol Gilligan that clients find easily accessible and useful.[7]

At the first moral stage (preconventional), we encounter behavior that is *self-interested and selfish*. This stage "looks out for Number One," with little concern for what this means for others. "I am the center of the universe, and I act accordingly."

The second moral stage (conventional) encounters behavior that expresses *care*. When my circle of concern expands, I see my self-interest as being directly tied up with the self-interests of others in my close-in tribes (based on some particular likeness, belief, or affiliation). "We're in this together—what helps you helps me. The group can count on me and I can count on the group for support." A tribe has an insular feel, with members identifying closely with other tribal members, and not with those of other tribes. It has both internal cohesion and a sense of insiders and outsiders, the chosen and the not chosen.

At the third moral stage (postconventional), we experience interconnections with people everywhere and with nature and its myriad life forms. This level is expressed by behaviors that spring from a sense of *universal or global care*. At this level, the entire global community and ecology are seen in an "I-Thou" relationship. "I'm part of everything and everyone and it all is an integral part of me." This stage acknowledges and behaves as if people anywhere are part of one tribe, inseparable, experiencing the joys and suffering of others as akin to their own. "I hold reverence for and an active stewardship with the ecological commons and the global human community."

Once I've introduced Gilligan's basic developmental distinctions to a leader, it is easy to introduce and contextualize other readings on moral and leadership developmental stages. I have found Joiner and Joseph's book, *Leadership Agility*, to be an accessible, effective framework for leaders to assess their current stage and undertake ongoing conscious development through the authors' framework and taxonomy. Coaches using stages as a framework for self-understanding learn where they have come from, where they are, and what their next areas of development are. When they use it with other leaders, those leaders benefit from insights into their mindset and how that mindset affects their view of leadership, power, possibilities, and social interactions.

BEARING WITNESS

When coaching, the concept of *bearing witness* entails holding active awareness of the current conditions of joy and sorrow, well-being and suffering, of stakeholders near and far. I can bear witness to the pain, confusion, and suffering as well as the joy, love, and satisfaction of the leader I'm with. At the same time I can bear witness to what I know is going on in the daily lives of people in other parts of the organization and the world, and at an appropriate moment I can introduce that broader awareness to the leader in front of me. And at other moments, I may bear witness to the impact of business actions (or inactions) on employees, the environment, on suppliers or the environment upstream or on consumers and nature downstream.

As leadership coaches, our professional obligations require us to be in continuous personal and professional development. With disciplined, active engagement in any dimension of development (somatic, emotional, cognitive, spiritual, social, humanities, social sciences, natural sciences, etc.), we expand the subtlety of the sensibilities that inform and shape our mindset and worldview. From that place of development, we listen with more complexity and openness, make distinctions, ask questions, and offer provocations for leaders. In broad terms, then, we coach and bear witness from predominantly one of three levels. We may coach and bear witness from a level that begins and ends with a focus on the leader's individual *self-interest* (and, perhaps, the coach's self-interest, as well). Or we may coach and bear witness from a perspective of *care* for the leader and the organization's stakeholders. Or we may coach and bear witness from a perspective of *global care* for the health and well-being of the global community.

What a holistic framework provides for leadership coaches and leadership coaching is a way to see the actual wholeness of the playing field we enter every time we engage in coaching relationships. By developing a framework that sees the leader within a much broader context, we can be more attentive, careful, and caring about what we listen for and inquire about with leaders. It enables us to have a balanced awareness and approach to supporting the broadest and deepest personal flourishing of leaders in service to the responsibilities and opportunities that accompany their position and ours.

NOTES

1. The books, authors, and thinkers referenced in this paragraph are listed, along with some of their seminal works, in the bibliography.
2. Esty and Winston, *Green to Gold*, 7–29.
3. Anderson, *Mid-Course Correction*, 149–181.
4. See note 2 above, 25, 126, 150–156, 229–233, 314.
5. US Environmental Protection Agency, "P3: People, Prosperity, and the Planet Student Design Competition for Sustainability," http://es.epa.gov/ncer/p3/fact_sheet.html (accessed November 13, 2007).
6. See note 4 above, 43–61, 139–181.
7. K. Wilber, *Integral Psychology*, 45–208.

BIBLIOGRAPHY

Anderson, Ray. *Mid-Course Correction*. Atlanta, GA: Peregrinzilla Press, 1998.

Benyus, J. *Biomimicry: Innovation Inspired by Nature*. New York: Perennial, 1997.

Capra, F. *The Hidden Connections: Integrating the Biological, Cognitive, and Social Dimensions of Life into a Science of Sustainability*. New York: Doubleday Books, 2002.

Cook-Greuter, S. "Making the Case for a Developmental Perspective." *Industrial and Commercial Training* 36, no. 7 (2004): 275–281.

Diamond, J. *Collapse: How Societies Choose to Fail or Succeed*. New York: Penguin Books, 2005.

Esty, D., and Winston, A. *Green to Gold: How Smart Companies Use Environmental Strategy to Innovate, Create Value, and Build Competitive Advantage*. New Haven, CT: Yale University Press, 2006.

Gilligan, C. *In a Different Voice*. Cambridge, MA: Harvard University Press, 1982.

Hawken, P. *The Ecology of Commerce: A Declaration of Sustainability*. New York, NY: HarperBusiness, 1993.

Hawken, P., A. Lovins, and L. Lovins. "A Roadmap for Natural Capitalism." *Harvard Business Review* 77 (May/June 1999), 78–81.

Hawken, P., A. Lovins, and L. Lovins. *Natural Capitalism*. New York, NY: Little, Brown, 1999.

HM Treasury. *Stern Review Report on the Economics of Climate Change*. 2006. http://www.hm-treasury.gov.uk/independent_reviews/stern_review_economics_climate_change/stern_review_report.cfm.

Intergovernmental Panel on Climate Change. *Climate Change*. 2007. http://www.ipcc.ch/

Jaworski, J. *Synchronicity: The Inner Path of Leadership*. San Francisco, CA: Barrett-Koehler, 1996.

Joiner, B., and S. Josephs. *Leadership Agility*, San Francisco, CA: Jossey-Bass, 2007.

Kegan, R. *In Over Our Heads: The Mental Demands of Modern Life*. Cambridge, MA: Harvard University Press, 1994.

Kohlberg, L. *The Philosophy of Moral Development*. San Francisco, CA: Harper & Row, 1976.

Maslow, A. *Toward A Psychology of Being*. Princeton, N.J.: D. Van Nostrand, 1962.

Nattrass, B., and M. Altomare. *The Natural Step for Business*. Gabriola Island, British Columbia: New Society Publishers, 1999.

Sahtouris, E. "The Biology of Business: New Laws of Nature Reveal a Better Way for Business." *VIA Journal* 3, no. 1 (2005). http://via-visioninaction. org/Sahtouris_BiologyOfBusiness-full_version.pdf

Senge, P. *The Fifth Discipline: The Art and Practice of the Learning Organization*. New York: Currency Doubleday, 1990.

Senge, P., B. Smith, S. Schley, and J. Laur. *The Necessary Revolution: How Individuals and Organizations Are Working Together to Create a Sustainable World*. New York: Doubleday, 2008.

Wheatley, M. *Leadership and the New Science*. San Francisco, CA: Barrett-Koehler, 1992.

Wilber, K. *Integral Psychology*. Boston, MA: Shambala, 2000.

Wilson, E. O. *Consilience: The Unity of Knowledge*. New York: Alfred A. Knopf, 1998.

Wilson, E. O. *The Creation: An Appeal to Save Life on Earth*. New York: Norton, 2006.

Worldwatch Institute. *State of the World 2012: Moving Toward Sustainable Prosperity*. Washington, D.C.: Island Press, 2012.

CHAPTER 23

THE THINKING PATH

ALEXANDER CAILLET

INTRODUCTION

The CEO of a bottling company toured a plant whose employees were demoralized. The tour proved extremely successful, and the CEO's approval of what he saw generated a visible lift of mood. Once the CEO had departed, the plant manager addressed the employees: "The boss really liked what he saw. He said it was the best he had ever seen. But why did you have the order of the products reversed in the coolers? It was embarrassing!" The employees' mood instantly slumped.

Afterward, my colleague asked the plant manager why he dwelled on the negative. He replied: "They won't be motivated toward perfection if you don't keep finding something they did that they can improve. You always have to find something wrong. Good feelings don't drive productivity and performance."

Sound familiar? Unfortunately, it is very common, and examples like this litter the organizational landscape.

This chapter presents a framework called the Thinking Path that is useful in leadership coaching and that can be used to help leaders understand and manage situations like the one described above.

The Thinking Path stipulates that people's conscious and unconscious thought processes (thinking) generate emotional/physical states (their feelings), which in turn drive behaviors (their actions) that produce outcomes (their results). Figure 23.1 illustrates the Thinking Path framework.

Figure 23.1 The Thinking Path
Source: Used with permission © Accompli, LLC, 2011.

Three questions inspired the creation of the Thinking Path:

1. How do human beings change?
2. What causes sustained change in human beings?
3. Why do some individuals succeed in changing their behaviors and results, and why do others fail?

The answers to these questions came to me after years of study, research, personal work, and client engagements all over the world. And the answers pointed to a deeper phenomenon called *thinking* and the impact of thinking on our moment-to-moment experience of life.

The Thinking Path provides a simple, yet powerful framework to help clients understand and work with their thinking in a way that can yield three outcomes:

1. Clients realize that their thinking is linked to their feelings and that by changing their thinking, their feelings also change.
2. Clients realize that their thinking and feelings drive their actions and results and that by changing their thinking and feelings, their actions shift and their results change.
3. Clients take greater responsibility for generating sustained improvements in their actions and results by intentionally shifting their thinking and their feelings.

FROM THINKING TO RESULTS

Most observers would agree that the plant manager's speech (his action) produced lower employee morale (his result). To the plant manager, however, the speech felt "right" and he delivered it intentionally to produce the exact outcome that was experienced and witnessed by all. Interestingly, a month earlier this same individual had received fairly negative feedback about these types of behaviors on his 360-degree performance review. And although this was the first time the organization had deployed a 360-degree feedback program, it was not the first time he had heard this feedback.

What could a coach do to help this plant manager and how could the Thinking Path be of service? The obvious answer is that the coach would help the plant manager avoid producing such negative results by shifting his actions. To achieve this, the coach would help him change the source of his actions and results: his thinking and feelings.

Consider that the origin of the plant manager's actions lies in his thinking. His answer to my colleague's question makes his thinking visible: "You always have to find something wrong. Good feelings don't drive productivity and performance." Furthermore, my colleague noticed that just prior to making his statement the plant manager appeared somewhat anxious and impatient. The Thinking Path framework suggests that these feelings of anxiety and impatience were a product of his thinking.

THINKING

Human beings think. We think all the time. It is a central factor in our lives; our experience of reality is shaped by the moment-to-moment flow of our thoughts. One way to define thinking is as the reception and processing of external and internal data in order to assess and interpret the world within and around us. Of course, thinking also encompasses the much broader phenomena of human consciousness or awareness. Because of my long study of neuroscience, however, I am inclined to emphasize the cognitive aspect of thinking and the mechanical functioning of the brain that underlies it.

It is said that the human body—not only the brain but also the nervous system and all the sensory apparatus connected to it—processes billions of bits of data every minute. These data are received through our senses and are immediately assessed so that we can interpret the world around us. New data are received and can be held as archival memory for later use. Familiar data are matched to the archival memory information in order to be interpreted.

The brain's primary function is to receive and store data within its networks and to activate specific networks once the data is presented. From the moment our brain is formed in the fetus, it uses the neurons resident within the brain to begin the process of coding the data it receives by creating neural pathways within predisposed regions of the brain. When specific units of data—such as a visual image, a sound, an odor, or a physical sensation—are received repeatedly throughout one's life, specific neural pathways corresponding to these units of data become stronger, creating hard-wired paths of neural circuits. From this point on, when data are presented to a human being, the brain responds by activating or "firing" specific neural pathways across the various regions of the brain that are predisposed to interpret these data. These neural pathways provide a perception of the data, which can then be interpreted and understood. This process occurs continuously in real time, providing us with the ability to make sense of our surroundings.

The advantage of thinking is that we can use what we already know to make sense of confusing and complex data instantly. As we do this, we create meaning, make decisions, and then take action. Thinking is what allows us to function and produce results.

Thinking is highly complex phenomenon, and it would be impractical to provide a comprehensive review of all that is known about it in this chapter. I also find that most clients are not interested in such a review and seek a simple and practical way to work with their thinking. To this end, I would like to introduce a short-hand, nonscientific, and practical term, *thought habits,* that allows clients to work with their thinking in terms of specific units of thought such as beliefs, knowledge, perceptions, assumptions, conclusions, etc.

From the moment we are conceived in the womb and throughout our lives, we constantly acquire new thought habits as a result of our ongoing experiences. The more we experience, the more data the brain codes. The more the brain codes, the more thought habits we have. The more thought habits we have, the more we can perceive and interpret. In the end, we develop a large storehouse of thought habits that allows us to process and interpret vast amounts of data.

In the case of the sales manager, the thought habit in play was: "You always have to find something wrong. Good feelings don't drive productivity and performance."

FEELINGS

One way to define feelings is as emotional and physiological manifestations experienced throughout the body. There is a great deal of debate as to which comes first, thinking or feelings. I believe thinking occurs first and feelings follow. This is supported by research that points to the fact that data is processed first in the brain and in the body triggering key organs within the center of the brain that, in turn, launch a series of chemical reactions that occur within the body to create emotional and physiological reactions.

As such, feelings provide the most reliable indicator of the characteristics of the thought habits we are generating. Insecure, chaotic, resentful thought habits generate feelings of anxiety, confusion and anger; secure, focused, composed thought habits generate feelings of clarity, calmness, and confidence.

Note that the plant manager had observable feelings—anxiety and impatience—prior to blurting out his statement. Upon further investigation, my colleague learned that as the morning went on, he began to feel anxious that the event was becoming "too much of a mutual admiration event," and he felt a need to reign in the group. To him, his feelings of anxiety were a normal consequence of the CEO's very positive remarks. This justified his negative statement to the workers. As he perceived the events unfolding, he was matching the incoming data to what he had archived in his brain from the past: "Good feelings don't drive productivity and performance." He did not realize that his own thought habit was triggering a feeling.

The challenge is that much of the time we do not notice our thinking. By contrast, we *do* feel our feelings as they become manifest as emotional and physiological reactions. So we may believe that our feelings are causing us to act in certain ways, but actually we are being driven by our thought habits.

It is important to understand that it is the *combination* of our moment-to-moment thinking and feelings that create what we experience as reality. Whether or not we have interpreted the data correctly does not matter; our inner experience feels like reality.

The Thinking Path helps clients understand the mechanism that generates what they perceive as reality. This is important because an individual's subjective reality may not reflect the objective situation. Instead, it might be based upon thought habits that are questionable, unnecessarily negative, or simply untrue. If a client's reality is based upon such thought habits, he/she may take actions that produce undesirable results.

ACTIONS AND RESULTS

One way to define actions is as the behaviors we manifest in the form of what we say and do. Our actions lead to results, which can be defined as the outcomes and achievements we produce. So each action we take produces results, and it is on the basis of our actions and results that we ultimately are assessed.

In the case of the plant manager, the action was a statement: "But why did you have the order of the products reversed in the coolers? It was embarrassing!" The result he produced was a mood of disempowerment and resignation among the workers. He may not have seen the connection between action and result, but it was unmistakable from the observer's standpoint.

COACHING WITH THE THINKING PATH

Coaches can use the Thinking Path in their coaching sessions to help their clients gain a much deeper and clearer understanding of what is at the source of the issues and challenges they are facing and to define different scenarios that will generate sustainable improvements regarding these issues and challenges. The Thinking Path methodology requires clients to explore what is happening in the issue and challenge they are facing by completing a Current State Thinking Path, including results, actions, feelings, and thinking. They then imagine a more desirable scenario and complete a Desired Current State Thinking Path.

To accomplish this, coach and client can use the Thinking Path template provided in figure 23.2. The instructions are simple:

1. The client selects a real issue or challenge.
2. With the guidance of the coach, the client identifies his/her thinking, feelings, actions, and results as they are occurring presently in the issue or challenge—this is the current state.
3. The client also defines his/her thinking, feelings, actions, and results as they could be—this is the desired state.
4. Coach and client may begin with either the current or desired state, and jump back and forth if they wish.
5. Coach and client may begin at any level of the Thinking Path within both the current and desired states and proceed through the other levels using any sequence they wish.
6. Coach and client may use the starter phrases provided above the blank lines in the template.
7. The client may choose to write his/her responses down in the blank spaces or simply speak them.

A coaching session using the Thinking Path may take 30 minutes to several hours and may occur over the course of several sessions. Figure 23.3 provides an example of an executive who completed both the current and desired states during several coaching sessions. This 38-year-old leader engaged in coaching due to recent criticism of his performance

Current State

I achieve/accomplish …
The outcome/result is …
_____
_____
_____
_____

I (verb) … I do … I say …
I behave like …
_____
_____
_____

I feel … My emotions are …
My state of mind is …
_____
_____
_____

My thinking/thought habits is/are …
My beliefs/assumptions are …
My reasoning is …
_____
_____
_____

Desired State

I would achieve/accomplish …
The outcome/result would be …
_____
_____
_____
_____

I would (verb) … I would do …
I would say … I would behave
like …
_____
_____
_____

I would feel … My emotions
would be …
My state of mind would be …
_____
_____
_____

My thinking/thought habits would
be … My beliefs/assumptions
would be …
My reasoning would be …
_____
_____
_____

Figure 23.2 The Thinking Path Template

Source: Used with permission © Accompli, LLC, 2011.

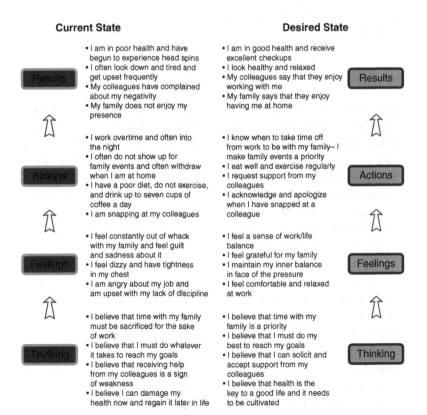

Current State

Results
- I am in poor health and have begun to experience head spins
- I often look down and tired and get upset frequently
- My colleagues have complained about my negativity
- My family does not enjoy my presence

Actions
- I work overtime and often into the night
- I often do not show up for family events and often withdraw when I am at home
- I have a poor diet, do not exercise, and drink up to seven cups of coffee a day
- I am snapping at my colleagues

Feelings
- I feel constantly out of whack with my family and feel guilt and sadness about it
- I feel dizzy and have tightness in my chest
- I am angry about my job and am upset with my lack of discipline

Thinking
- I believe that time with my family must be sacrificed for the sake of work
- I believe that I must do whatever it takes to reach my goals
- I believe that receiving help from my colleagues is a sign of weakness
- I believe I can damage my health now and regain it later in life

Desired State

Results
- I am in good health and receive excellent checkups
- I look healthy and relaxed
- My colleagues say that they enjoy working with me
- My family says that they enjoy having me at home

Actions
- I know when to take time off from work to be with my family– I make family events a priority
- I eat well and exercise regularly
- I request support from my colleagues
- I acknowledge and apologize when I have snapped at a colleague

Feelings
- I feel a sense of work/life balance
- I feel grateful for my family
- I maintain my inner balance in face of the pressure
- I feel comfortable and relaxed at work

Thinking
- I believe that time with my family is a priority
- I believe that I must do my best to reach my goals
- I believe that I can solicit and accept support from my colleagues
- I believe that health is the key to a good life and it needs to be cultivated

Figure 23.3 The Current and Desired States

Source: Used with permission © Accompli, LLC, 2011.

as a manager with the organization and due to his deteriorating health. He found the sessions challenging but made the discovery that underlying his actions and results was a set of thought habits—which he called core beliefs—he had never before seen with such clarity.

As stated above, coaching with the Thinking Path can yield solid results. Yet, it is important to remember that this is only a framework, and like any framework, it best serves those who invest in study and practice, and it will not be appropriate in every situation. Therefore, give yourself time to learn how to use the Thinking Path. Try it on yourself first or with a person in your life who is not a client and who is willing to experiment with you. When you try it for the first time with a client, apply it to an issue or challenge that is not too complex; you can apply it to more complex issues later on after you have gained experience with the model.

When you begin using the Thinking Path with clients, remain alert to the client's responsiveness and reactions. If the client seems disinterested or is resisting the approach, be ready to let go of the framework. You may choose to come back to it later or drop it altogether. The key is to remain flexible and to always meet your client where he/she is.

CHANGING THINKING

Up to this point, the Thinking Path has provided us with an effective approach to understand our current state and define our desired state. It has allowed us to peer into our thinking and identify the thought habits that we use today and those we wish to use tomorrow. But is this enough to help our clients really change their thought habits? The answer is no. In my experience, most clients need something more to help them change their thought habits in a sustained manner. What is needed is an action plan comprised of a set of goals and practices that transform the desired state into reality.

Most coaches know how to build action plans and most clients appreciate action planning. However, when building action plans, most coaches focus primarily on behaviors and results and construct a set of goals related to the new results and a set of behaviors to achieve these results. For most coaches and clients, this may feel like it is enough. I believe this is not enough as too often simply setting a new goal and identifying new behaviors to reach the goal leads only to short-term, unsustainable shifts. The New Year's resolution is the most glaring example of these types of shifts. What is needed is another action plan aimed at sustaining the new thinking described in the desired state—an action plan that can ensure that the necessary change in thought habits actually does occur. We call this action plan a Thinking Path Plan; it is a combination of traditional planning oriented toward behaviors and results and planning focused on the thought habits in order to enhance the possibility of sustained change.

Fortunately, we can make changes to our thought habits if we choose to do so, and we can do so throughout our entire lives. New research in neuroplasticity confirms this statement. We now understand that the brain's primary function of receiving and storing data within its networks continues throughout our lives. As such, the brain can create new neural pathways within predisposed areas of the brain based on new data. These new pathways can be built in addition to the original neural pathways and over time can become stronger than the old pathways, providing us with alternatives. These alternatives are critical for a very important reason: the brain does its work extraordinarily quickly, and it is impossible to intercept the firing sequence of specific neural pathways in response to data. As such, our interpretations are almost immediate. That said, we *can* choose to keep or change the thoughts we have made, once we have made them. And if we choose to change the thought habit, we can select the alternative. And if we consistently choose the alternative, we have the possibility of building this alternative as a new pathway and quieting down the original pathways or extinguishing them altogether. As long as we can learn, we can acquire new thought habits and even change or eliminate old thought habits.

A question now emerges: How do we encode the new thought habits from the desired state into our neural pathways so that they become viable alternatives the next time the original pathways fire? Not surprisingly, we must engage in an activity most of us experience throughout our lives: learning. It is through learning that we acquired most of our thought habits. And it is through learning that we can encode new thought habits into our neural pathways so that they become viable alternatives

There are many approaches used in learning, and everyone has a preferred approach that works best for the individual. When using the Thinking Path, there are five approaches that are particularly helpful in creating new and sustained neural pathways: (1) repetition, (2) education, (3) visualization, (4) writing, and (5) conversation. Most clients will want to use more than one approach, but may not use all five at once.

REPETITION

Repetition, also known as *affirmation*, involves repeating new thought habits like mantras. In the same manner we memorized our multiplication tables, the act of repeating a thought habit increases the chances that it will be encoded in our brains. In neuroscience, this is called long-term potentiation and can be described as a long-lasting period of signal transmission between two neurons, and this increases the strength of their connection to one another and thus also the probability that they will fire together in the future. Long-term potentiation is widely believed to be at the basis of learning and memory building and has led to the well-known adage that neurons that fire together wire together.

With this in mind, a coach might suggest that as part of a client's Thinking Path Plan, he/she could quietly affirm a new thought habit several times a day. The client could continue to do this until he or she experienced greater facility in choosing the new thought habit as an alternative to the original, and/or began to feel or act differently when he/she affirmed the new thought habit. Let's now take the case of the executive in figure 23.3 and focus for the rest of this chapter on building a Thinking Path Plan to encode and sustain one of his four new thought habits: "I believe that health is the key to a good life and it needs to be cultivated." If we focus on repetition, one part of his Thinking Path Plan could be to affirm this thought habit every morning, afternoon, and evening for a period of time.

One challenge to be aware of is that some clients will give up on repetition because it may seem artificial and shallow to them. The new thought habit may seem foreign, questionable, or simply untrue, and affirming it over and over again may not yield tangible results. As such, repetition works best when it is coupled with other learning approaches that will give the thought habit a greater chance of becoming encoded as a new neural pathway and become the basis for a new reality.

EDUCATION

I define education broadly to include any active engagement in activities such reading, watching TV, videos and film, listening to experts, going to events and shows, and attending workshops and courses. It goes without saying that one of the essential components of learning is the acquisition and processing of new data and information either individually or in collective settings. From a neuroscience perspective, when we actively engage in educational activities related to a new thought habit, we experience a significant increase in neural activation relative to that thought habit. The more complex and collective the activity is, the more neural landscape we use, the more neural pathways are formed, and the greater likelihood that new thought habits are encoded and sustained.

With this in mind, a coach might suggest that as part of a client's Thinking Path Plan, he/she could read articles or books related to the thought habit, watch a specific documentary or film that incorporates the thought habit, or attend a specific lecture, course, or workshop that further expounded upon the thought habit. In the case of the executive in the example, another part of his Thinking Path Plan could be to read articles on exercise and fitness, watch a documentary on the adverse effects of stress, attend a course on stress management, or consult a nutritionist. If these practices were coupled with daily affirmations, the probability that the thought habit would be sustained would be increased.

VISUALIZATION

Visualization, also known as *mental rehearsal*, involves quietly thinking about a thought habit and imagining how it might play out in real life. Recent research has revealed that the brain responds similarly to the thought of an action and to the real action. Athletes who have submitted themselves to electromyography have demonstrated that when they mentally rehearsed their moves, the electrical currents sent to their muscles by their brains were similar to the impulses sent when they were physically performing the moves. These experiments demonstrate that whether an activity is mentally imagined or is actively performed, the same neural pathways are stimulated, the same physiological changes are present, and the neural pathways are ultimately strengthened.

With this in mind, a coach might suggest that as part of a client's Thinking Path Plan, he/she could take a few minutes during the day or evening and quietly visualize how a thought habit could play out in real life. This is especially powerful if the client has been doing daily affirmations of the thought habit and has engaged in various educational activities. In the case of the executive in the example, another part of his Thinking Path Plan could be to take a few minutes each day for a week to quietly visualize being at the gym, engaging in stress management practices, or living a joyful and happy life. The executive would effectively be imagining prior to acting. This would strengthen the impact of the affirmations and educational activities.

One challenge to be aware of is that most clients prefer to close their eyes when performing visualizations in order to avoid distractions. As a consequence, many may feel uncomfortable closing their eyes and performing visualizations during the workday or even during a coaching session in the workplace. It is important to allow clients to perform visualizations when they feel most comfortable and this may be in a place other than the workplace.

WRITING

Writing, also known as *journaling*, involves writing about the thought habit. The client can use the Thinking Path framework to write about the thought habit including where it comes from, what it means, what it feels like to use it, and what behaviors and results emerge when it is used. Much has been written on the benefits of journaling as a meditative and reflective practice, including enhancing self-awareness and self-understanding, discovering meaning in specific events, making connections between different ideas and events, gaining perspective and clarity, and developing critical thinking skills. From the perspective of neuroscience, the act of writing activates a broader neural landscape and causes a multitude of neural pathways to form and fire around the new thought habit. Writing also translates the thought habit into a motor skill by activating a sequence of neurons that ultimately fire motor neurons that activate the skeleton and muscles of our shoulders, arms, and hands. This not only strengthens the original thought habit but encodes the sequence within the broader landscape of the body.

With this in mind, a coach might suggest that as part of a client's Thinking Path Plan, he/she could take a moment each week to journal about a particular thought habit using the Thinking Path framework as described above. In the case of the executive in the example, another part of his Thinking Path Plan could be to take half an hour every week to journal about the thought habit. The subject of the journaling could be specific to one aspect of living healthy lifestyles or it could be general. As you can imagine, if journaling is added to daily affirmations, educational activities, and occasional visualizations, the probability that the thought habit would be encoded and sustained is even greater.

One challenge to be aware of is that some clients do not enjoy writing, and many shy away from the practice of journaling. It is important to allow clients to find their own approach and rhythm, including the frequency and duration of their journaling periods. It is also important to accept that some clients will simply not do it.

CONVERSATION

Conversations with others about a specific thought habit can generate a remarkable amount of learning quickly. From the perspective of neuroscience, conversations, like writing, activate a broader neural landscape and cause a multitude of neural pathways to form and fire around the new thought habit. Conversations also translate the thought habit into a series of motor skills by activating several sequences of neurons that also ultimately fire motor neurons. This also encodes the sequence within the broader landscape of the body and strengthens the original thought habit. We often remember great conversations and their content. And if the client is willing to remain curious and open and to use inquiry and actively listen, he/she can only enhance the number of new neural connections that can be made relative to the thought habit.

With this in mind, a coach might suggest that as part of a client's Thinking Path Plan, he/she could select certain people in both the personal and professional spheres to have conversations with. These conversations could be about the thought habit itself or about applications of the thought habit in everyday life. In the case of the executive in the example, another part of his Thinking Path Plan could be to have specific conversations about his desire to live a healthy lifestyle with his wife, several friends, his doctor, and one or more of the experts he listened to in his education activities. He could also have conversations or even work sessions with his boss and his team about what it would take to engage in a healthy lifestyle at work. Conversations are an excellent way to transform affirmations, educational activities, visualizations, and journaling into an interactive experience. They can be powerful in their ability to sustain change.

One challenge to be aware of is that some clients are more reserved, may lack conversational skills, may be uneasy having these types of conversations, or may have issues speaking with certain people. It is important to gain a clear understanding of any reservations a client may have and to strategize accordingly. There are many different ways to have conversations and many different types of people with whom to have conversations.

THE THINKING PATH PLAN

Let's now examine how the Thinking Path Plan actually did support the executive. Figure 23.4 provides one of the Thinking Path Plans developed by the executive and his coach. This particular plan focuses on the executives health and lifestyle. When the executive and his coach began the action planning process, they completed a first level of planning focused on establishing a set of goals (results) to achieve the desired state and a set of actions to achieve these goals. These goals and actions are located on the left-hand side of the plan. The executive and his coach then selected the thought habit "I believe that health is

THINKING PATH PLAN

GOALS (RESULTS)

1. Reduce my weight to 180 pounds
2. Improve my lipids profile:
   - Total cholesterol = 190
     - LDL = < 125
     - HDL = 35 – 80
3. Get a full 7 hours of restful sleep at least three nights a week
4. Eliminate my emotional hijacks
5. Feel more joy and happiness in my life

ACTIONS

1. Go the gym at least twice a week for one hour
2. Eat a low-cholesterol diet as prescribed by my physician
3. Leave work at 6:00 p.m. at least twice a week
4. Go for a bike ride or a hike once every weekend
5. Get to bed before 11:00 p.m. at least three nights a week
6. Engage in my meditation practice at least twice a week for 15–20 minutes each session
7. Listen to my favorite music on the weekends

NEW THOUGHT HABIT: I believe that health is the key to a good life and it needs to be cultivated.

LEARNING PRACTICES

AFFIRMATIONS
- Repeat '*A good life is a healthy life*' several times upon waking, at lunch and before bed

EDUCATION
- Read: Cholesterol Down by Janet Brill
- Attend NYU course on Stress Management
- Read Meditation by Eknath Easwaran

VISUALIZATION
- Visualize going to the gym the morning of each day I plan on going to the gym
- Visualize feeling joy and happiness as often as possible

WRITING
- Journal 30 minutes each week on the benefits I am experiencing from shifting to a healthy lifestyle

CONVERSATIONS
- Speak with my team at work about what it would take to promote a healthy lifestyle at work
- Speak with my wife about changing the way we eat as a family
- Speak with a nutritionist about the right diet for me

Figure 23.4   Partial Thinking Path Plan

the key to a good life and it needs to be cultivated" and developed a set of learning practices designed to fully encode and sustain this thought habit in order to more powerfully support the fulfillment of the actions and the achievement of the goals. These are located on the right-hand side of the plan. The full plan took two coaching sessions to complete.

And although it only took two sessions to complete the plan, it took several years for this executive to fully live a healthy lifestyle. The change was not immediate, and there were many relapses. Although neuroplasticity informs us that as long as we can learn, we can acquire new thought habits and even change or eliminate old thought habits, it does not inform us on the time it takes to do so. Changing our thinking can and, in most cases, will take time.

The good news is that the executive ultimately did change, and when he did, he was not just acting out a new healthy lifestyle; he was being a new healthy lifestyle. He believed in living a healthy lifestyle, and this new way of thinking led to significant changes in his life and had an impact not just on him, but also on his team at work and ultimately on his personal life at home. He continues this lifestyle to this day, making continuous improvements and enjoying the benefits he receives.

CONCLUSION

How do human beings change? What causes sustained change in human beings? Why do some individuals succeed in changing their behaviors and results, and why do others fail? These were the three questions that inspired the creation of the Thinking Path over 20 years ago. Today, hundreds of coaches and a multitude of clients from around the world have benefited from this simple yet effective framework. Many coaches describe it as an essential component of their coaching toolkit and one of the lenses through which they engage with their clients. Many clients speak of the deep insights they acquired and the sustained thinking and behavioral changes they made using it.

I have personally witnessed deep and lasting transformation in many leaders who have used the Thinking Path in their coaching work. Whether working in large corporations, small businesses, government institutions, NGO's or nonprofit organizations, these leaders were able to clearly understand the current source of their limitations. They were able to recognize that their thinking is linked to their feelings and that by changing their thinking, they also change their feelings. They realized that their thinking and feelings drive their actions and results and that when they change their thinking and feelings, their actions shift, and their results change. And they took greater responsibility for generating sustained improvements in their actions and results by intentionally shifting their thinking and their feelings and creating new realities that better serve them and the people they serve.

BIBLIOGRAPHY

Arntz, W., B. Chasse, and M. Vicente. *What The Bleep Do We Know!?* Deerfield Beach: Health Communications, 2005.

Berns, G. *Iconoclast: A Neuroscientist Reveals How to Think Differently.* Boston: Harvard Business Press, 2010.

Charles, J. P. "Journaling: Creating Space for 'I.'" *Creative Nursing* 16, no. 4 (2010): 180–184.

Childre, D., and B. Cryer. *From Chaos to Coherence.* Boulder Creek: Planetary, 2004.

Claxton, G. *Hare Brain, Tortoise Mind.* New York: HarperCollins, 2000.

Claxton, G. *Noises from the Darkroom: The Science and Mystery of the Mind.* London: HarperCollins, 1994.

Csikszentmihalyi, M. *Finding Flow.* New York: Basic Books, 1997.

Demasio, A. R. *Descartes' Error: Emotion, Reason, and the Human Brain.* New York: Putnam's, 1994.

Goleman, D., R. Boyatzis, and A. McKee. *Primal Leadership: Realizing the Power of Emotional Intelligence.* Boston: Harvard Business School Press, 2002.

Greenfield, S. A. *Journey to the Centers of the Mind: Toward a Science of Consciousness.* New York: Freeman, 1995.

Humphries, N. *A History of the Mind: Evolution and the Birth of Consciousness.* New York: Simon and Schuster, 1992.

Kandel, E., J. Schwartz, T. Jessell, S. Siegelbaum, and A. Hudspeth. *Principles of Neural Science.* 5th ed. New York: McGraw-Hill Professional, 2012.

LeDoux, J. *The Emotional Brain: The Mysterious Underpinnings of Emotional Life.* New York: Simon and Schuster, 1996.

LeDoux, J. *Synaptic Self: How Our Brains Become Who We Are.* New York: Penguin Books, 2003.

Mills, R. *Realizing Mental Health: Toward a New Psychology of Resiliency.* New York: Sulzburger & Graham Publishing, 1995.

Ornstein, R., and D. Sobel. *The Healing Brain: Breakthrough Discoveries About How the Brain Keeps us Healthy.* New York: Simon & Schuster, 1987.

McTaggart, L. *The Intention Experiment.* Harper Element: London, 2007.

Rock, D. *Your Brain at Work.* New York: HarperCollins Publishers, 2009.

CHAPTER 24

COACHING FOR LEADERSHIP PRESENCE

CLARICE SCRIBER

LEADERSHIP PRESENCE IS a common coaching concern for aspiring leaders in organizations where technically savvy leaders—and even brilliant ones—climb the corporate ladder and find that they are navigating unfamiliar terrain and that the stakes are high. To succeed at this level, leaders must develop a strong leadership voice with peers, superiors, and subordinates. Many also must round off sharp edges that make them ineffective.

Valued and rewarded for their subject matter expertise and their ability to achieve results, these rising stars frequently have neglected the people skills necessary for success in the executive ranks. When newly promoted leaders get feedback in their initial performance review about their own lack of leadership presence, more than a few are perplexed by the fact that it's not just the work that counts. After all, mastering their domain was the hallmark of their success so far. These leaders are mystified about feedback critical of the way they engage and show up. Here, many realize they are facing the challenge of "executive presence."

The difficulty in meeting this challenge is that executive presence is an elusive concept, shaped by an organization's culture and presence in the marketplace and by its region and reach. From my perspective, presence is a mélange of a number of qualities, including awareness of self and others, courage, passion and commitment, clear, resonant communication, energy that inspires and motivates, and connection and focus. Few leaders exemplify all these qualities at any one time. What seems to be important is for the leader to intuitively know and understand when these characteristics are needed and to embody the quality that is needed. In any one organization, one or more of these qualities may be prized more than others, and leadership presence is often defined by how the organization views itself and characterizes leaders who are successful. For example, in company A, a leader with presence may be defined as one who is authoritative and decisive. In company B, the prototype may be openness, ease of engagement, and the capacity to enroll and influence others. In company C, presence may be defined as the leader's ability to think well on his or her feet and to demonstrate grace under pressure in stressful times.

In this chapter, I will examine the qualities that support a leader's effectiveness, ones that I have noticed and assessed when engaging with leaders regarding their executive presence.

The qualities I've mentioned above are not the only ones a leader must embody by any means, and they are not always the ones a company measures in the year-end review. However, I do believe that these are ones that emanate from leaders who have developed mature relationship skills and who have thought carefully and intentionally about how they want to lead. These qualities support leaders' stance and are among the soft skills that—when missing—can derail leaders. These qualities are frequently among those traits I am asked to help leaders develop. To develop them, we sometimes have to look at how they show up in the leader's day-to-day life.

CLIENT READINESS

When I receive a call from a leader to initiate coaching, I listen deeply so that I can understand the leader's commitment to coaching that will require him to examine some issues that may fundamentally speak to that person's identity. Unlike coaching to enhance management skills, coaching to change one's way of being in the world involves ego development, and a shift in perception of one's being in relationship with others. That change is transformative. Can the leader commit to regular reflection and self-observation to understand how he or she is showing up? Can the leader scrutinize long-held beliefs about his or her ways of being in the world and how he or she is in the workplace? Can the client engage in a reflective conversation and take on practices that may upend his or her self-image?

All these are questions clients and coaches alike are wise to consider. Why? Some clients are ready to do this work; others may not see the need. When the client is ready, the coaching alliance can be productive and satisfying for both client and coach.

MAXINE

Take Maxine for example. A quiet, introverted thinker, Maxine was well respected and liked by the people who worked with her, particularly by direct reports. She was great at delivery, and enjoyed rallying her team to partner IT projects. Maxine was eager to progress to the next level in her organization. However, the feedback she received at review time indicated that her boss's peers and other superiors weren't sure she was ready. Although her company appreciated her work ethic and ability to perform, her bosses wanted more. In meetings, her boss wanted her to speak up more, speak strategically, and engage more robustly in conversations. What was Maxine's point of view, they wondered? How did Maxine think about the work? When there was controversy, where did she stand? Where was her passion? These questions pointed to the level of leadership Maxine's company wants its leaders to demonstrate. For Maxine's company, it is important for leaders to show they have some skin in the game.

Until this point in her career, Maxine had been a good lieutenant, largely carrying out the vision of others. Now, the requirements had changed. Maxine was being asked not only to articulate her vision but to do this on a more public stage. She was now being asked to engage in dialogue with others without the benefit of having the time to think things through; she had to respond in the heat of the discussion. Finally, there was an observation about Maxine's level of energy. No matter what the event, Maxine was always calm and collected. Maxine believed that appearing calm was a strength, especially during a fire drill. However, others viewed it as a lack of passion and conviction on her part.

In our coaching sessions, Maxine proved curious about the feedback and was eager to explore possibilities for building her leadership capacity. "I chose you because I was intrigued by your comments about 'developing my leadership voice,'" she said. At the end of coaching, Maxine was more comfortable speaking up about her vision for the organization. With a great deal of practice and by using visual imagery, she was able to manage her energy to express greater enthusiasm when situations warranted it.

Maxine may never be an ebullient leader. She realized that grace under pressure was an asset. To be authentic, she needed to keep integrity with herself. At the same time, she was able to confidently express her opinion in meetings, which put her on the road to changing her colleagues' perception of her as a wallflower. She took the time to flesh out her point of view, and she practiced speaking about her thoughts until it became easier for her to express them.

JACK

My coaching conversations with Jack had a very different tenor from my conversations with Maxine, although both were deeply immersed in the tactical approach to leading. Jack was an up-and-coming, twentysomething midlevel executive. He was considered brilliant by peers as well as by colleagues senior to him. By training, he was an economist, responsible for creating sophisticated analytical models. Energized by his work and by the intellectual conversations that occurred when he was engaged with his colleagues, he was oblivious to whether the client or colleague was able to keep up with his thinking or the concepts he was trying to convey. He saw himself as an intellectual and equal to those in positions higher in the chain of command, and he did not defer to hierarchy. This quality set him apart from peers and helped him to earn the respect of superiors. Some managers thought it was refreshing and useful for Jack to challenge their views.

Jack did not suffer fools gladly—an assessment his staff, his peers, and his boss all made. Jack's manner was often abrupt, even curt, particularly when he was under pressure. A mentor said: "When you encounter Jack and his energy and appearance, you might think, 'Oh, a grad student or a professor.'" He does not look like an up-and-coming leader; what matters most to him is thinking about ideas, solving problems, and getting the work done.

The company regarded Jack as having "high potential," someone who would climb the ladder more quickly than others because of his knowledge, contribution, and creativity. At the same time, his sponsors recognized Jack's manner was not always welcome, and they noted that he needed to adapt his communications style, his appearance, and his interpersonal style to be less abrasive and more open to others' opinions and ideas. The reality is that what had served Jack well in the past could derail him at the next rung of the career ladder. To help him, Jack's boss offered him the opportunity to work with a coach.

Jack's story has a different ending from Maxine's. From the start, Jack knew he wanted something more for himself, but in the end he was not developmentally ready to take on the kind of practice required to change the way he engaged with others. Although he acknowledged that he was getting in his own way and recognized the desirability of change, he wanted the coach to give him a template of behaviors he could adapt. Ultimately, it was the work product that intrigued him, not changing his way of working and engaging with others, particularly with peers and subordinates. At this time in his development, Jack was not ready to let go of the person he believed himself to be. The call to commit to self-reflection was secondary to his tendency to *do* and his reliance on *being* the expert. In time, Jack could decide to connect, collaborate, and be more humble and engaged with peers and reports.

These two illustrations deal with the readiness of clients to engage in changes that affect how others view them. Early in the coaching alliance, both coach and client should be satisfied that the client is clear about the "why" of the coaching—the larger consideration. Who am I as a leader, and how do I want to show up as a leader?

UNPACKING THE INSTITUTIONAL FEEDBACK

Once the client-leader and I forge a coaching alliance, we engage the client's manager or sponsor in a conversation to further clarify the feedback. Just as the conversation with the client-leader must be utterly candid, the one with the boss must be so also. Here, I work with the client to help him make sense of the intangibles. The clearer the feedback, the more specific we can be identifying what should be addressed in the coaching.

To begin, I want clients to understand what is at stake and what differences will occur when they transform their style. I often ask clients and also their managers about the nature of success and what it looks like to the organization. In other words, I press for a concrete picture of what the sponsor or boss is looking for and make sure the client believes that the new way of showing up meets both parties' perception of who the client is striving to be. A total picture is not always easy to obtain, but in many cases clients have an idea of what is missing. What is most important is for the client to have a clear sense of what change the sponsor needs to see as a signal that the desired leadership qualities have been achieved. The skillful coach will ask for clear examples and expectations and will ask about the support the client-leader can expect from the manager and from those within the client-leader's sphere of influence.

Finally, a coach's conversation with the sponsor might result in greater clarity about what is at stake for the client-leader and discern what the client-leader truly needs to demonstrate to broaden that leadership capacity. Another effective way (which also leads the client to powerful discovery) is to get a read on how the client-leader is doing by interviewing peers and other stakeholders to see where the client's leadership style is working and what changes need to occur. Peers and subordinates can provide specific feedback about the client-leader's ability to articulate a vision, to influence without formal authority, and to motivate effectively.

When leadership presence is an issue, the most important feedback often comes from superiors or seasoned peers. For example, if the issue is around presence with groups, the coach might inquire about how the leader is showing up in meetings.

Observations from colleagues can include, but are not limited to, questions like these:

- Does the leader have a vision that is elegant and easily conveyed?
- Does the leader communicate strategically about matters concerning the organization?
- Does the leader take a stand and articulate a point of view?
- Does the leader manage his or her energy well?
- Does the leader command the room when speaking?
- Does the leader look the part? In some organizations, the right tie and sleeve length, hair cut, and color choices for attire matter and signal whether the leader is part of the team or not.

Although such matters may seem superficial to the client-leader, the question remains: how do these factors affect the leader's ability to connect and to be viewed and accepted as a member of the executive team?

When the coach interviews multiple stakeholders and peers, those interviews can help clarify whether the feedback is an idiosyncratic preference on the part of the boss or whether others hold the same perceptions. Thus, having a conversation with the boss about what the boss is seeing and which leadership issues should be addressed can be critical in helping the leader determine which goals to address.

COACHING THE LEADER

Because of the tender nature of coaching for presence, it's critical for the coach to hold the space without judgment and to inspire trust in the client-leader. When that happens, the client becomes a more connected, inspirational, committed, and intentional leader. Making that choice will be life-enhancing if it is meaningful. Then, the client takes charge of enhancing his or her leadership voice or presence or both when dealing with colleagues and those he or she wants to influence.

When you begin with the premise that your clients are competent and whole, the opportunity to broaden their capacity provides an immense opportunity for both leadership and personal growth. It is essential for the leader to retain integrity with personal values as the leader changes. Coaching for leadership presence works best when wholesale change is not required. We assume here that our clients are competent to do their job. With coaching, the coach and client reimagine and reshape the way the leader relates to others, influences, communicates, or self-manages to have greater effect in the organization.

MARTIN

When Martin began working with me as a coach, he had been leading teams for five years. He was organized, precise, and authoritative in his approach to getting the work done. His last couple of projects had broad impact on the organization, and his sphere of influence spanned multiple divisions instead of just one. Managing down, he'd always been directive. Managing across, he found that his "just do it" style was not as effective. His peers ignored his calls, waited until the last minute to weigh in on decisions, and were lackadaisical about his requests and his desire to meet established deadlines. At the same time, Martin's new boss valued collaboration and was assessing Martin's performance, not only by the quality of the deliverable, but also by how he worked with his peers.

When I started working with Martin, he was indignant about his peers, casting blame and feeling frustrated by his inability to get things moving. He just wanted his colleagues to "get off the dime" and work as hard as he did, be as invested in the work and "deliver the goods." Feedback interviews with Martin's boss and his peers revealed that his colleagues viewed him as a leader who was distant until he wanted something and then relentless in trying to get it; they thought he was extremely bright but unappreciative of input from others and a micromanager with his subordinates.

As you might imagine, Martin had a totally different interpretation of the situation. He viewed himself as capable, committed to the task—driven by a strong work ethic and strong desire to change things within the organization. In the feedback conversation, we talked about how we see ourselves and how others see us—how others and we might interpret the same data differently. We discussed how strengths when overused can derail us. We discussed intention versus impact. I asked Martin what leadership meant to him, how he wanted to lead, and what his peers had to offer in the accomplishment of work. He said, "You know, I thought it was my job to delegate the work and deliver on the project. It never occurred to me that I might have to take a different approach with my peers. They are right. I don't know them, and they probably don't know me. I never thought that really mattered. We're here to get the work done. Not to be social."

It took time for Martin to digest the data and to accept that his assumptions about his leadership might not be well grounded. In the end, he reexamined not only his relationships with his peers, but also his relationships and leadership with subordinates. When we started our work together, Martin was entirely focused on getting things done. On the basis of a carefully crafted development plan shaped by Martin's desired outcome to work collaboratively with others, Martin made changes. He took responsibility for his part in the dynamic between himself and clients. As he began to extend himself more to peers, his peers came to know him, and they were able to see how much he cared about the work. He started to listen to what they wanted and to notice their strengths and what mattered to them. The work became easier, and Martin's energy shifted from tightly wound to greater ease. The use of 360-degree feedback, self-observation, clear goals, willingness to examine and let go of old assumptions as well as practices and support, all contributed to Martin's growth as a leader. An introvert, he had to make an effort to reach out and build relationships, but he now is seeing the payoff. His boss has taken note and encouraged him to go beyond his comfort zone. Martin began spending time engaging his team to seek input. He has developed listening skills. Martin reported that it was stressful trying to get everything done all by himself. Now that he sees himself more as a part of the team, he enjoys his work in a way he had not before.

Working with a client-leader who is challenged with developing or modifying his or her leadership presence is more effective when the coach is knowledgeable and experienced in adult developmental theory. It helps when the coach is cognizant about how leaders grow and change and when she or he understands emotional intelligence and can offer practices that engender intentionality, awareness, and change. The works of Kegan, Basseches, Torbert, Cook-Grueter, Laske, and others can help the coach become more conversant in the stages of adult development.[1]

The leader is often required to adapt a leadership stance to fit the challenges at hand. Changing how we are requires us to be attuned to the organization in a way that is different from the way the leader previously perceived it. Thus, coaching occurs in the space between leaders' current locus of control, their assumptions and story, and their desire and capacity to change. Martin believed he had the wherewithal to change and to interact with his peers differently. On the other hand, Jack needed to manage his energy, listen, and enroll others so they understand his vision, and he did not feel it was important to do so. Another leader might need the flip side of the coin: to speak with greater authority and conviction.

To make an authentic change, leaders must buy into the notion that their way of being—their identity in the organization—can be a means of accomplishing more than the current reality. That is, their role is only part of the equation. This concept is often difficult for a leader to fathom, especially one who depends on hierarchy to influence. What may make the issue even more difficult is when leaders have relied on their commitment to work and have given scant attention to developing relationships and an astute view of the political aspects of organizational life.

In the initial conversation, I want to understand how the client-leaders are motivated, whether their perception of who they are matches how others see them and whether they are ready to examine how their style affects their relationships. Does the leader see the value in finding a voice and a strategy for leadership that reflects that stance? Does the leader view the feedback as an opportunity to work more easily and successfully with colleagues? Does the leader feel diminished or supported in such efforts because the coach is in the mix? Can the leader take charge of his destiny, or does he or she see the organization's request as threatening?

At the heart of leadership presence is authenticity and genuine respect for oneself and for others. Knowledge, technical ability, experience, and accomplishment are important, but the ability to connect with others and to be genuinely present is an essential part of strong leadership. When respect is present and consistently demonstrated, others can receive us more fully, and this creates space for a genuine exchange of ideas. The new leader can be more emboldened to articulate ideas and to elicit the truth from others. The goal should be to articulate vision, challenge current thinking, contribute to the conversation regarding future possibilities, move action forward, make difficult decisions public, and lead. Listening is a key ingredient in this mixture because it keeps the leader in touch with what is going on; listening also provides a way for gathering new ideas from others. Listening keeps the leader in touch with the reality. It says to others that "I" do not have all the answers, and it offers relief from being solely responsible for information and solutions.

It takes courage on the part of the coach and the client-leader to engage in coaching with a focus on presence. Often clients who are striving to find their leadership voice are new leaders who prefer time to think before they speak, who find they cannot get a word in when in a group setting, or who are at a loss for words when they are questioned about a topic they don't know.

SUMMARY

It is crucial for both leader and coach to be clear about the overarching goal of coaching when presence is the issue. When coaching concludes, we've been successful if the client walks away from the engagement feeling whole and intact and more confident about his or her impact on the organization and colleagues. The balance between the organization's request that the client-leader shifts and adapts a stronger leadership presence and the leader's capacity to be more comfortable and skillful in navigating in the organizational setting is not always easy to achieve. At the end of the day, leaders want to retain integrity and remain in harmony with their own core values and sense of themselves. The ultimate goal is not only about results the client will get from a change in behavior. If coaching is successful, the client-leader will grow and understand a great deal more about his or her purpose of having greater impact on the organization.

NOTE

1. Robert Kegan, *The Evolving Self: Problem and Process in Human Development* and *In Over Our Heads: The Mental Demands of Modern Life*; Laske, *Measuring Hidden Dimensions: The Art and Science of Fully Engaging Adults*; Torbert and Cook-Greuter *Action Inquiry: The Secret of Timely and Transforming Leadership*.

BIBLIOGRAPHY

Kegan, Robert. *The Evolving Self: Problem and Process in Human Development*. Cambridge, MA: Harvard University Press, 1982.
————. *In Over Our Heads: The Mental Demands of Modern Life*. Cambridge, MA: Harvard University Press, 1994
Laske, Otto E. *Measuring Hidden Dimensions: The Art and Science of Fully Engaging Adults*. Medford, MA: Interdevelopmental Institute Press, 2006.
Torbert, Bill, and Susanne R. Cook-Greuter, et al. *Action Inquiry: The Secret of Timely and Transforming Leadership*. San Francisco, CA: Berrett-Koehler, 2004.

CHAPTER 25

COACHING FOR LEVERAGE: HELPING CLIENTS TO MANAGE PRIORITIES, TIME, ENERGY, AND RESOURCES

KATHERINE EBNER

The young woman is perched on the edge of her chair in my office. Her face is pale, shoulders slumped. She emanates stress as she describes a crushing list of deadlines and commitments, and I have the sense that she might jump up any minute and run out the door to get back to work. "The worst part," she tells me, looking distraught, "is that I fainted at work last week and again during the weekend. I went to the hospital for blood tests, but they didn't find anything. The doctor said that I have to deal with my stress." As I listened to her, I noticed that, when she finished speaking, she held her breath. I counted silently to see how long she would hold it. After about ten seconds, she spoke. "I don't know what to do. I need this job, but I have no work/life balance." Again she held her breath. "Are you aware that you're holding your breath?" I asked her. "No!" she said, startled. As I described my observation, she began to smile. "Are you telling me that the reason I fainted is that I'm holding my breath?" "Could be," I said. "Would you mind observing this to see if it is happening consistently?" Three days later, she called. "Yes. I'm holding my breath all the time. I have so much going on at work and outside of work that I seem to just keep bracing myself by holding my breath."

THIS EXAMPLE SEEMS EXTREME, yet many people who describe their commitments do so in the same kind of breathless rush, running through lists of "to do's," creating mental piles of commitments. As coaches, we meet people like this young woman frequently—high achievers who have gotten far in life by exceeding expectations. Eventually, they achieve a level of challenge that forces them to face up to the limitations of time, energy, and resources. There are too many priorities. Everything is urgent. Nothing can be set aside or removed from the towering stack of "must-do's." At this point, an individual realizes that something is terribly wrong. "I can't go on like this," one of my clients said recently. "Even when I accomplish something important, there are three more things I haven't gotten to. I need help sorting out my priorities and finding some work/life balance."

For the coach, the goal of "work/life balance" may seem at first simply like a call for help with time-planning. Indeed, this is an important skill for leaders to master. However, to truly help a client make a transformational shift in the way she manages herself, the coach must also help the client to look at behavior and attitudes in three other areas: priorities, energy, and resources. In this chapter, we explore concepts and strategies for helping clients to move from a state of being overwhelmed to a healthier way of living and working.

PRELIMINARY CONVERSATION

Before beginning to work with a client who is overwhelmed, the coach and the client must have a preliminary conversation in which the coach invites the client to tell his story and describe his current challenges. During this conversation, the coach listens for:

- the external requirements and standards that the client currently faces, with attention to areas that need the client's immediate attention;
- the client's contribution to the situation, including history, beliefs, and personal standards that may be contributing to the situation;
- the client's emotional, mental, and physical state, which provides information about what is realistic for the client to undertake in the near term, as well as where the client may need to attend to his own needs;

- ideas the client may already have about how to identify top priorities and work for better balance.

This conversation may also give the coach an opportunity to address the mistaken belief—not uncommon among high achievers—that the habit of overwork is one of the key reasons for their success. Many people believe that they risk losing rewards, status, and the support and admiration of others if they do not exhibit this type of "work ethic." Choosing to live a more balanced life feels like the first step *off* the fast track—an invitation to relinquish control of career success. To coach such a client, the coach first must help the client to become aware of the debilitating consequences of overwork—including diminished performance over time, loss of perspective, loss of stamina and health, and the inability to demonstrate self-mastery. Thus, the client's call for coaching on "work/life balance" is an invitation to work with clients, not simply at the level of tactics, but also at the deeper level of self-awareness and self-mastery.

COACHING FOR LEVERAGE

The concept of "leverage" is well known in business, where it is associated with strategies that achieve equal or better results with less effort and stress. Designed to help the client "work smarter, not harder," the *Leverage Coaching Model* (figure 25.1) looks at the client's life through four interrelated lenses: priorities, time, energy, and resources.

To gain the full picture of the client's immediate challenges and options, the coach asks the client a series of questions in each quadrant (table 25.1). Typically, the coach will select the four or five questions from each quadrant that seem most appropriate for the client, rather

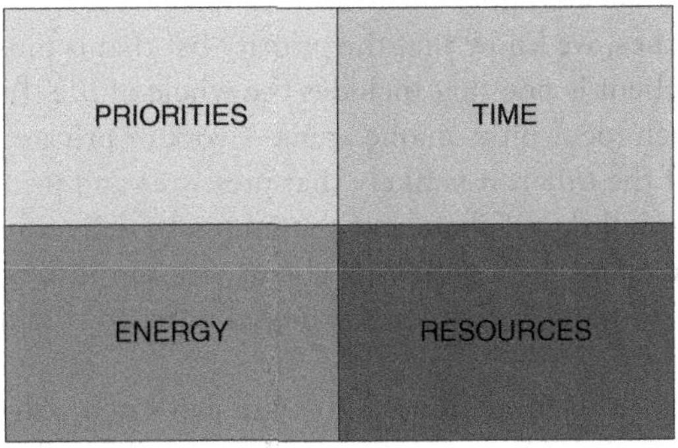

PRIORITIES	TIME
ENERGY	RESOURCES

Figure 25.1 Leverage coaching framework

Table 25.1   Priorities interview—Sample questions

- What has heart and meaning for you in your life?
- Who are the most important people in your life? How do they factor into your daily life right now? Are you satisfied with how it is working?
- Identify the priorities in your private life and in your work life.
- Rank the priorities in each category and then explain the ranking.
- What prevents you from focusing on these priorities?
- For each priority, indicate:
  - what is important to you about this priority,
  - what you will have accomplished if you achieve this priority,
  - how your days would be different if you were observing this priority faithfully.
- If you could only do two things in each category, what would they be?
- If you don't allow yourself to set priorities, what will happen?

than putting the client through a long questionnaire that may feel like an interrogation.

By developing an understanding of the relationships among these four aspects of the client's life, the coach can readily assess what is foremost in the client's mind and what the internal and external pressures are.

Our priorities are the commitments that we believe deserve our most immediate and constant attention. Busy professionals juggle an astonishing mix of work and life priorities every day. They feel responsible for delivering "results," not only at work, but also in their personal lives. Moreover, as businesses struggle to meet quarterly goals under the scrutiny of shareholders, the pressure on employees at all levels mounts. High achievers internalize the expectations of their employers and add them to their own personal standards and life goals. The result is a continuous sense of urgency and responsibility, with little differentiation between major priorities and minor ones and with little or no time to celebrate accomplishments.

As coaches, we know that the priority list that is most meaningful for the client is one that includes the whole of life. In fact, if client and coach focus only on one arena—work or private life—to the exclusion of the other, it is likely that pressures and priorities in the other arena will derail the client's attempts to deliver on priorities. When we explore priorities with clients, we tap into several levels of commitment and beliefs, from the daily "to do" list to the entire life plan.

The chance to think about all of life can catch a driven professional by surprise. One executive made a startling discovery when she wrote down her priorities during a recent coaching session. In less than 10 minutes, she generated a list of 20 priorities at work. When she worked on listing her priorities for her personal life, however, she became confused. "Are these priorities or goals?" she asked. "Does it matter if I'm not actually doing any of them?" Slowly, she produced a list of priorities for her private life that included time with her husband and with each of her two children, time to practice yoga, and a work schedule that allowed her to be home by 6:00 p.m. to have dinner with her young family. "I'm not doing it, though," she said, thoughtfully. "Every single day I get up at 5:00 a.m. to get to work, so that I can supposedly leave by 5:15 p.m. and have dinner with my family. The truth is, I rarely leave the office before 6:30. The kids are already in bed by the time I get home. My real priority must be work. I am not acting like family is a real priority, even though I say it is." Looking at priorities with a client invites a moment of truth.

A good way to get a clear picture of what someone's priorities actually are is to ask them to track how they are spending time for one week (table 25.2). Since there is a difference between intentions and actual behavior, by collecting the "data," the true priorities become clear. Once the client has done this self-observation, she is usually ready to talk about how to make changes to live in a way that truly reflects her personal values.

For high achievers, one particular barrier that may stand in the way of changing their behavior is a highly developed sense of responsibility to others (company, family, and colleagues), which often causes them to put their own needs last. They believe they are only allowed to give attention to what matters to them after they have satisfied the needs and expectations of their boss, their workplace, and their family. In the coaching conversation, when these clients

Table 25.2   Time interview—Sample questions

- Describe an ideal day/week.
- What prevents you from having that kind of day/week?
- What deadlines are you facing in the next six weeks?
- How do you budget time for projects and priorities?
- How do you use your calendar to manage your time?
- Look at this week's calendar. Is it realistic?
- Does your calendar reflect your top priorities? If not, how will you find time for important work?
- Is your personal life included in your calendar?
- If you could make three changes in how you expect to spend your time this week, what would they be?

identify their priorities and actual daily experience, they are often revealing to themselves deeply held beliefs about what success means. Their actual behavior reveals what they are willing to do—and sacrifice—to achieve it.

A client who puts her own needs last is often out of "sync" with her values and suffers not only from overcommitment, but also from trying to achieve success on terms that are important to other people rather than to herself. When prioritization leaves out considerations of the health and well being of the person making the priorities list, that person is working long and hard, with dwindling energy, motivation, and hope. For the client to place herself at the top of the list takes courage and a willingness to make substantive changes in the commitments she makes—and the leaders who do this are held up as "authentic" and as admirable role models for the rest of us.

Executives at all levels of the organization experience problems with saying no to unrealistic workloads. I notice that many of my clients believe that, if they could just manage *time* better, they could succeed more easily. A conversation about how they spend their time reveals the rationale behind the work habits. Some confess to staying late to micromanage the work of others ("I just can't trust anyone else to do the job right.") or to being a perfectionist who procrastinates on complex projects because it seems that "there isn't enough time to do it properly."

As the coach works with the client on time-planning and matching priorities with time allocation, the coach will be able to observe the client's "mode of operating"—what she believes is necessary for her to *do* and to *be* in order to succeed. The coach will also see where the client may be sabotaging herself as a result of unrealistic (or nonexistent) planning.

By attending to time-management early in the coaching process, the client will experience a greater sense of control and focus and will most likely deliver better results in the days ahead. These early wins build credibility for coaching as a helpful learning process and for the coach as someone who can provide real value and benefit for the client.

People focus on mastering many competencies on their way to "the top," but the most successful senior executives—those who have learned to sustain high performance over years and who have a confident, energetic presence—know that the key to success is to pay attention to energy (table 25.3). By doing work that is energizing and by making time for activities that refuel their energy, these leaders are able to sustain their focus and to thrive.

Table 25.3 Energy interview—Sample questions

- What gives you energy?
- What drains your energy away?
- What do you love about your work?
- What do you love doing when you aren't at work?
- What are your top work priorities this week?
- Which things on the list do you look forward to?
- Which ones give you a sense of dread? What could you do to increase your enthusiasm and energy for those you dread?
- What is your typical energy level in the morning? Midday? Evening?
- What do you do to refuel your energy? What are your daily habits?
- Do you take care of your health through diet, exercise, and sleep?

To discover what is energizing to the client, the coach and client must examine what truly motivates him. We are most motivated to work on challenges that are aligned with our values. Thus, this conversation is a critical part of linking personal values and life vision with priorities.

When the client sees the difference between where he has passion and where he is just tolerating his existence—and understands how passion is linked with energy—he will begin to use as a criterion in managing his responsibilities, "does this give me energy or take it away?" This key distinction can lead the client to see new possibilities and to let go of old responsibilities, relationships, and habits that are unproductive and unsustainable.

As the coach helps the client appreciate the importance of managing energy to sustain performance, stamina, and health, the client will be able to make heartfelt commitments to improved health and stick with those commitments. He will make adjustments to take care of his health and energy with the new awareness that peak performance requires attention to passion, health, and energy. He also is likely to feel better physically, which increases motivation and well-being in all areas of life. This attention to the physical self often addresses a long-held regret in a busy person, who knows that he needs to change his habits but hitherto has not had a strong enough rationale to commit to it.

Busy people often tell me that "it would take too much time" to delegate work to others or to renegotiate deadlines. Instead, they apply themselves to the tasks at hand, working in isolation to keep all the balls in the air. By overlooking the available resources (table 25.4) or not taking the time to use them effectively, a leader is on a course to fall short of expectations and burn out in the process.

Table 25.4 Resources interview—Sample questions

- Make a list of your commitments. For each item, identify your responsibilities and others' responsibilities.
- What special knowledge/information/skills are needed to complete each item? Do you know anyone with these skills who can help you? What would you need to do to get that help?
- Is there anyone on your team who has a passion for one of these projects and would benefit from taking on a bigger piece of it?
- What keeps you from delegating?
- What do you need to request from your family right now to handle this situation?
- If you tackle a project by yourself, can you describe what is likely to happen?

The question "What resources are available right now?" signals to the client that help is available—or at least, it could be. In the Leverage Coaching Model, the concept of "resources" includes:

- *people* who can provide support at work and at home;
- published resources, such as books and articles;
- *experts* or *consultants* who can provide specialized assistance;
- *technologies* that can make work processes more efficient;
- financial resources; and
- competencies, experiences, and skills of the client himself.

As the client's situation is made clear to the coach in the "Resources" portion of the Leverage Interview, the coach can begin to test the client's assessment of the situation, to determine how much support is actually available to the client. Often, the client realizes that he hasn't actually made others aware of his challenges and has not made a clear request for help. The Resources Interview helps the client think more creatively about his current use of resources and about available resources that may have been overlooked.

Occasionally, a client will demonstrate that he is truly alone in having to handle a big responsibility. In this case, coach and client might work together to frame requests that enable the client to deliver on commitments or to renegotiate expectations.

Paying attention to available resources whenever possible will free up time and energy for the priorities that matter most.

SUMMARY AND STRATEGIES FOR USING THE LEVERAGE COACHING MODEL

After completing the four-part Leverage Interview, the client and coach have a solid, richly detailed body of information and plenty of areas where the client can begin self-observation and practice. Coach and client can continue to work together to design practices and actions that give "leverage" to the client and dramatically improve the way that he functions at work and in life in general.

There are many other applications of the model. Its usefulness relies on the coach's creativity in integrating the activities and ideas from each quadrant.

The following strategies provide examples of how a coach might work with the Leverage Coaching Model. These approaches can be used independently or simultaneously, depending on the client and the situation.

STRATEGY ONE: FOCUS ON THE CALENDAR

The purpose of this strategy is to encourage the client to use the calendar to reflect priorities accurately and manage resources efficiently. The coach begins by reviewing the client's priorities with him and then asking him to block out time on the calendar for priority projects and goals. For example, if the client's goal is to sell $1 million in consulting services within the next six months, he needs to map out the steps necessary to achieve that goal and then plan the time needed for each step, blocking out appropriate periods in the calendar to accomplish each.

Focusing on the calendar should get the client thinking well beyond the next month. It is possible, and frequently desirable, to ask the client to plan as far out as twelve or eighteen months. At minimum, the client should look ahead three months to anticipate future deadlines. The calendar should reflect such things as travel plans, important meetings, performance assessments of staff, personal appointments (dentist, doctor, school events, accountant, etc.), management meetings with staff, and vacation plans.

As the client begins to treat the calendar as a helpful tool for achieving priorities, she will begin to experience a sense of relief. The calendar exercise will also show the client when her commitments add up to "impossible," forcing her to a moment of truth about her definition of a successful life.

STRATEGY TWO: FOCUS ON ENERGY AND PASSION

Building on the Energy Interview, the coach can provide resources and encouragement to the client to invest in increasing his energy and passion. The first step is to educate the client about the demonstrable difference that passion and energy make in performance. *The Power of Full Engagement: Managing Energy, Not Time, Is the Key to High*

Performance and Personal Renewal[1] by Loehr and Schwartz, or the article "The Making of the Corporate Athlete"[2] by the same authors, are outstanding resources for helping the client to understand this link. In these works, the authors share their research on what distinguishes top performing athletes from average athletes, and they apply their findings to the performance of executives in the corporate environment.

Once the client has accepted the idea that managing energy is the key to sustaining performance, coach and client can begin to explore how passion (or lack of it) is affecting performance. As the client begins to observe his energy level and its link with passion, the coach can ask the client to give priority to activities that bring him energy.

The focus on energy also opens the door to a discussion about health and happiness, allowing the coach to talk about the domain of the body. I frequently ask my clients to commit to at least one practice that fosters physical health. Clients quickly sign up for the yoga class or resolve to jog three times per week—activities that they have wanted to do, but previously saw as superfluous rather than essential.

To make room for this new activity, the coach and client must revisit priorities and time-planning, a conversation that strengthens the client's understanding of the relationships among the quadrants of the Leverage Model.

Additionally, the coach can work with the client to identify his life mission, values, and personal needs. This work reveals the client to himself in a way that gives the current challenges a larger, more meaningful context. The mission and values exercises will help the client to understand what his passion really is, while the personal needs exercise will show him what "hooks" distract him from acting with passion and integrity.

STRATEGY THREE: FOCUS ON REDUCING PRIORITIES

When someone suffers from overcommitment, reducing the number or scope of priorities is essential.

Once the client has identified personal and professional priorities broadly, the coach can work with her to select those that are most urgent or perhaps are the foundation for achieving other goals. The client is able to find a good starting point for progress by prioritizing the priorities.

The coach's first question might be, "What is on this list that *only* you can do?" encouraging the client to accept the idea that not everything must be "owned" by her. Next, the client could begin to narrow the list by assigning each priority a number in terms of its importance to her well-being. The coach might then suggest that the client set priorities within a specific timeframe (the next week, month, six months, etc.), narrowing the list even more. Suddenly, the path forward is clear and better organized. It is time to identify the tasks related to achieving each priority and slot them into the calendar— including the time needed to enlist the right resources.

At the end of this exercise, the client should have a focused and streamlined picture of what must be accomplished in a defined time period and at least a preliminary plan for accomplishing it.

CONCLUSION

As it examines four aspects of performance—priorities, time, energy, and resources—the Leverage Coaching Model gives the coach an excellent opportunity to work with the client on three levels—tactical, strategic, and transformational. Of particular value is the inclusion of an energy assessment, which allows the coach to call attention to the crucial relationships among health, energy, and performance. By focusing on the ways in which the client determines priorities, manages time, maintains energy, and uses resources, the Leverage Coaching Model can make a critical difference in whether the client can achieve his goals, stay focused on his priorities, and have a fulfilling private life. A client who understands the relationship between priorities, time, energy, and resources—and can manage these variables effectively—is well on his way to mastering essential skills for leadership and sustainable high performance.

NOTES

1. Loehr, Schwartz, *The Power of Full Engagement*.
2. Loehr, Schwartz, "The Making of the Corporate Athlete," *Harvard Business Review*, January 2001.

BIBLIOGRAPHY

Covey, Stephen R. *The 7 Habits of Highly Effective People*. New York: Simon and Schuster, 1989.

The Grove Consults International and Joan McIntosh. *Personal Compass: A Workbook for Visioning and Goal Setting*. San Francisco, CA: Grove Consults International, 2002.

Loehr, Jim and Tony Schwartz. *The Power of Full Engagement: Managing Energy, Not Time, Is the Key to High Performance and Personal Renewal.* New York: Free Press, 2003.

Strozzi-Heckler, R. *The Anatomy of Change: A Way to Move through Life's Transitions.* Berkley, CA: North Atlantic Books, 1993.

Watkins, Michael. *The First 90 Days: Critical Success Strategies for New Leaders at All Levels.* Boston: Harvard Business School Press, 2003.

CHAPTER 26

ACTION LEARNING: AN APPROACH TO TEAM COACHING

JENNIFER WHITCOMB

AS SOMEONE WHO COACHES INDIVIDUALS, you might be intrigued to learn about an approach that uses your existing skills to coach a group or team effectively. Organizations all over the world are using action learning as a group-coaching method to develop teams, enhance leadership skills, solve complex problems, and improve organizational efficiency. Action learning is fast becoming a popular group-coaching method as groups work on real-time challenges and apply learning and action at the same time.

ACTION-LEARNING OVERVIEW

Action learning is a group-coaching approach that uses real people to solve real problems, in real time, to obtain real results. It is a process that brings people together to solve challenges, learn through reflection, and take action. Action-learning groups can work on a single problem or challenge that affects the entire group or on several problems presented by individual group members.

Reg Revans first introduced this approach when working with coal mine managers in the United Kingdom in the 1940s. Miners became involved and energized by solving their own problems and were successful at solving problems at each other's sites. The miners who participated in the action-learning process found their mines' performance increased, compared with the mines that did not participate.

This method emphasizes defining the problem accurately so the actual problem is solved. The group focuses on what it is learning, and how this learning applies to the group's individual members and to the organization. Action learning helps people look at the way they analyze a problem, work together as a team, take action, and get results. Given our rapidly changing work environment, action learning can be considered a just-in-time approach to leadership and team development that individuals may not get in a training program. A training program may not be offered at the right time or provide the relevant content.

Action learning uses many of the same skills that are used in individual coaching: asking powerful questions, creating reflection, enhancing learning, and taking action. With this group-coaching approach you will be able to use and transfer many of the individual coaching skills that you have honed.

The role of the coach is to use the process of listening and asking questions to help the group optimize its performance. An action-learning coach intervenes at various points to help the group improve its process, take action, and capture group learning.

COMPONENTS OF ACTION LEARNING

Action learning has six components and two ground rules. The six components are:

1. problem or challenge
2. group or team
3. questions and reflection
4. focus on learning
5. action
6. the coach

For a conceptual view, see figure 26.1.

The two ground rules are these:

1. Statements can be used only in response to questions.
2. The action-learning coach can intervene at any time.

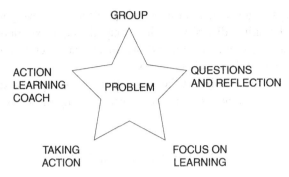

Figure 26.1 Components of action learning

PROBLEM OR CHALLENGE

Ideally, the presenting problem should have these qualities:

- It should be urgent.
- It should not be a puzzle.
- It should be complex.
- It should be solvable.
- It should be something that has not been worked on already.

The types of problems, challenges, or opportunities that can be explored include improving a process, creating a new product, cutting costs, increasing business, resolving difficult workplace dynamics, handling leadership challenges, creating a new structure, improving communications, and so forth. For an individual presenting a problem, it can be anything meeting the earlier criteria that are keeping him or her up at night.

A number of people can present individual problems in a session, or one problem can be taken on by the entire group. At an action-learning session offered for executive directors of nonprofits, each executive director came to the session with a problem important to that director. The schedule allowed three people to present their problems during each session. Another organization using action learning for leadership development had two teams work on two different organizational issues.

GROUP OR TEAM

An action-learning group or team ideally comprises six to eight participants. Groups smaller than six may not generate enough participation, and groups larger than eight may make it difficult for everyone to participate. Bringing diversity to the group through experience, background, age, gender, culture, and organizational level will generate a variety of viewpoints and perspectives.

At least one member of the action-learning group should have the authority to implement solutions discovered during the action-learning sessions.

QUESTIONS AND REFLECTION

One of the ground rules in action learning is that statements can only be used in response to questions, thus making questions the major tool in this approach. The group works together by asking questions of each other, and the coach intervenes by asking questions at various points to help facilitate the process.

As with individual coaching, questions can be a powerful tool to gain clarity, build dialogue, create shared understanding, and enhance awareness. Questions help the group focus on the problem to gain clarity, get to the nut of the problem, and avoid the temptation to rush to a solution too soon and potentially solve the wrong problem. Questions help create an opportunity for reflection and for group members to step back and think. By creating this pause, group members can challenge their own assessments, open up perspectives, and possibly think about the problem in a different way. It's very common for the presenting problem to shift and be reframed after the group has started to ask questions. The group is responsible to ask questions either of the problem presenter or of each other. Group members often develop better coaching skills themselves as they begin to ask better questions and to listen more. Asking better questions is a skill that often gets transferred back to the work environment as group members learn the benefit of inquiry.

FOCUS ON LEARNING

Being engaged in solving a complex problem creates individual, group, and organizational learning. Individuals learn about themselves: how they tackle a problem, how they assess themselves, and how they operate in a group. They may develop and strengthen a leadership competency, enhance awareness of their behavior in a group, or become better at solving problems. One person in an action-learning session realized he was monopolizing the process after the action-learning coach asked, "What are we doing well?" and "How could we be better as a group?" By reflecting on those questions, this person realized he tended to monopolize the process at other points in the workplace and in his personal life. He became more attuned to listening to others, and at work he became more likely to ask questions than to offer his opinion, thus helping improve his work relationships.

The group learns to improve and enhance its functioning. Group members begin to slow down their questioning process by listening more to other questions and building on those questions.

ACTION

Taking action is a key component in action-learning coaching, as it is with individual coaching. Group members take action by testing and implementing ideas. Taking action can involve doing research, gathering information, designing a process, or trying out a new idea or piece of a process. Individual team or group members take action on the problem between meetings. This is what makes action learning different from other problem-solving methods because the group is responsible for more than providing recommendations or reports. When the group has the authority to take action on its ideas, it remains committed and energized to solve the problem. Taking action provides a great opportunity to learn what action steps work and what needs to be improved. These action steps will form the basis for implementing the solution.

THE COACH

As when working with an individual, the action-learning coach is a neutral party who creates the spirit of inquiry, reflection, learning, and action. The action-learning coach does not comment on the content of the session; otherwise, the credibility and neutrality may be lost and the group then may grow too dependent on the coach.

The coach intervenes at various points in the process, when he or she sees an opportunity for the group to learn about its process. One of the ground rules is that the action-learning coach has the authority to intervene at any time. Often the coach will sit a bit removed from the group and move in to intervene.

THE ROLE OF THE COACH

The action-learning coach acts in four main areas of the process:

1. helping the group define the problem
2. enhancing the group process
3. taking action
4. capturing learning

HELPING THE GROUP DEFINE THE PROBLEM

The action-learning coach asks the person presenting the problem to describe the problem in a couple of minutes. If the presenter speaks much longer than that, he or she begins to get into too much detail or begins to solve the problem.

When the problem has been described, the group can begin asking questions about the definition. The time for the coach to intervene is when the group uses statements rather than questions, asks leading questions, asks solution-embedded questions, or when the group seems challenged. The first time the coach intervenes is usually approximately ten minutes into the session. The kinds of questions to ask toward the beginning of a session are:

- How are we doing as a group?
- What is the quality of our questions so far?
- What is the balance between statements and questions?
- How could we be better?
- What questions have been useful so far?

After the group has spent some more time asking questions, the coach may intervene to see whether the group has clarity on the problem. This step often works best when the coach says, "Write down in a couple of sentences what the problem is." This gives each person a moment to pause and reflect, and gives the group an opportunity to see if it is in agreement on the problem definition so far.

Debrief by asking each participant to read his or her statement. If there is one problem presenter, you may ask that person to go last. Ask the group if there is agreement on the problem. Most of the time, the group is either not clear about the specific problem or lacks agreement. Have the group ask questions again; then intervene again by repeating the exercise of writing down the problem statement and reading each statement to the group.

At this point, ask, "Do we have agreement on the problem?" If there is more than one problem for consideration, ask which problem the group would like to focus on.

ENHANCING THE GROUP PROCESS

The action-learning coach intervenes when needed to improve the functioning and effectiveness of the group. However, it's just as important to intervene when things are progressing well to keep that momentum going as it is to intervene when things are not going well. The approach to the interventions with the group is often more appreciative in nature, focusing on making things better and improving its process. For example, the coach will ask, "What's working well?" versus "What's not working well?" When someone in the group says, "That's a great question," it is a good time to intervene to find out what made that a good question so that the group can continue in that line of thought. The action-learning coach can intervene when one person is dominating, when the rate of questions is not allowing for enough reflection time, when the questions are not building on one another, or when the group is not making progress. Here are some questions that the coach can ask:

- How are we doing as a team?
- What would improve our process?
- Are we building on each other's questions?
- What's working well?
- What could we do better?

The interventions are done by asking these very simple questions. It sometimes can be tempting to comment on the process or ask a longer question, but these simple, tried-and-true questions really help the coach and the group.

TAKING ACTION

When the group has agreement on the problem statement, it can move into this phase. The coach needs to make sure that the group has enough time in the session to come up with strategies and action steps. The coach may need to intervene to remind the group of the session's timeline, or to tell the group to begin developing strategies and action steps.

Group members will begin suggesting strategies and action steps— what to do and how to do it. When one individual presents a problem, the group develops suggested strategies and action steps for that person to consider. When the group is working on a problem affecting the entire group, it needs to come to agreement on what strategies will be helpful, how action will be taken, and who will take responsibility between now and the next meeting.

As in individual coaching, the coach will ask what action steps will be taken as a result of the session. This question may be asked of the individual presenting a problem or of the entire group. This question typically is asked at the end of the session in the phase focused on capturing learning. Each group member will volunteer to take on specific action steps between sessions. The coach typically begins by asking, "What action steps are you going to take as a result of today's session?"

Ideally, each group member will take some responsibility for an action between meetings. Group members need to capture these action steps because the coach will ask what progress has been made on these steps at the next meeting.

CAPTURING LEARNING

The coach needs to plan for enough time to capture the group's learning adequately. Reminding the group that he or she will be stopping the process to allow for this will make the coach's job easier. Sometimes it's hard to bring the group to a close when it is making progress, but it's just as important to capture the learning as it is to solve the problem. It's advisable to plan at least fifteen minutes for this step.

Questions can be tailored to the purpose of the action-learning session. If the focus of the sessions is leadership development, then there may be more questions on the requisite skills and qualities of leaders. The action-learning coach needs to choose which questions will be most valuable to the group and will provide the most learning.

If there is one person presenting the problem, then the first three questions will be asked of that individual initially. If the group is working on a problem affecting the whole group, then these questions can be asked of the entire group. Here are questions to capture the lessons learned from the experience:

- What actions are you (we) going to take as a result of today's session?
- Were you/we helped? How?
- What did you learn about yourself?
- What did you learn about the problem?
- What did you learn about problem solving?
- What did you learn about leadership?
- How did we do as a team?
- What did we do well?
- What could we do better?
- What helped us make progress?

- What might we do differently next time?
- How can we transfer today's learning to us personally or to other parts of the organization?

TIMING AND LOGISTICS OF THE ACTION-LEARNING PROCESS

Action-learning groups may meet once or twice a month over a six-month stretch or may meet for longer sessions over a couple of days. Most groups work well for up to a two-hour period. The length of time the group meets may depend on the complexity and the urgency of the problem.

Action learning tends to work best when members can meet face to face; however, many groups are composed of members in diverse locations. When working with groups whose members live in different locations, it's possible to use teleconferencing or videoconferencing; but at least for the first session, the group should meet in one location. When working with a group of executive directors for non-profits, we hosted the first meeting in a retreat center. At our opening session in the afternoon, we introduced the concept of action learning, and we provided an overview and initial practice. The evening offered time for group members to get to know each other. The next morning three people volunteered their problems in forty-five-minute sessions. Half an hour of each session was dedicated to the problem, and 15 minutes were given to capturing learning. This group met for a period of six months using a balance of face-to-face meetings and teleconferences, with group members rotating the presentation of their problems. We noticed that providing the initial face-to-face meeting and allowing time for the group to get to know each other helped the group bond well. The group was very willing to help individual group members.

BENEFITS OF USING THIS COACHING APPROACH

Some benefits resulting from this coaching approach include:

- greater diversity of ideas
- improved employee collaboration and engagement
- solutions to complex problems
- potential cost savings from solving complex problems
- group ownership of the problem

- leadership development
- team building
- transfer of individual coaching skills to group-coaching skills

CONCLUSION

Action learning may be one form of coaching that you wish to try to expand your portfolio of coaching skills. Many of the skills that you already have will help you with this method of coaching.

Your ability to be a neutral presence is the skill that transfers most easily to group coaching. Your staying objective and neutral helps the group become much more self-sufficient and productive. Another skill that easily transfers to group coaching is the use of powerful questions and reflection. Your familiarity with these kinds of questions will make it easier for you to create space for the group to reflect on both its process and its progress. Another skill that we learn in individual coaching is to facilitate learning and create awareness in our clients. As the action-learning coach intervenes at various points within the process, the group members learn about themselves, problem solving, teamwork, and transfer of learning to other parts of the organization. Of course, the ability to help our clients take action and move forward is another skill that transfers to group coaching. Without this critical step, we would not be able to help our clients learn from the actions they have taken or to help them implement the solution in the organization.

BIBLIOGRAPHY

Adams, Marilee G. *Change Your Questions Change Your Life: 7 Powerful Tools for Life and Work*. San Francisco, CA: Berrett-Koehler, 2004.

M.J. Marquardt. *Action Learning in Action: Transforming Problems and People for World-Class Organizational Learning*. Palo Alto, CA: Davies-Black, 1999.

————. "Harnessing the Power of Action Learning." *Training and Development Journal*, June 2004, 26–32.

————. *Leading with Questions: How Leaders Find the Right Solutions by Knowing What to Ask*. San Francisco, CA: Jossey-Bass, 2005.

————. *Optimizing the Power of Action Learning: Solving Problems and Building Leaders in Real Time*. Palo Alto, CA: Davies-Black, 2004.

For more information on Action Learning: The World Institute of Action Learning, www.wial.org

CHAPTER 27

COACHING NEW TEAMS
PATRICIA A. MATHEWS

SUCCESSFUL TEAMS, WHETHER NEW OR EXISTING, need continuing support from the leader and the organization. A team coach can intensify this support by observing the team's current functioning, assessing the team's strengths and weaknesses, and, in collaboration with the leader, developing a plan for addressing any needed changes. Brand new teams in new situations require extra care and feeding.

There are various "new" team categories. For example, an existing team with a new leader is a team that has already been formed and worked together when a new leader is appointed and enters the mix. If members join an existing team and/or a new leader is appointed, the hybrid team is actually an existing team gaining new members and/or a new leader. In either case, the end result is a "new" team—different from the original team.

A third example is the brand new team. Here the team is new to the organization and/or its members who may have never worked on a team before. This chapter discusses the specific strategies a team coach can use when working with brand new teams.

THE BRAND NEW TEAM: A CASE STUDY

Meet John Post. He's just been hired as the superintendent of a large public school system. He wants to form a team of senior staff to work together to accomplish great things for the school district. John is new to the area and in the first weeks of his job he observes that there is not a true senior leadership team in place. He spends several weeks observing staff members who serve in administrative roles and determines which staffers should be part of the senior team. After he identifies the members of the team, he decides to hire a team coach to work with him and the team to get them all off to a good start. John interviews me and decides that I would be right for the job.

John and his team are a good example of the benefits of utilizing team coaching with a brand new team. John was committed to leading this team to produce results in a school district where the previous leader had been in place for more than twenty years. Previously, the administrative staff members had never worked together as a team and they did not understand John's expectations of them. He brought a different leadership style to the school district and the potential team members had no experience working as a team or with their new leader.

Workplace teams are not new and have been part of organizational culture for years. What is becoming more apparent is that *how* new teams are managed can make the difference between successful teams and those that fail miserably. John was committed to making his brand new team one of the success stories.

One of the critical distinctions between successful and unsuccessful teams is the role of the leader. Some team leaders act like "bosses" and tell team members what to do and how and when to do it. Others maintain a "hands-off" policy and believe that this approach is best for the team. In our initial conversations, John confided that he was quick to make decisions, was great at vision, urged people to act quickly, and that he often floated ideas to team members, but wasn't good at following up on whether team members took action.

We discussed my role as team coach. John wanted help for himself as leader and for the team members to form a cohesive and productive team from disparate individuals. In our initial meeting, we discussed how I might help him with three of the most critical indicators for team success:

1. Focus on performance
2. Define a set of goals
3. Agree on methods to achieve the goals

INITIAL CONTRACTING AND COACHING THE LEADER

In the case of a brand new team and before meeting with the team members, the team coach spends time with the leader to chart the team course. This includes:

- Team mission and goals
- Roles and responsibilities of team members
- Ground rules for the team

When I met with John initially to help him clarify these important foundational items, I asked him the following:

- Why should this new team exist?
- What does the team have to do to accomplish its purpose?
- What kind of decisions can the team make?
- How will the team make decisions?
- How often and how long will the team meet?
- Where and when will the team meet?
- What have you learned from leading other teams that you want to bring to this one?
- What do you already know about the team members?
- What do you need to know?
- How will you get the information you need?

Once John identified his answers to these questions, he decided to use some of the questions in this vital formative work with his team. In addition, John and I discussed the role of the team coach distinguishing between team coaching and team building. My role in working with his team would include some teaching, consulting, and coaching and would focus on helping the team to work together to achieve their goals, as well as on strengthening John's role as leader. We were clear about the distinctions between team coaching and team building. We were not planning simulations, games, or other means of building his team. We decided on a four-month initial contract with continued team coaching to be contracted after evaluating the first four months.

TEAM MEMBER INTERVIEWS

Once John and I had completed several meetings and he achieved some clarity about the team's purpose, I scheduled an interview with each member of the team. I often do these interviews via telephone, partly because of geographic and schedule concerns, and because team members may feel more comfortable on the telephone. I stress that these interviews are confidential and that the information helps me to understand each member better. I also clearly indicate that the overall results of the interviews will be shared with the leader and the team at our first joint meeting, explaining that I give this feedback in the form of general themes, never using direct quotes or indicating which team member contributed the information.

The questions I used for this interview were:

- What do you think will be the strengths of this team and leader?
- What strengths do you personally bring to the team?
- What weaknesses do you think the team and leader might have?
- What areas would you personally need to improve to be a good team member?
- What do you hope will be the results of working with a team coach?
- Is there anything else that I have not asked, by way of background or information gathering, but should know to help me do my job better when I work with you?

I compiled the results of the interviews and shared general feedback with the leader before the first team event.

USING ASSESSMENTS DURING THE START-UP PHASE OF A TEAM

The next step I take in coaching new teams is to have each team member complete the *Success Insights*[1] team assessment. This statistically valid and reliable instrument uses the DISC model, and it is completed by each team member and the leader via an Internet delivery system. Each team member signs on and completes an assessment. I use it with team leaders and members for several reasons: it identifies their natural style of behavior, it highlights challenges they might have with people of a different style, and it gives me as the team coach a foundational understanding of how to coach the leader and the team. I print all the reports so that they are kept confidential until the first team meeting. I also compile a team report that maps each individual profile on a team wheel.

Applications for this assessment in coaching a new team include identifying team and individual strengths (and comparing them to the interview answers), uncovering stress areas for individuals and potential conflicts between team members, identifying potential blind spots among team members, providing a neutral tool for self-discovery of natural talent and behavior and providing a behavior-based tool for assessing behavior shifts.

There are other assessments that are constructive for those teams that have already been working together because they assess the current state of the team, but I find that the *Success Insights* team version is the most beneficial for brand new teams as they have not yet experienced how the team works together. Later in their development as a team, other assessments may be used.

When the team is new, it is helpful for members to complete an assessment that advances each member's understanding of his/her own behavior and how it fits with the rest of the team. This is important during the start-up phase because it helps members understand that their intention (based on their style) may not be showing up in their behavior.

This team assessment contains the following sections:

- Basic characteristics
- Work characteristics
- Value to the team
- Value to the organization
- Effective communication
- Team effectiveness factors
- Perceptions
- Descriptors
- Action plan

Before I met with the entire team, I debriefed John's assessment with him. This step both helped John understand his style and also established the foundation for him to use the results of the instrument when working with the rest of the team. I did not share the results of the individual assessments with the leader.

I coached John to conduct the portion of the team meeting that utilizes the results of the assessment. He would facilitate a conversation about these specific topics:

- Similarities and differences in behavioral style
- How the similarities and differences affect team behavior

THE FIRST TEAM MEETING

Once the background work with the leader and the interviews with the team were complete, John scheduled the first team meeting.

At this meeting, John reintroduced me as the team coach and stated that I would be working with him and with the group both collectively and individually during this meeting and in the coming months. Explaining how the first meeting helps the team to recognize their strengths and to identify objectives for their work together, I shared the general results of the interviews and talked about my role as both coach and occasional facilitator for this first meeting.

I distributed all of the assessments and conducted a brief session about the *Success Insights* assessment to help the team members first understand their individual styles and then to determine their team composition. The value of the assessment is not in the results alone. The true value comes from the feedback conversations, acknowledgement of styles and strengths as well as the follow-through on the commitments of just how the team will work together.

First team members read their individual reports. I conducted another short session on understanding behavioral styles and the interpretation of the graphs in the report. Then, in small groups, the team members answered a series of questions, posed by the leader. John and I agreed on these questions before the meeting:

- What three to five things from your report should other team members remember to do/not do to best communicate with you?
- What are some of the similarities and differences you are discovering in your group?
- Based on these similarities and differences, how/when do you see conflicts and misunderstandings in communication occurring between team members?
- What are three to five words you think other people would use to describe you?
- How would you check these perceptions out to see if they are on target?

John facilitated a conversation among the team members about their answers. I observed how he conducted this part of the meeting and recorded my observations, but I did not intervene during this exchange.

After team members had a chance to work in the initial small group conversation, I did another brief teaching piece—sharing the graphic depicting the team members' behavioral styles so that they could see the style of each member in relationship to each other. I then had them reform into small groups according to their styles.

John resumed leadership of the team. He asked these new groups to discuss the following questions:

- What six to eight general characteristics do you all have in common?
- List six to eight things you believe people value about all of you.
- Name three to five ways you believe people have difficulty working with all of you.
- Pick one or two of the behaviors in your DISC analysis. How are these behaviors demonstrated at work?
- How have these behaviors made you successful?
- Have any of these behaviors created problems for you or your staff? How?
- How do these behaviors match up with the other team members?

John facilitated a conversation in which team members shared their discoveries with each other. Again, I observed his facilitation. During this portion, I noticed that John was allowing too much side conversation (people were excited about their learning). Requesting permission to coach, I asked John how he thought the meeting was going. He turned the question back to the team, and several members identified that they thought the team was off track. He asked their help in staying on task and proceeded with the meeting.

I could see that some of the team members were surprised by this exchange. Later one of them told me that she was encouraged by John's method of handling the question and the team. Encouraging these conversations between the leader and the team is part of the role of the team coach. For a team to establish the trust that it takes to work together to accomplish their goals, team members, beginning with the leader, must be willing to step up and be vulnerable. Once team members see that the leader is willing to be vulnerable, they are more likely to express their own opinions and consider others' points of view.

Following this conversation, John worked with the team to develop the mission, roles, responsibilities, and ground rules. This phase of team development allowed me to serve in a traditional coaching role, observing the leader and the team members, asking for permission to share observations and asking key questions.

Katzenbach and Smith[2] define a team as "a small number of people with complimentary skills who are committed to a common purpose, set of performance goals and approach for which they hold themselves mutually accountable." Helping the team get clarity about mission, roles, responsibilities, and ground rules is important formative work for the leader. Teams that operate with a solid understanding of these critical elements produce significantly better results than teams who must find their way without the right foundation.

John worked with the team to establish a set of group norms. The group decided to meet weekly on Monday mornings from 7:30 a.m. and finish by 9 a.m. Norms included the following:

- Start and end meetings on time.
- Submit agenda items the Friday before the meeting.
- Include the time needed and the expected outcome for each agenda item.
- Recap action items at the end of the meeting.
- Evaluate the meeting at the end and course correct for the next meeting.
- Keep meeting information confidential.
- Discuss how to cascade communication to the rest of the organization at the end of each meeting.

Each team member agreed to hold each other to these norms. My role as coach was to coach the team to follow through on their commitment to the norms and to each other. I got permission to step in both to have them notice when they were doing this well and when they needed to relook at how they were honoring their norms. The team members became more comfortable with giving each other feedback and realized that by holding back, they were hurting the team and also their teammates.

CONTINUING WORK WITH THE NEW TEAM

My ongoing work with a new team consists of attending team meetings, continued coaching with the leader, and coaching individual team members. In this case, after the initial team session, I attended weekly leadership meetings for three months, coached the leader every two weeks, and met with individual team members every month. I was also available between meetings for conversations with the leader and team members. After the initial three months, I attended occasional leadership meetings and continued coaching the leader and several team members.

During the team meetings, I helped John pose well-structured questions rather than offering definitive answers as he initially stated he had a tendency to do. John's style is fast paced, results oriented, and competitive as well as visionary. In the past, he said he lost the support of coworkers when he became impatient and moved ahead with his own agenda. During our individual coaching sessions, John recalled the times he had been successful in team meetings—realizing he had more success as a leader when he enabled the team members to develop their own ideas instead of directing them to his.

A major piece of work for this new team was focusing on their results and not the next "great idea" that the leader (or another team member) came up with. John asked the team members to each identify the most important initiative in his/her department. He then facilitated a group discussion of how each team member would need to contribute to these initiatives for organizational results. Each member committed publicly to what the team needed to achieve, and John is in the process of developing a scorecard to review progress against the expected achievements.

Successful teams focus on both task and process. The task of the team is the specific work the team does toward defined objective—the "what" question. The way the individuals work together to complete the work process is the "how" question. To keep success in focus, John has two questions posted on his wall that he asks the team to consider at every meeting:

- Are we working on *what* we should be working on (mission, strategy, goals, and objectives)?
- Are we working *how* we should be working (roles, responsibilities, and following ground rules)?

CONCLUSION

As the case study shows, team coaches need to shift into consulting, teaching, and facilitation to help the new team understand its behavioral dynamics, maintain open communication, productivity, and effectiveness. The purpose of team coaching, however, doesn't change. As noted by Alexander Caillet,[3] team coaching strives to increase the performance level of a team as it works toward a specific outcome. It strives to promote the individual growth of team members along the way with the intention of creating capacity within the team for sustaining quality and generating excellence.

John's team is certainly not typical of all teams and the coaching approach is not the only model that could be used for a brand new team. There are many approaches to team coaching and many types of teams that may contract for team coaching. Workplace teams enable groups of people to respond to workplace challenges and goals in unique and creative ways, but they can be challenging to manage in the best of circumstances and can easily develop into a quagmire if things go wrong.

Coaching is often used as an effective means of helping new teams draw out the wisdom and experience of each individual while helping them take responsibility for collectively achieving results for the organization. When coaching new teams, it is critically important to coach the leader to create a safe environment for open communication and to support the team members in their own individual development as well as to meet the team's task-related goals. Remember, many leaders are skilled at focusing on task (what), but not on process (how). A masterful coach helps the leader and the team pull together to clarify the goal, develop a plan of action, and overcome the barriers along the way.

NOTES

1. Target Training International, Ltd., *TI Success Insights (team assessment program, 2007).*
2. Jon R. Katzenbach, and Douglas K., Smith (March–April 1993), "The Discipline of Teams," *Harvard Business Review*, July 2005, 162.
3. Alexander Caillet, "Coaching Teams and Groups in Organizations" (manuscript, 2007).

EDITORS AND CONTRIBUTORS

EDITORS

Beth Bloomfield is the founder and principal of Bloomfield Associates, LLC. Beth is an experienced certified executive coach, strategic consultant, and former senior executive whose clients include leaders in the business, nonprofit, and public sectors. Beth received her coach training through the Newfield Network and also earned a certificate in organizational learning from George Mason University. Beth has earned the distinction of professional certified coach (PCC) from the International Coach Federation (ICF), and she serves on the leadership team of the New Mexico chapter of the ICF. Beth graduated from Barnard College and earned an MA from Columbia University. She is a learning circle adviser in the Georgetown University Leadership Coaching Program.

Clarice Scriber, president and CEO of Clarity Consulting, has more than a dozen years of experience coaching executives and leaders in the corporate, public, and private sectors who want to enhance their interpersonal skills and executive presence. Clarice holds the master certified coach designation from the International Coach Federation, a certificate in coaching from the New Ventures West Professional Coaching course and a certificate in adult development from the Interdevelopmental Institute. Clarice earned her coaching certification through the New Ventures West Professional Coaching Course. She holds an MS degree in clinical psychology from Loyola University in Maryland, and an MA in communications from the Annenberg School of Communications, University of Pennsylvania.

Christine Wahl, founder of Miro Group Consulting, is a master certified coach with the International Coach Federation. Her coaching practice spans numerous industries and is focused on coaching leaders and their teams as well as on helping organizations build internal coaching cadres in their human resource departments. She holds a BA in psychology and an MA in counseling. Christine is the creator and former director of the Georgetown University Leadership Coaching Certificate Program, where she continues to teach. Christine is a certified professional effectiveness coach (New Ventures West) as well as a certified developmental coach (Interdevelopmental Institute). She is a frequent contributor to journals and a speaker about coaching, and she teaches courses for coaches on the topics of transitions, coaching teams, and working with the stages of adult development.

CONTRIBUTORS

Frank Ball has been an independent executive coach and organizational consultant for more than 10 years. Before starting his own practice, he was manager and leader in a number of large organizations for more than two decades. Frank holds a BA in economics from Davidson College, an MS in financial management from George Washington University, and a certificate in organization development from Georgetown University. He completed the yearlong professional coaching course presented by New Ventures West and shorter, more focused professional coaching courses presented by the Newfield Network, the Strozzi Institute, the Interdevelopmental Institute, and the Gestalt Institute of Cleveland. He has been designated a master certified coach by the International Coach Federation.

Alexander Caillet is the founder of One21Five, Inc., an organizational consulting and coaching firm dedicated to helping leaders in organizations around the world achieve significant transformations by balancing the business and people aspects of change. In addition, Alexander is on the faculty of Georgetown University's Leadership Coaching Certification Program and is a guest lecturer at several US universities. He is a frequent international speaker on the subjects of change, teams, coaching, and leadership. Alexander completed his BS in psychology at the University of Michigan and his MA in organization psychology at Columbia University.

Randy Chittum is the vice president for leadership development at PSS/World Medical in Jacksonville, Florida. In this role, he coaches executives and other leaders, provides learning opportunities for all leaders, and manages the succession management program. Prior to taking this position, Randy managed a consulting and coaching practice that was primarily dedicated to developing leaders. Randy has a

PhD in psychology from the University of Northern Colorado. He has taught leadership at multiple universities, including the MBA program at Georgetown University. At the core of Randy's coaching philosophy is a belief in creating a new perspective, using lightness and play, and tapping the fundamental human urge to "be" more.

William Courville is an executive coach, consultant, and educator with extensive managerial and executive experience. He is on the adjunct faculty at Georgetown University, American University, the University of Maryland University College, the National Leadership Institute, and the Center for Creative Leadership. Bill has a PhD from the University of Ottawa (Ontario, Canada). His dissertation examined the role of meaning, value, and purpose in executive coaching. He holds an MEd in counseling from Loyola University (New Orleans). He received his BA in philosophy from Loyola University and his BS in business administration from Louisiana State University. He currently focuses on executive coaching and leadership development.

Karen Curnow is managing director of Compass International, a consulting company helping corporate and federal clients develop their leaders, work effectively across cultures, and manage individuals and teams internationally. With over 30 years of experience, Karen coaches senior leaders and managers, facilitates team development, and provides training and consulting services, all to inspire transformative change built on authenticity, respect, and collective wisdom. Having worked and lived in France, Turkey, Kenya, Austria, and New York prior to her work in the DC area, Karen earned her MBA in international management and marketing from US International University and her BS in business administration and French at Houghton College and at the Sorbonne/University of Paris. She received her certification in coaching and organizational learning from the Newfield Network-USA and George Mason University.

Katherine Ebner is the founder and principal of the Nebo Company, a leadership development firm based in Washington, DC. Katherine helped found the Institute for Transformational Leadership at Georgetown University and serves as the institute's codirector. Katherine earned a BA in English/creative writing from Middlebury College in 1987 and has completed graduate work in English literature at the Bread Loaf School of English. She holds a certificate in leadership coaching from Georgetown University.

Margaret Echols has been assisting individuals, groups, and organizations in taking steps toward transformation for nearly 20 years. Before creating the Development Consortium, Margaret was a senior manager in executive development at PricewaterhouseCoopers. Margaret's academic background includes an MBA from George Washington University with concentrations in international business and organizational behavior and BA and MA degrees in education and administration from the University of Florida. She is a master certified coach (International Coach Federation), a certified professional effectiveness coach (New Ventures West), and has completed a graduate coaching program with the Newfield Network. Margaret also has extensive training in somatic coaching and is certified as a somatic coach by the Strozzi Institute.

Karen Gravenstine has been a master certified coach and organization effectiveness consultant, engaged in coaching and development of executives, rising leaders, and members of boards of directors and their teams for over 25 years. She is a founding faculty member of Georgetown University's Leadership Coaching Program, where she continues to teach. Karen holds the International Coach Federation's master certified coach designation, a mentor coach certificate from Invite Change, an advanced ontological coaching certificate from the Newfield Network, and a personal effectiveness coach certificate from New Ventures West. Karen earned an MA from the Catholic University of America in Washington, DC.

Steve Heller is an independent leadership coach whose clients have included corporate executives, entrepreneurs, public sector leaders, educators, nonprofit executives, attorneys, scientists, coaching students, and established coaches. In addition, Steve is on the faculty of Georgetown University's Leadership Coaching Certificate Program. He holds a BSE from Johns Hopkins University, an MSE from the University of Pennsylvania, and a certificate in leadership coaching from Georgetown University. Steve is a past president of the board of directors of the Washington, DC, chapter of the International Coach Federation (ICF), and holds an ICF professional certified coach (PCC) credential.

Roselyn (Roz) Kay is managing partner of New Heights Group, a strategy and leadership development firm working with corporate, nonprofit, and government organizations. She seeks to help her clients embody the change they seek. Roz was a senior leader in banking and financial services before transitioning into the fields of organization development (OD) and executive coaching. She holds an MS in OD from American University and a certificate in leadership coaching from

Georgetown. Roz is a faculty member of the Georgetown Leadership Coaching Program and a Practicum Advisor for American University's MS in Organization Development program. Roz is a professional certified coach with ICF and a master somatic coach with the Strozzi Institute.

Kelly Lewis is the founder and principal of The Bounce Collective, a leadership development firm based in Richmond, VA. In 2011, Kelly was honored as one of Workforce Management's Game Changer award recipients for a cutting-edge learning model that provides a meaningful way for leaders to develop while bringing communities together. Before starting Bounce, Kelly spent 15 years as an executive and change leader at Capital One. Kelly earned her coaching certification through Georgetown University and is a professional certified coach (International Coaching Federation). She holds a BS in business management from Virginia Tech University.

Patricia (Pat) A. Mathews is a master certified coach (International Coach Federation) and president of Mathews Associates, her leadership and executive coaching and consulting business. Pat is dedicated to supporting leaders as they build productive partnerships, teams, and workplaces. Her work as a coach includes leaders in all fields, and she is especially drawn to health care. Her health care experience includes clinical, management, and educational roles in acute care, outpatient, and educational settings. She is a registered nurse and has an MA in health administration from Jersey City State College and a certificate in leadership coaching from Georgetown University. Pat currently serves as program director of the Georgetown University Leadership Coaching Program and is a member of the Global Board of Directors of the International Coach Federation.

Sue E. McLeod is a professional certified coach (International Coach Federation), is a certified professional co-active coach (The Coaches Training Institute), and a certified mentor coach (InviteChange). Sue brings 12 years of experience in coaching and leadership development and over 20 years of experience in leadership in high-tech consulting to her work with leaders and organizations. She has held numerous leadership and management positions in technology consulting firms, run her own consulting company, and worked as a consultant with Hay Group, a global management consulting firm. Sue holds a BA in mathematics from Colby College, Waterville, ME.

Sandy Mobley, founder of the Learning Advantage, LLC, has been providing leadership and team coaching for over 25 years. Before starting her company in 1992, she worked as an executive at Hewlett Packard, Watson Wyatt, and McKinsey. Sandy has an MBA from Harvard Business School and an MA in mathematics. She was a founding faculty member of the Georgetown University's Leadership Coaching Program. Her book *Juicy Work: Creating Fruitful Careers and Cultivating Nourishing Workplaces* was published May 2012. Sandy is designated a master certified coach (International Coach Federation), a master somatic coach by the Strozzi Institute, and a professional effectiveness coach by New Ventures West.

Eric de Nijs coaches executives and coaches to become better leaders. His specializations include leadership presence, talent development, coaching, relationship building, and training. He focuses on helping leaders establish their personal brand and presence within their organizations and articulate their business strategies and models. Eric is principal of the de Nijs Company, a management consulting company, and serves as a program codirector and instructor for Georgetown University's Leadership Coaching Program. Eric has a PhD in human resource development and two master's degrees. Eric also holds a certificate in coaching from Georgetown University and a certificate in corporate coaching from Corporate Coach University. He is the author of *Playing in a Bigger Space* (2011).

Lloyd Raines is a seasoned executive master certified coach (ICF), leadership development consultant, and educator. As principal of Integral Focus, he brings a holistic, systems-oriented approach to "leadership as stewardship" in service to the financial, social, and ecological sustainability of vital resources. Lloyd was a founding faculty mentor in the Federal Judicial Center's Leadership Program and a founding faculty member of Georgetown University's Leadership Coaching Program, where he continues to teach. He helped conceive and launch Georgetown's Institute for Transformational Leadership. He has an MA in justice from American University and a BA in psychology from the University of Maryland.

Neil Stroul is a professional psychologist, who left the therapy world for organizational consulting and training in 1979. A partner in Kenning Associates, Neil has devoted his entire career to helping organizations foster a developmental culture. Focusing on leadership coaching during the past 10 years has been his most recent discovery about how to help organizations become more developmental.

Julie Shows is the president and founder of the Coaching Connection. She focuses on coaching midlevel and senior managers who have been identified by their companies as having high potential. Julie is recognized as a master certified coach, a designation awarded to the most experienced coaches by the International Coach Federation. She has completed coaching certification programs from Georgetown University and Success Unlimited Network and is a certified mentor coach. She holds a BA from Miami University in Ohio. She has been on the faculty of the Georgetown Coaching Certificate Program since 2003 and is currently program director.

Jennifer Sinek has over two decades of experience working with individuals, teams, and organizations, helping them see and be excited by the possibilities open to them—and then make them happen. Utilizing conversational and somatic practices, she helps clients step into their power as leaders—and authors—of their professional and personal lives. Jennifer earned her MA in public and private management from Yale University and her BA in psychology from Colgate University, designations of MCC from the ICF, master somatic coach from the Strozzi Institute, and CPEC from New Ventures West.

Dave Snapp was a union organizer for more than 20 years before becoming a consultant and coach. As part of his practice, Dave is a core faculty member of the SEIU Institute for Change. He holds a BA from Brown University and an MPH from the University of Michigan. He has completed certificate programs in organization development, change leadership, and leadership coaching at Georgetown University.

Jennifer Whitcomb, a master certified coach (International Coach Federation), is principal of the Trillium Group, a firm focusing on helping leaders bring their best self forward. Jennifer is an executive, team, and group coach. She has an MA in human resource development and certificates in coaching from Newfield Network and the Coaches Training Institute. She is a certified action learning coach and certified mentor coach. She is a previous director of the Organization Development Certificate Program at Georgetown University.

Lee Ann Wurster-Naefe brings a practical managerial perspective to her work as an organizational consultant and leadership coach. She has 30 years of experience in first-line through senior-level leadership positions in insurance and financial services, health care, education, and the federal government. Lee Ann has an MA in business administration from Frostburg State University and certificates in leadership coaching and organization development from Georgetown University. She is a professional certified coach (ICF) and certified somatic coach™ through the Strozzi Institute.

INDEX

Note: Page numbers followed by an "f" or a "t" indicate a figure or table, respectively.